AVIATION ASSAULT
BATTLE GROUP

It's the Jock fighting spirit within everybody in this compound and within the whole Battalion. You can't take it out of the man, it's always in there. And once the bullets start flying and the bombs start landing, the blood starts rising and the hairs and the hackle starts to come up, that's it. You want to go and do your business, live life to the limits.

Sergeant Gus Millar, Mortar Platoon,
Op PANCHAI PALANG, Luy Mandeh Wadi, 22 June 2009

In memory of

Sergeant Gus Millar
Sergeant Sean Binnie
Corporal Tam Mason
Private Kevin Elliott
Private Robert McLaren
Bombardier Craig Hopson

AVIATION ASSAULT BATTLE GROUP

THE 2009 AFGHANISTAN TOUR OF THE BLACK WATCH 3RD BATTALION THE ROYAL REGIMENT OF SCOTLAND

FOREWORD BY HRH THE PRINCE CHARLES, DUKE OF ROTHESAY

Pen & Sword

MILITARY

First published in 2011 by
PEN & SWORD MILITARY
an imprint of
Pen & Sword Books Ltd
47 Church Street
Barnsley
South Yorkshire
S70 2AS

Copyright ©
The Black Watch, 3rd Battalion The Royal Regiment of Scotland, 2011

ISBN 978 1 84884 536 7

Typeset and design by
L S Menzies-Earl, Chic Media Ltd
Printed and bound by Printworks International Ltd. in China

Pen & Sword Books Ltd incorporates the imprints of
Pen & Sword Aviation, Pen & Sword Maritime, Pen & Sword Military,
Pen & Sword Family History, Pen & Sword Discovery, Wharncliffe Local History,
Wharncliffe True Crime, Wharncliffe Transport, Pen & Sword Select,
Pen & Sword Military Classics, Leo Cooper, The Praetorian Press, Remember When,
Seaforth Publishing and Frontline Publishing

For a complete list of Pen & Sword titles please contact
PEN & SWORD BOOKS LIMITED
47 Church Street, Barnsley, South Yorkshire, S70 2AS, England
E-mail: enquiries@pen-and-sword.co.uk
Website: www.pen-and-sword.co.uk

CONTENTS

PART 3 – D (Light) Company

PART 4 – Final Strands

ACKNOWLEDGEMENTS

This book has been written by a wide selection of individuals from across the Battle Group. I am extremely grateful for everyone who has contributed. However two individuals are worthy of particular praise; Captain David Mack and Major Gillian Shaw. David, the Mortar Officer, spent many hours developing the book structure and writing the introductions for each operation, sifting through all the operational paperwork and records. Gillian, the Regimental Administrative Officer, had the original idea for the book and has overseen the whole project, including tireless work with capturing the individual written contributions, as well as leading the selection and coordination of all the photographs. She left the Battalion in August 2009, but has remained the project officer throughout, dealing with the extensive bureaucracy required to produce a military book. Without these two individuals, we would have only had a small photographic journal as the memory of an exhilarating, challenging and rewarding operational tour.

Lastly my thanks go to Henry Wilson and his staff at Pen and Sword who have persevered with the project. All the royalties from the book will go to the Royal Regiment of Scotland's Welfare Fund. This fund provides financial support to all those serving and retired soldiers from The Regiment and their immediate dependants that require welfare assistance.

SJC
October 2010

This book tells the story of The Black Watch, 3rd Battalion The Royal Regiment of Scotland's seven month tour to Afghanistan in 2009. Unlike the vast majority of military books that have been written in the last few years covering this campaign, this one is written by the officers and soldiers of the Battalion themselves, not by an author or journalist. As such it is not just about military history, but more about the individuals who collectively come together and produce a team, a fighting infantry battle group. From the leadership of the Commanding Officer, through the tactical experience of the Company Commanders and the enthusiasm of the young platoon commanders on their first operational tour, to the courageous young non-commissioned officers and private soldiers, many still teenagers, this was a team effort that consistently produced excellent results in a most demanding environment against a determined and ruthless foe.

The Black Watch Battalion's contribution to the UK's military effort in Afghanistan in 2009 was unique. In its role as an aviation assault battalion, supported by many helicopters from the Coalition, it was used extensively throughout Southern Afghanistan to reassure the local population, in the more remote areas, that the Government of the Islamic Republic of Afghanistan was their future, and that the Taliban were not. This often meant that they had to take the fight to the insurgents, which they did with courage, restraint and compassion.

The Battalion's success on operations came at a considerable cost and I can only say that my heart goes out to those families who have lost loved ones, together with my deepest condolences. There were terrible injuries inflicted as well and I salute all those who are recovering so well, together with those who provide such dedicated service to the recovery of our wounded personnel. My admiration goes to all the families who were left behind to deal with the uncertainty and responsibility that military service brings; a hugely important part of the collective team effort.

For me, it is the greatest possible privilege to be the Royal Colonel of The Black Watch Battalion. I need hardly say that everyone who served in this Battle Group is an immense credit to their own Regiments and to this country of ours, which is more fortunate than it realizes in having such dedicated and professional people serving in its Armed Forces.

This is their story.

Introduction

LIEUTENANT COLONEL STEPHEN CARTWRIGHT
Commanding Officer

BACKGROUND

The Black Watch, 3rd Battalion The Royal Regiment of Scotland, deployed to Afghanistan as part of the force structure that made up Operation HERRICK 10 (HERRICK being the UK's operational name for operations in Afghanistan) in the period of April to November 2009. This book seeks to capture the personal story of a remarkable human effort over this period, a snap shot of life as an infantry soldier serving far from home in a foreign land, in support of an international campaign. The book is not written by a 'third party' author or journalist; it is a frontline view of what everyone serving in the Battalion at the time assessed as being the most intense and challenging operational tour of their generation. Some of the more experienced members of the Battle Group have seen service in Gulf War 1, Bosnia, Northern Ireland, Kosovo and more recently Iraq. The intensity of the fighting, the physical and mental pressure on everyone over a sustained period and the implications of tactical defeat place Afghanistan 2009 in a different league.

The Commanding Officer, Lt Col Stephen Cartwright. (Maj G Shaw)

During this deployment, the Armed Forces had the most outstanding support from the public, but the Afghanistan campaign itself was much less popular. It is not the aim of this book to present Government policy, but the extracts, comments and interviews should provide a picture of what was happening on the ground. As the tour drew to a close, it was recognized that although much progress had been made, there was much to be done and many problems to be solved.

LCpl Ratakalou assists in the raising of the Battalion flag in Camp ROBERTS to mark the change of command from 42 Cdo Gp to 3 SCOTS BG. (MOD – Sgt C Halton)

There was however a collective belief that Afghanistan was not a lost cause, and from a military perspective, our aims could be achieved.

The UK Government has deployed its military to Afghanistan to improve the security of the UK. At the time of writing, 44 contributing troop nations are supporting the Government of the Islamic Republic of Afghanistan (GIRoA) in its fight against a Taliban inspired insurgency. It was a Taliban-run Afghanistan that provided a safe haven from which Al Qaeda planned, trained and directed major terrorist attacks across the globe. Afghanistan has faced decades of conflict and it is not an easy task to develop it into a stable, peaceful and more prosperous country.

There are 3 strands to the UK's strategy; development of the Afghan Security Forces, credible Afghan governance at national and local level and economic development. The primary role of the UK's Armed Forces in Afghanistan is to assist in the development of the Afghan National Security Forces (ANSF). This is being done as a partnership as all International Security Assistance Forces (ISAF) and the ANSF together fight an insurgency across parts of Afghanistan.

UK military success will be achieved when the Afghan Forces can sustain this fight without our assistance, in that the Taliban will never be able to return to power through force. There is no sense that the UK will be in Afghanistan until it has the western equivalent of a stable and democratic state that we would recognize here in the UK. The GIRoA, supported by

ISAF, are making considerable progress and the UK's military endstate is assessed as being achievable.

In late 2001 the United Nations Security Council authorized the creation of an ISAF composed of NATO troops. ISAF has 6 Regions currently and the UK's commitment has been firmly targeted at the South. The UK announced intentions to go to Helmand in the second half of 2005 and the first troops of the main deployment arrived in April 2006. In 2007, the MOD approved the deployment of a UK Regional Battle Group (South), a second echelon force[1] to assist in Regional Command (South)'s operations across Southern Afghanistan, rather than just leaving each contributing Nation to conduct operations within their own areas. 1 Royal Ghurkha Rifles were the first to serve in this role, followed by the 3rd Battalion The Parachute Regiment and 42 Commando Royal Marines. The Black Watch, 3rd Battalion The Royal Regiment of Scotland (3 SCOTS) took over this role in April 2009. The task was formally known as the Regional Battle Group South (RBG(S)) and was the only battle group not committed to ground holding in the Regional Command (South). Ground holding battle groups provide a constant security presence on the ground, in that they provide the permanent security for the governance and development to prosper. RBG(S) was the only NATO force not committed to ground holding, with the exception of Special Forces, in the whole of Afghanistan. The UK's commitment to Op HERRICK 10 was based on 19 (Light) Brigade: in the UK, 3 SCOTS is commanded by 19 (Light) Brigade. In Afghanistan 19 (Light) Brigade, less 3 SCOTS, formed Task Force Helmand.

FORCE STRUCTURE

The 3 SCOTS Battle Group consisted of 2 rifle companies, a fire support company, an artillery tactical group, a logistics company, and a variety of specialist troops. The Battle Group numbered over 540, 450 of which were provided by 3 SCOTS personnel. 3 SCOTS also provided a company of 50 personnel to the Operational Mentoring and Liaison and Training (OMLT) Battle Group based in Musa Qal'ah, 12 soldiers to the Brigade Recce Force (BRF), and 10 personnel in a variety of posts including the Non Commissioned Officers Training Team in Kabul. Within the RBG(S) establishment, there were a number of appointments that were filled with considerable support from 51st Highland, 7 SCOTS, our sister Territorial Army Battalion. These posts included Company Intelligence Officers, a Non-Kinetic Effects Team Officer, watch-keepers, a medical liaison officer and intelligence analysts. Afghan National Security Forces were always involved in the operations and included the Afghan National Army, Afghan National Police and officers from the National Directorate of Security. Other assets assigned to the Battle Group were dependent on the task and included the Brigade Reconnaissance Force, an armoured company (including a troop of Leopard 2 tanks), counter-IED teams, military working dogs, biometric advisors, Military Stabilization Support Teams (MSST), female searchers and mobile air operations teams.

---

1 Second echelon forces are units not commited to permanent security tasks and therefore free to conduct a variety of proactive and reactive operations. First echelon forces are ground holding units providing a permanent security presence to the people so that governance and economic development can take place.

THE ROLE OF RBG(S)

Commander RC(S)[2] was very clear about how RBG(S) could be used. Whilst the mission set was broad[3], he deployed his manoeuvre force in support of his operational design: support to the Presidential Elections, support to the freedom of movement and support to the US expansion in the South. The Battle Group was tasked with operations in areas less frequented by ISAF with the aim of disrupting the insurgents in depth. He sought to disrupt the insurgents' command and control, their safe-havens, their IED logistics nodes and the confluence of narcotic and insurgent activity. The 3 SCOTS Battle Group also deployed on first echelon type operations such as providing security for engineer construction.

As the only reserve force in southern Afghanistan, the Battle Group had a commitment to be ready to deploy a company group within 6 hours of a task, with the remainder of the Battle Group following in 12 hours. This reserve tasking was only used once during the tour, when A Company responded to a downed US Chinook helicopter.

---

2 *Major General de Kruif, Netherlands.*
3 *Deliberate clearance and exploitation operations, strike and interdiction operations, support and influence operations, disruption operations.*

PREPARATION FOR DEPLOYMENT

The Battle Group had a traditional training progression. Exercise GRAND PRIX, an expeditionary exercise to Kenya in September and October 2008 was an excellent opportunity to improve basic infantry skills while operating in an austere environment and dealing with extreme temperatures.

The key training priorities the Battle Group faced in preparation for deployment on operations in Afghanistan were fitness, driver training, medical and radio signals communications training. Cultural awareness was also key; a deep understanding by the soldiers of what is acceptable cultural behaviour was just as important as a few basic Pashtun words. Physical fitness proved to be a chief concern prior to deployment. The cold and wet winter months in Fort George and the surrounding mountains of the Scottish Highlands is an ideal training environment for arduous activities, however, southern Afghanistan is an arid region where intense dry heat reaches 50 degrees Celsius during the summer months. As a result, once in theatre, the Battle Group conducted acclimatisation training in order to fully prepare itself for the operations that were to follow.

EXECUTION

Operations for ground holding forces are by their nature restricted to their area of operations: ground in the vicinity of Forward Operating Bases (FOBs). For the RBG(S), operations were conducted at significant reach from Kandahar and were always coalition in nature. The majority of the operations were aviation assault, using coalition Chinook helicopters, but some operations also included subsequent ground link up of protected mobility vehicles and logistic support vehicles. The Fire Support Company (consisting of Javelin Platoon, Machine Gun Platoon and Sniper Platoon) was used either as an independent company (dismounted or in 22 Jackal Vehicles) or integrated into the 2 aviation strike companies. Command and control was dispersed as the controlling headquarters remained in Kandahar and the tactical Battle Group Headquarters (the Commanding Officer and a small support team) deployed into the field to command the strike companies.

---

4 *Javelin is an anti-tank missile system.*

RBG(S) conducted 13 Battle Group operations and 8 company operations during the 7 month tour. The Battle Group attracted considerable military resources: helicopters, aircraft, divisional intelligence and intelligence gathering assets. If our task was in direct support to first echelon forces then it was easier to assess the effectiveness of operations. However, if tasked at the Regional level to achieve 'Regional effect', the measurement of effectiveness proved to be harder to judge. In a slow moving campaign it may be several months before the effects of a particular tactical engagement might be best judged.

The Battle Group worked directly to a Multinational Regional HQ, but had UK logistic support from the UK Joint Force Support based in Kandahar. There was no traditional support from a Brigade Headquarters and as a result the Battle Group punched well above its weight. The Intelligence Cell became the Battle Group Intelligence Fusion Cell, as it was responsible for fusing information from a number of disparate sources. The Battle Group also planned operations up to 3 weeks out that often involved 3 separate and different phases.

The key moment of the tour was the Battle Group's contribution to Task Force Helmand's Operation Panther's Claw in June and July. The whole Battle Group conducted a single wave aviation assault to start the Brigade operation and securing key crossing points in the north of Babaji. B Company then held the position for 2 weeks, and subsequently conducted another aviation assault in support of the Light Dragoons Battle Group. The last act was another aviation assault by the Battle Group, with a link up of armoured vehicles into the heart of the Babaji area.

Indirect Fire Support and intelligence gathering assets have been critical to the success of all the Battle Group operations. The Battle Group enjoyed unrivalled support in this area and seldom operated without coverage from a combination of assets normally associated with much larger formation level operations . The integration of these assets started at the earliest stage of planning with intelligence gathering platforms, in particular totally embedded within the Battle Group Intelligence Fusion Cell. To meet the demands of the deployment the Battle Group developed its own image analysts and nurtured a strong relationship with operational and strategic level collection agencies.

The tactical integration of intelligence gathering assets and artillery on the ground was conducted by the Fire Support Teams, consisting of both Royal Artillery and 3 SCOTS personnel who, critically, had worked together for over a year. The Battle Group delivered ordinance from many different platforms. The key factor that linked all engagements was the assessment of proportionality and need to use force within the rules of engagements; assets were withheld many more times than they were committed to ensure that the right effect was achieved and that civilian casualties and damage to property were avoided.

Offensive operations against a virile insurgency sadly come at considerable cost. The 3 SCOTS Battle Group suffered 8 killed (Sergeant Gus Millar, Bombardier Craig Hopson, Private Kev Elliott, Private Rab McLaren, Corporal Tam Mason and 3 ANA soldiers) and 29 wounded in action. Additionally Sergeant Sean Binnie was killed in action with D Company in their operations in support of the Afghan Security Forces in Helmand. In total 51 soldiers were evacuated back to the UK for various medical reasons.

As a predominantly aviation battle group we have contributed to the equipment debate in order to reduce the weight carried by the dismounted soldier. Whilst first echelon

companies may typically deploy on an 8 hour patrol, the Battle Group deployed up to 6 days away from ISAF FOBs, living in the desert and in compounds. Everyman carried in the region of 100–160 lbs. Nonetheless, the Jocks became battle hardened very quickly and coped extremely well with the intensity of the fighting, the heat and the austere environment. The equipment currently provided to our service personnel is of the highest quality.

The detailed chapters of the book describe briefly each operation, with personal contributions bringing life to the events at the time. The old adage that military conflict is 95 per cent boredom and 5 per cent excitement holds true; the majority of the comments and interviews focus on the most dangerous and exhilarating parts of the memory bank – the 5 percent. In the remaining 95 per cent, the less reported activity is taking place: engagement with the Afghan people, development of the Afghan Security Forces and the UK's wider contribution to campaign success. It is these less glamorous activities that are slowly bringing Afghanistan to a better place and making our military mission increasingly successful.

The dawn extraction of the Battle Group on Op TORA ARWA. (MOD – Cpl R Freer)

3 SCOTS REGIONAL BATTLE GROUP (SOUTH) OPERATIONS

April – October 2009

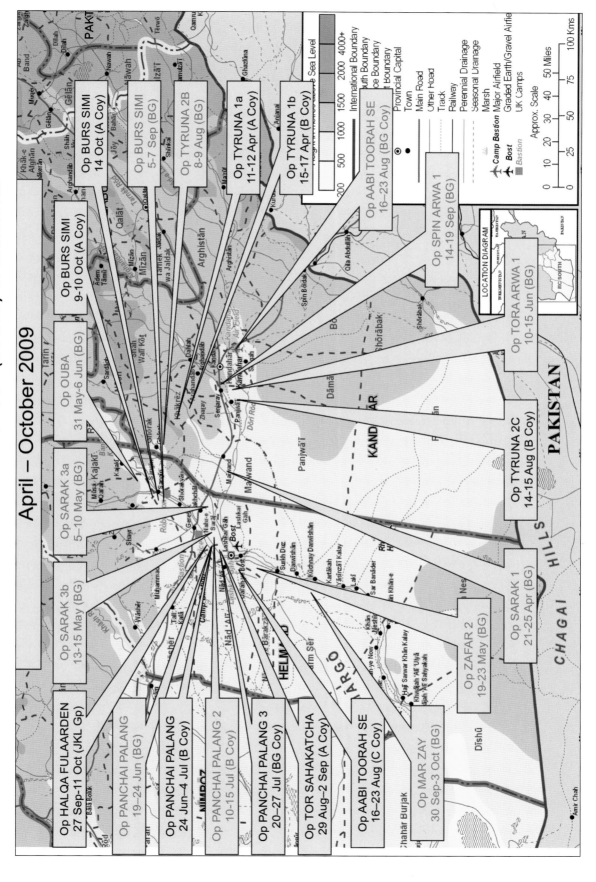

Op HALQA FULAARDEN 27 Sep–11 Oct (JKL Gp)

Op PANCHAI PALANG 19–24 Jun (BG)

Op PANCHAI PALANG 24 Jun–4 Jul (B Coy)

Op PANCHAI PALANG 2 10–15 Jul (B Coy)

Op PANCHAI PALANG 3 20–27 Jul (BG Coy)

Op TOR SAHAKATCHA 29 Aug–2 Sep (A Coy)

Op AABI TOORAH SE 16–23 Aug (C Coy)

Op MAR ZAY 30 Sep–3 Oct (BG)

Op ZAFAR 2 19–23 May (BG)

Op SARAK 1 21–25 Apr (BG)

Op SARAK 3b 13–15 May (BG)

Op OUBA 31 May–6 Jun (BG)

Op SARAK 3a 5–10 May (BG)

Op BURS SIMI 9–10 Oct (A Coy)

Op BURS SIMI 14 Oct (A Coy)

Op BURS SIMI 5–7 Sep (BG)

Op TYRUNA 2B 8–9 Aug (BG)

Op TYRUNA 1a 11–12 Apr (A Coy)

Op TYRUNA 1b 15–17 Apr (B Coy)

Op AABI TOORAH SE 16–23 Aug (BG Coy)

Op SPIN ARWA 1 14–19 Sep (BG)

Op TORA ARWA 1 10–15 Jun (BG)

Op TYRUNA 2C 14–15 Aug (B Coy)

LOCATION DIAGRAM

m above Mean Sea Level

200 500 1000 1500 2000 4000+

International Boundary
Province Boundary
District Boundary

Provincial Capital
Town

Main Road
Other Road
Track
Railway
Perennial Drainage
Seasonal Drainage
Marsh

✈ Camp Bastion   Major Airfield
Bost   Graded Earth/Gravel Airfield
Bastion   UK Camps

Approx. Scale

0 10 20 30 40 50 75 100 Kms
0 25 50 75 100 Miles

REGIONAL BATTLE GROUP (SOUTH) OPERATIONS – OPERATION HERRICK 10

DATE	OPERATION	LOCATION	TYPE	REMARKS
11 – 12 Apr 09	TYRUNA 1 / A Coy	Nasser, TFK	DISRUPT (avn)	No kinetic engagements.
15 – 17 Apr 09	TYRUNA 1 / B Coy	Bagkak, TFK	DISRUPT (avn)	Mission aborted due to weather on insertion
21 – 25 Apr 09	SARAK 1 / BG	Band-e-Timor, TFK	INTERDICT C2 and IED (avn)	Disruption achieved with enhanced local situational awareness.
5 – 10 May 09	SARAK 3a / BG	Nahr-E-Saraj, TFH	INTERDICT C2 and IED (avn and PM)	Culvert denial. Dislocation of insurgents, enhanced freedom of movement along Hwy 1. Armr Coy from Danish Battle Group TACOM
13 – 15 May 09	SARAK 3b / BG	Nahr-E-Saraj, TFH	STRIKE (avn and PM)	BRF included during operation following intelligence gather on Sarak 3a.
19 – 23 May 09	ZAFAR 2 / BG	Aynak, LKG, TFH	DISRUPT 1st Ech, UNDERSTAND (avn and PM)	Build of check point, 1 x IED Strike (Mastiff).
31 May – 06 Jun 09	OUBA 3 / BG	Upper Sangin Valley, TFH	STRIKE, CN (avn)	2 x BG aviation raids against the narcotic insurgent confluence.
10 – 15 Jun 09	TORA ARWA 1 / BG	Nalgam, Zhari District, TFK	DISRUPT (avn)	3 x KIA (2 x ANA, 1 x UK). ANA Recce Coy involved with operation.
19 – 24 Jun 09	PANCHAI PALANG / BG	Luh Mundeh Wadi, TFH	SECURE iot BUILD: 1st Ech (avn and PM)	BG aviation assault. 1 x KIA (ANA). Movement control procedures implemented, insurgents disrupted. BG orbat: 2 Aviation Coy, 1 Mobile (JACKAL) Coy.
24 Jun – 04 Jul 09	PANCHAI PALANG / B Coy	Luh Mundeh Wadi, TFH	SECURE iot BUILD & HOLD: 1st Ech (avn and PM)	Insurgents disrupted.
10 – 15 Jul 09	PANCHAI PALANG 2 / B Coy	Babaji, TFH	BLOCK (avn)	Aviation assault into depth. Working to Light Dragoon BG. No kinetic engagements.
20 – 27 Jul 09	PANCHAI PALANG 3 / BG	Loy Adera, TFH	SECURE (avn)	1 x KIA (UK). BG aviation assault. Obj seized. 2 Royal Welsh Armr Inf Coy and Assaye Tp Light Dragoon BG TACOM
08 – 09 Aug 09	TYRUNA 2b / BG	Malmand Chinah, TFK	DISRUPT (avn)	Narcotics and detainees seized. Operation against narcotic insurgent confluence.
14 – 15 Aug 09	TYRUNA 2c / B Coy	Panjwayi, TFK	DESTROY (avn)	Insurgents disrupted prior to elections.

1 PM – Protected Mobility: combination of MASTIFF, VIKING and JACKAL vehicles.
TFK – Task Force Kandahar; a Canadian led Brigade.
TFH – Task Force Helmand; the British Brigade.

DATE	OPERATION	LOCATION	TYPE	REMARKS
16 – 23 Aug 09	AABI TOORAH SE / BG	RC(S)	SECURE (avn and PM)	Regional Reaction Force across Southern Afghanistan during election period.
29 Aug – 02 Sep 09	TOR SAHAKATCHA / A Coy	Shamalan Canal, TFH	SCREEN and DISRUPT (avn)	2 x KIA (UK). Aviation assault in support of Welsh Guards BG.
05 – 07 Sep 09	BURS SIMI / BG	Karlz Kukah, TFH	DISRUPT (avn)	BG aviation assault.
14 – 19 Sep 09	SPIN ARWA 1 / BG	Sangsar, Zhari District, TFK	DISRUPT (avn)	3 x WIA (1 x UK, 2 x CDN). Significant attrition to ins; 2 x prestige weapons. Tp CDN Leopard 2 tanks.
27 Sep – 11 Oct 09	HALQA FULAARDEN / JKL Group	Nahr-E Burgha, TFH	ISOLATE and DISRUPT (PM)	Support to BG(C).
30 Sep – 03 Oct 09	MAR ZAY / BG	Lakari Bazaar, TFL	CLEAR (avn)	BG Avn Aslt in support of TFL (USMC) in Lakari Bazaar.
09 – 10 Oct 09	BURS SIMI / A Coy	Sangin, TFH	DISRUPT (avn)	Coy Gp aviation assault.
14 Oct 09	BURS SIMI / A Coy (Reserve)	Sangin/ TFH	SECURE and PROTECT (avn)	Coy Gp secure of damaged Chinook.

(left to right) Capts Brian Cooper QM (Forward) and David Harvey, Battle Group Liaison Officer (BGLO), Majs David Bruce QM and OC Rear Operations and Barney MacAskill, Air Operations Officer. (Maj G Shaw)

Training for War

CAPTAIN SAMUEL NEWSON
Second in Command, Alpha (Grenadier) Company

During our preparations for operations in Afghanistan we trained in many and varied locations. We constructed forward operating bases on the banks of the Moray Firth, practiced for explosive method of entry in and around the Officers' Mess at Fort George and raided Afghan villages constructed in the Kenyan bush. Some training was more relevant than the rest, though not always that which you might imagine. The build up to operations is a long one as there is a great deal of work to do before getting anywhere near the official Pre Deployment Training period. As with all this the foundations need to be well established from the beginning.

I arrived back at Battalion in March 2008, to briefly take over Alpha (Grenadier) Company as acting Officer Commanding, with one platoon commander, a Company Sergeant Major heading out the door and around 40 Jocks: we were pretty undermanned. The company staff formed up over the next couple of months and the number of Jocks steadily increased. We were not starting from scratch but we did have a fair bit of work to do to get the company up to speed.

The Fire Support Group deployment of a Javelin during a live firing exercise in Archers Post, Kenya. (Maj G Shaw)

Sgt Scott McLeod along with the rest of Delta (Light) Company helps the Kenyan Army deal with 'Civpop' during the final exercise in Kenya. (Maj G Shaw)

Lt Alex Philips briefs members of his Platoon during a lull in the battle, Kenya. (Maj G Shaw)

Our first opportunity for prolonged and intense training was on our overseas exercise in Kenya. With our new Company Commander, Major Matt Munro we could start to shape the company as we wanted it. Away from the distractions of home and the temptations of Inverness everyone began to focus on soldiering. Basic infantry skills were honed and we all became accustomed to living in austere conditions.

We had time to practice the basics, to drill and rehearse, we used satellite technology and lasers to review our performance and identify where we needed to improve. We had space to manoeuvre as a company and space to practice live firing at every level. This training culminated in a company attack that was supported by artillery and helicopters. Kenya gave us the opportunity to develop and perfect those conventional tactics on which everything else is based.

One of the most important things for the company was having time in which to build the command relationships which would see us through the next 12 months, be it from company commander to platoon commander or section commander to private soldier. The command structure may be based on rank but it is trust that holds it together. Our time spent in Kenya gave us time to learn to trust one another to understand what we were capable of: how to get the best out of each other.

On return to the Fort we began to turn our attentions to more theatre specifics, understanding the cultural aspects of life in Afghanistan, the threats we would face and the unique way in which we would measure success. We learned how to apply those skills and tactics we had refined in Kenya in the more complex world of full spectrum counter insurgency operations in order to prepare for the ever present threat of IEDs, the mercurial nature of the enemy and the need for clinical levels of precision.

The time for fighting in Afghanistan is not yet passed and the company has fought many actions in various circumstances, what remains constant is the setting in which these actions

Capt Harry Hood the Regimental Careers Management Officer with Capt David Anderson the Padre at the end of the final exercise phase in Kenya. (Maj G Shaw)

LCpl Millar and Cpl Rock receive 'Quick Battle Orders' from Lt Alex Philips. (Maj G Shaw)

are fought. The civilian population is never far away and must always be accounted for; nothing is gained by simply destroying the enemy if the good opinion of the people is lost.

What was critical in preparing for such complexity was again time; time to understand the culture, the problems and the environment; time to experiment with different solutions to each new problem; time to go over each eventuality again and again until it was understood at every level; time to develop contingencies, alternates and fallbacks.

Even in our 7 months in Afghanistan the theatre changed, the enemy evolved as did our tactics; the challenge of war will ever change. As such the most important thing in preparing for operations is to develop a team. Be it a fire team, platoon or company, it must be a tight knit group, agile and able to react rapidly to the changing environment.

We live in a technologically advancing world, we have become used to flying into battle in waves of Chinooks, tracking our enemy with multiple layers of ISTAR and prosecuting targets with a vast range of weapon systems. Who is to say how the battlefield will change over the next few years. What will remain critical is the ability to shoot straight and find cover and most importantly, for the men and officers of the fighting company to work together toward a common goal. What therefore is the most valuable resource in training for war: simply time.

Time to foster trust and understanding, to forge the relationships and the spirit that will see a company through half a year of operations in a complex and often hostile land.

Chapter One

Operation TYRUNA 1A

11–12 April 2009

INTRODUCTION

The first operation the 3 SCOTS Battle Group conducted was Operation TYRUNA 1A. Task Force Kandahar instructed the Battle Group to conduct disruption operations into the insurgent safe havens of Nasser and Baghak in the Khakrez District of Kandahar. Intelligence suggested that these areas were insurgent command and control nodes as well as logistical centres. The Battle Group planned to launch 2 separate company level pulses into the area over 2 separate periods in order to interdict insurgents. However, due to a change in weather, only the first pulse, led by Alpha (Grenadier) Company, was conducted in Nasser.

EXECUTION

11 April 09 (D Day)

On 11 April 09, Alpha Company deployed on Operation TYRUNA 1A in Chinook helicopters and landed at 0516 hrs. Initial assessments by Officer Commanding Alpha Company, Major Matt Munro, suggested that the pattern of life in the area was normal except for some suspicious movement in the vicinity of one of the compounds. Very few adult males were seen in the village of Nasser as the majority of the population was involved in the poppy harvest at that time. Minimal finds were made consisting of small amounts of opium, copper wire, circuit boards and a radio control device that could be used to build an IED. Major Munro's impression of the day is recorded in the operational logbook:

'. . . the enemy has the capability to do harm but has yet to do so. We have been regularly dicked throughout the day and possible smoke signals have been observed. Recent intelligence suggested the enemy approach will be to sit tight until we leave the area knowing that previous ops in the area have been around 36 hours in duration. The atmospherics have been that the local nationals are compliant and neutral with no overt support for either coalition forces or insurgents. When questioned about insurgents in the area there was a consistent trend of a sketchy story with vague details.'

12 April 09 (D+1)

The following day was similar to the first with the majority of the village harvesting the poppy fields. Throughout the day, our intelligence revealed that the insurgents continued to observe the company but were reluctant to launch any form of an attack.

The company made finds of 3 anti-personnel mines, 2 rocket propelled grenades, and 2 mortar rounds and extracted from the region at 1646 hrs.

Members of Minden Platoon outside the QM's department in Camp Roberts – they were attached to 3 SCOTS from The Royal Scots Borderers 1st Battalion, The Royal Regiment of Scotland. (Maj G Shaw)

One down – members of Alpha (Grenadier) Company return to KAF after the 1st operation of a 7 month tour. (Maj G Shaw)

SUMMARY

Although Operation TYRUNA 1A did not uncover significant finds or cause significant attrition to the insurgents, it nonetheless served 2 important functions. Firstly, the operation successfully launched a company into a region that had lacked the presence of coalition forces for a marked period of time. Secondly, it gave the Battle Group a chance to operate in an aviation role and adapt to the complexities of this role; an important experience that would become the model for the entirety of 3 SCOTS Battle Group throughout Operation HERRICK 10.

Observations Op TYRUNA 1A – Major Matt Munro (36), from Hampshire, Officer Commanding Alpha (Grenadier) Company

E-Mail home to friends and family . . .

Our first operation was in support of Task Force Kandahar, the Canadian-led mission in Kandahar Province. We deployed to Kakrez, an insurgent logistics node and staging post. Although our preparation, which had begun in Kenya some 9 months prior, had been

A soldier of the Afghan National Army – this one is armed with a Rocket Propelled Grenade or RPG.

comprehensive there was a degree of apprehension. Planning and battle preparation was necessarily lengthy; we were still feeling our way. Some of the Jocks were noticeably rather 'wide-eyed'. My company group numbered about 200 personnel and included a platoon of Afghan National Army and their French Canadian Mentors, an Afghan Intelligence Agent, Sniffer Dogs, an American bomb disposal team and Field Engineers. We were flown in pre-dawn by 2 waves of Chinook helicopters and rather gratifyingly, had some British Apache helicopters and numerous ISTAR platforms overhead.

Unsurprisingly, the whole experience was fascinating and very rewarding. The insertion was particularly adrenaline-fuelled; running off the back of the helicopter ramp in the grey pre-dawn light into the (relative) unknown was exciting to say the least. The sights, sounds and smells are hard to describe accurately. Much of what we saw appeared pretty medieval or even pre-historic. The landscape is very harsh; most of it is desert and mountains. The villages are often irrigated to create little oases of 'green-zone' (which is typically very close-country and not easy to soldier in). The population live in compounds made from straw and sun baked clay. They mostly subsist by farming (wheat, maize, grape or opium) or trail around after skinny goats all day. The more affluent may have a well, a plough and perhaps some livestock but we saw no evidence of mains electricity or running water. We noted that all the compounds have a distinctive smell; perhaps a mix of human faeces and wood smoke. The compounds are usually guarded by mangy and aggressive mongrel dogs and whilst the kids seem comfortable with our presence the burkha-clad women hasten away at the earliest opportunity. We stayed overnight in these compounds (having first asked or evicted the owners and given them local currency to compensate them). Despite the smell, the compounds are at least secure (particularly by the time that we put various weapon systems and sentries on the roof). We assessed that the majority of the locals that we met were Taliban sympathisers (or just plain Taliban?) hence were not terribly hospitable. One old 'grey-beard' explained that he last saw foreign soldiers when the Soviets were here in the eighties.

The weather was bizarre; although the days were really heating up (about 35 degrees) we suffered two incredible storms. The first was a hail storm of almost bruising proportions and the second involved some sudden high-winds and driving rain. It was as bad as anything I have experienced in Sennybridge or Salisbury Plain; we were not really dressed for it. None of the boys had kit for this sort of weather (we only have space or, more realistically, the strength to carry 'essential kit'; batteries, radios, water, ammunition etc – the weight is crippling); we found ourselves shivering through a pretty cold night. That night I was busy and managed only a couple of hours sleep; I was cold enough to be persuaded to use a likely flea-infested and mal-odorous Afghan blanket.

Although the 'atmospherics' were pretty hostile in the village and it was clear that the Taliban were manoeuvring to try to hit us, there were no fire-fights. We had after all, turned-up 'mob-handed'. This particular village is in the middle of the desert and has a population of about 300.

The Taliban are pretty well organised; we found a Taliban medical facility complete with stores of saline, antibiotics and adrenaline (all packaged and from Pakistan we think), a cache of various munitions, bomb making components and also assorted documents of intelligence value.

It was a relief to get this first operation under our belt. It bodes well for what is bound to be a busy summer.

Op TYRUNA 1A – First Foot on the Ground – Lieutenant Rob Colquhuoun (26), from the Isle of Skye, 2 Platoon, Alpha (Grenadier) Company

At last there is no more time to prepare and I have no choice but to accept that we are ready. As we move down to the flight line to get on the waiting Chinooks I know my guys know what they'll be doing; I just hope that I do too. Will I cope if things start to go wrong? Will I be what I want to be or fail myself and them? I smile and calm myself knowing that I'm as ready as I'll ever be and this is why I've been training for the best part of 2 years; possibly much longer. It's still strange to think that I'll be telling people to load their rifles with rounds intended for live targets, telling people to risk their lives on the basis of my decisions. I hope it doesn't come to that. I'm getting ahead of myself. Need to think about one thing at a time. As I look round at the faces of the nearest Jocks I realise all eyes are on me, with looks of nervous excitement seeking reassurance from my composure. I give a look of confident, steely determination (I think) before I do something I've not done in a long time and say the words of the Black Watch Collect.

The Chinooks touch down with a thump that almost knocks the standing Jocks off their feet and as the ramp goes down the pressure releases and the Jocks pour out into the dust cloud on the ground. As soon as I have checked our location we set off, positioning ourselves as I had briefed on to the target compounds and before I know it all my fears

Lt Rob Colquhoun – 2Pl Comd – on arrival back at KAF after his first Op, (Maj G Shaw)

have subsided. Corporal Welshman breaks into the first compound, I move forward, snipers onto the roof, signaller establishes communications, Corporal Boila stacks up by the second compound while Corporal Koro covers our flanks. We roll through the village clearing many compounds, searching for weapons caches while always poised to deal with what happens when it happens.

As the dawn continues to brighten the sky, I start to become aware of the simplistic beauty of this landscape. The stark and jagged mountains in the distance, rolling desert slopes of hills nearby and the basic mud-built compounds of the Afghans nestling together on the edge of their green fields of grapes and poppy. The people themselves are intimidated by our arrival but we reassure them through our behaviour and the use of an interpreter and local Police Agent. They stare at us wide eyed with a shy curiosity I suppose to be a combination of fear and wonder. I wonder what it'd be like if foreign soldiers swooped on my village back home.

The Jocks are earning their money with a dedication and professionalism they never showed in training. The metal detectors swing, the Jocks rummage and the search dog scampers about on the scent of a conviction: the search is thorough and no stone is left unturned. As the sun rises further though the weight of the kit becomes more and more debilitating. We're all carrying well over 100lbs of body armour and kit, and young Private Stevens only weighs 120lbs after a good meal. We have to stop to rest the backs and eat some breakfast before going on so we find another high walled compound, set out sentries and relax. It's only 8 o'clock.

As the day goes on no shot is fired, but I have an uncanny feeling that someone is watching. In the afternoon despite the heat of the morning and against all the odds it starts to hail! Hailstones the size of soft mints pelt us from on high and the temperature plummets. We rush to find shelter and stand under the porch of a bemused Afghan farmer. Despite the cultural and language barrier we still manage to laugh about the weather. We continue the search and man a cordon for a helicopter resupply. By the time dusk turns to night my back and shoulders are screaming from the weight and my blistered feet are now soaked through as well. I can barely keep my eyes open long enough to eat my dinner.

After another full day's searching we fly back to Camp ROBERTS just before dusk, jealous of another platoon unearthing mortars and anti-personnel mines. Despite our lack of finds I'm glad for the 'run out' and glad nothing serious has happened. The guys have performed excellently and kept their sense of humour through 2 long days. The training has paid off and they grafted hard. We will need to look at what we ask the guys to do in the heat under all that weight on future ops, but at least we can do that more familiar with the environment we'll be working in having already achieved our first foot on the ground.

Members of the Mortar Platoon – the man on the left is carrying an 81mm Mortar Barrel in one hand and a "greeney" in the other, a greeney is simply 2 mortar rounds held together in a green, plastic container. (Maj G Shaw)

Cpl Shelly Pardoe, Royal Signals, glad to be back after the 1st outing.
(Maj G Shaw)

Op TYRUNA 1A – Personal Account – Private Aaron Black (20), from Blairgowrie, 2 Platoon, Alpha (Grenadier) Company

We arrived in Afghanistan at the end of March 09 excited about the role our Battle Group was about to undertake for Op HERRICK 10. The aviation assault aspect was new to all of us. The prospect of running off the back of a Chinook into the darkness, possibly under fire, was nerve racking as well as exciting!

After briefs from NCOs from the Royal Marines, who had just completed their successful tour, and rehearsals up at the flight-line using the choppers, Alpha (Grenadier) Company were ready to deploy on their first operation, Op TYRUNA 1A.

It's hard to describe the feeling when you are down at the Chinooks waiting for 'wheels up'. A lot of the lads sat around chatting about what lay ahead of them. A few preferred to sit with their own thoughts and listen to their iPods. I was part of the latter, whilst going through a packet of 20 cigarettes in no time!

The hail storm that caught us off guard.

What we were to discover over the next 36 hours maybe wasn't what we expected or even hoped for as it turned out not everywhere in Afghanistan was overrun with anti-ISAF insurgents. A few of the lads even claimed that this was the next stage in training: a better OPTAG village than the one in Stanford, Norfolk. The op was a good way to hone our skills and get used to the massive burden that is the weight we have to carry around with us. If anything it eased us into a tour that was going to be more physically and mentally challenging than anything we had ever done before.

Op TYRUNA 1A – Personal Account – Private Graham Johnson (22), a Territorial Army soldier from Inverness, Mortar Platoon, Charlie Company

The most difficult part of an op both mentally and physically is getting to the airhead. Hauling yourself and your fully loaded kit on and off a variety of transport until you are in your chalk awaiting to load your chopper is in itself a minor feat of human endurance. Feeding your body with fluids as it sweats in an effort to stave off dehydration even before you arrive at the landing site (LS); fighting the tiredness that tries to take over you at those hours in the morning no matter how much rest you have had; toiling to keep your body in as a comfortable position as possible while resisting the natural sickness that builds within you as you are swayed and shaken in the cramped confines of the Chinook, in semi-darkness. I remember on the first flight we were filling all the seats and the floor space available right up to the ramp. For all these reasons it was perhaps not surprising that one member of the FSG had an attack/fit of some sort on this first insertion.

LSs can be confusing, everyone attending to radios/ECM/kit, taking up fire positions, orientating themselves to the ground, confirming if the choppers have dropped you off at the correct grid or not, under-slung loads coming in — all the while aware of the possibility of becoming caught up in a contact. I remember thinking on that first LS — it was exactly as we had been briefed; whilst much of Afghanistan might look the same, every LS was unique and often looked very different from that you are expecting even given the aerial and satellite imagery. As organisation began to take shape, it was both cold and the air damp and then something else became noticeable. As we prepared to move off it struck me what it was…. something familiar, to hill walking, to home… sheep. Turning to a friend from 7 SCOTS originating from Stornoway he concurred. Sure enough as daylight grew we observed the droppings of many small beasts and then as the op continued we watched the workings of shepherd boys and men walking their assortment of sheep and goats about their course. Such was the rural scene and the relative green growth clinging to the stony ground.

The op itself was a success but taught us many things including not underestimating the weather in Afghanistan; living in Inverness, and training at Fort George, Otterburn, Sennybridge et al I try not to underestimate the weather and consider myself well practiced in not doing so. On the morning of the first day, it began to warm up, and at the altitude we quickly began to wither in the strength of the sun and the increasing temperature. Then a wind picked up and after turning overcast, storm clouds on the distant mountain range were visible. What followed for a couple of hours was light rain, turning to heavy rain, turning to hale. Hale of a normal proportion turned to hale the size of golf balls. We had no shelter from the sun and its debilitating effects, and now we had even less protection from this onslaught of a frozen hell. Those that had wet/warm kit shared it out between detachments. The landscape turned into a wintry Christmas scene — no wonder we did all our build up training in the snow storms of February/March. Sited in a shallow piece of dead ground between two hills for best defence, worse was to come. The surface water/ice mix headed down stream by its natural course — straight through our position, running through more than one of our base plate locations. We struggled to keep the water away from our kit and from keeping the kit from being washed away completely.

A cold night was followed by a few hours of sunshine sufficient to thaw and dry out — only for the weather cycle to repeat itself.

I remember the extraction as being the stuff of Commando action comics. Always glad to be leaving the ground and your safety transferred into the hands of the Chinook pilots. As the airframes hovered over us I was amazed — amidst all the noise, dust and being pelted with stones flung up from the downdraught — that 3 such craft could land so close, the pilots do an admirable job overlapping rotors. Returning over a number of mountain ranges, clinging to the sides of the mountains before skimming the ridges and hurtling down the other side was my single most memorable moment. To see the accompanying Chinooks travelling at such amazing angles and speeds only heightened the experience.

Operation SARAK 1

21–25 April 2009

INTRODUCTION

Operation SARAK I was the first Battle Group level aviation assault conducted by the 3 SCOTS Battle Group. Like Operation TYRUNA IA, Operation SARAK I was situated in Task Force Kandahar's area of operation and along the Arghandab River. The Battle Group was given the mission to interdict insurgents in the region of Band-E Timor in order to increase security along Highway I (the main southern highway that connects Gereshk with Kandahar City and Kabul). Intelligence reports indicated that Band-E-Timor was an area in which insurgents enjoyed freedom of movement and exercised a shadow government. Also, the region was believed to be one of the principal narcotic transit nodes between Kandahar, Helmand and Pakistan. At the time of the operation, the poppy cultivation was at its peak and there were numerous Kuchi nomads employed to harvest the fields.

The operation was supported by a troop of mechanized armoured Vikings, manned by the Royal Marines Armoured Support Company, which transported the Mortar Platoon. Prior to D Day, the Viking Troop established a laager north of the area in order to conduct a ground link up with the remainder of the Battle Group on D Day.

A Viking Troop from the Royal Marines Armoured Support Companies drove from Camp BASTION to link up with the BG on the ground. (MOD – Sgt C Halton)

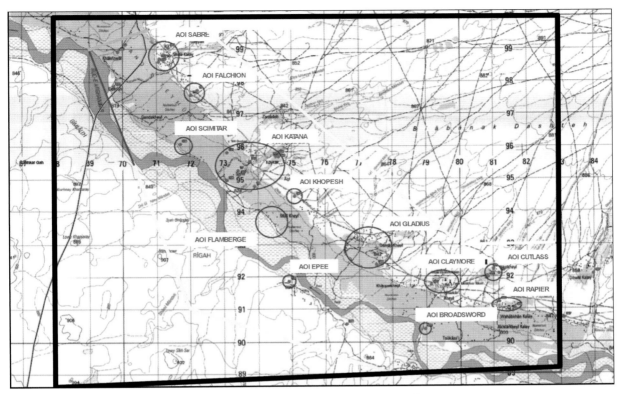

The map for Op SARAK 1. The map shows the AoI – Areas of Interest.

EXECUTION

21 April 09 (D Day)

The operation began with the lead elements of Alpha Company touching down at 0300 hrs and the Viking Troop, loaded with the Mortar Platoon, moving from its laager north of Band-E-Timor. By 0400 hrs, Alpha Company was complete on the ground and Bravo Company likewise complete by 0440 hrs. Alpha Company moved on to its objective of the village of Zarzadeh and Bravo Company patrolled into the village of Koykak. On Bravo Company's insertion Apache helicopters observed a number of *squirters* (suspect individuals) running from the compounds. It was believed that these *squirters* could be insurgents, however, engagement with local nationals suggested that they were simply individuals who were frightened by the helicopters. Both Alpha and Bravo Companies searched through the compounds in their areas of responsibility and the pattern of life of the local nationals remained friendly. Early in the day, Bravo Company uncovered 4 grenades and a small amount of drugs.

22 – 23 April 09 (D+1 – D+2 Day)

Both Alpha and Bravo Company continued compound searches in their areas of responsibility and established company locations in the close vicinity of Objective GREENIE. Objective GREENIE was initially secured by the Viking Troop and occupied by the Mortar Platoon and in turn became the resupply location for all the troops on the ground.

The following day, the Royal Engineer Search Team conducted a thorough search of a compound after the discovery of a Russian grenade and commercial detonator as well as a small bag of wet opium. The medic, Lance Corporal Vorster provided first aid to a number of injured workers and Bravo Company was thereby able to engage with local nationals in a non threatening way.

24 – 25 April 09 (D+3 – D+4)

In the early hours, the Reconnaissance Platoon led Bravo Company to their target area while Alpha Company pushed west of Objective GREENIE to conduct searches of compounds. Soldiers from the Afghan National Army attached to Alpha Company found 2 pressure plates. Both companies returned to Objective GREENIE. Extraction of troops began at 0730 hrs on the 25 April and the Battle Group was complete back in KAF by 1030 hrs.

SUMMARY

Operation SARAK 1 provided the Battle Group with an excellent opportunity to refine its role as an aviation assault Battle Group. The Battle Group was well received by local nationals and the positive influence in the area caused local elders to prevent any insurgent engagement of ISAF forces.

LCpl Jurica Vorster, from South Africa, RAMC speaks to a local national woman – female soldiers like LCpl Vorster were trained to be female searchers as well as their primary job. (MOD – Sgt C Halton)

Two soldiers carry out a detailed search of a motorbike – the insurgents used motorbikes a great deal, either to gain intelligence on our movements or to move IEDs. (MOD – Sgt C Halton)

A shura – shuras are like council meetings only they happen at all social or political levels. By attending shuras we could identify and better understand the local nationals' needs and show them that we were committed to helping them. (MOD – Sgt C Halton)

Capt Ian Bunce – the BG Non Kinetic Effects Team Officer speaks to a local national. (MOD – Sgt C Halton)

A US Black Hawk – call sign "Shocker" landing on an emergency HLS and evacuating a heat casualty to be flown back to KAF. Our predecessors, 42 Cdo, spoke very highly of Shocker who were later relieved by the "Pedro" call signs. The Pedro call signs also extracted casualties from anywhere, even during the fiercest of fire fights. (MOD – Sgt C Halton)

Although some minor finds were made, the lack of significant finds indicated the transitory nature of insurgent presence in Band-E Timor. Nonetheless, post mission reports suggested an effective dislocation and disruption of insurgents in the region.

Op SARAK 1 – Initial Run Out – Major Al Steele (33), Officer Commanding Bravo Company

The company's first operation was aborted in the air so it was with great relief when we approached our helicopter landing site even given the particularly unsociable hour. It was a strange feeling immediately prior to landing; a healthy mix of excitement and anxiety that focuses the mind. Excitement about the mission with an acute desire to escape the confines of the musky helicopter rammed full of men and equipment. Anxiety about exactly what, if anything, was going to 'greet' us on the ground at our most vulnerable and whether we would be dropped off in the right place. With 2 minutes to go we heaved up the soldiers who were sitting in the centre aisle, turned on the night sights attached to our helmets and checked our handheld GPS. We touched down and within 30-40 seconds were on terra firma. The helicopters lifted off, leaving us a parting gift of dust that coated us from head to toe. We then had only a couple of minutes to orientate ourselves and try to regroup the 200 or so men who, by now, were scattered across the landing site.

I pulled my command team together and headed off to a group 100 m to my right; it was

Members of Bravo Company sorting out their re-supply.
(MOD – Sgt C Halton)

pitch black. Frustratingly I discovered that it is the other company and the helicopter had dropped me 800 m from my own! This is unusual as the pilots are excellent, but it does happen. We got moving quickly to link up, the speed of the march getting rid of some of our nervous energy. I passed the other Company Commander en route who had been dropped off at my location! Then, with minimal fuss we linked up with the remainder of the company.

By now it was beginning to get light and despite having pored over air photography it is only now that we were able to get a feel for the land. Afghanistan is a truly medieval place. We were in a rural area where it was believed insurgents transited and mounted attacks. The locals, mostly tenant farmers bound by feudal and tribal law, were stuck in the middle. Unable to commit to ISAF, because we don't have the capacity to provide them permanent security, they hedged their bets. This has always been the Afghan way and power has regularly changed hands throughout centuries past. The rural landscape is split between the green zone and dasht (desert). The former extends out from the major river systems and is sustained by an intricate latticework of irrigation. Karezs, deep underground streams, provide the main flow of water from which smaller channels run. Developed over centuries these are visible at ground level by

Sgt Ian Carlisle taking a knee – Sgt Carlisle was Bravo Company's FAC. Forward Air Controllers were trained in talking to pilots of all air frames of all nationalities. They could ground command re-supply CH47s, Black Hawk casualty evacuations or even fast jet strafing runs. (MOD – Sgt C Halton)

A rifle platoon moves into an Afghan Compound with the Viking Troop providing cover.
(MOD – Sgt C Halton)

huge wells every 50 or so metres that can go on for kilometres. Generally 5-6 m across and up 10-15 m deep they need to be seen to be believed. Within the green zone poppies and wheat fields are broken only by the occasional compound or hamlet. The compounds vary in size but common to all are the thick sun baked walls usually 3-4 m in height. Inside, the more affluent will have several basic buildings, crops, a water pump and a whole host of animals. Most aren't this fortunate. The interface between the green zone and the dasht is stark. Vegetation is stopped in its tracks giving way to a vast expanse of nothingness.

We surrounded the compounds that were of specific interest to us and positioned the rest of the company. Within this I included a platoon of Afghan National Army (ANA), essential to the work we do. Most of their commanders were schooled in the eighties by either fighting for the Mujahedeen or against them in the Soviet Army. While not as capable in modern military terms the ANA are good. They immediately gain local consent, spot changing atmospherics and are fiercely brave. There are similarities to our soldiers too. If given a boring task they tend to do it badly! I tend to push them up front to talk to the locals and reassure them of our intentions.

They remain at times unpredictable. At one point during this operation I heard a burst of gunfire too close for comfort. As I gingerly peered around the corner I saw the ANA platoon commander chastising one of his men who had fired at a local dog that was moving towards him. Before casting judgment you should understand that 'dog' is misleading. These beasts would be front page news if seen on Bodmin moor and are very aggressive. Besides, the soldier had missed and the dog thought better of his advance and skulked off!

On another occasion I was about to begin a night march when the ANA Commander explained his men were too weak to continue. On close inspection I discovered that the halal rations we had provided them with weren't going down well. The only solution I could find was to buy them a goat that they butchered right in front of one of my sentry positions, much to the young Jock's amusement. The impact was immediate and morale soared.

Once we had secured the main compound and searched through it, we discovered a number of minor items of interest but nothing significant to speak of. The insurgents had melted away, although remained close by and watching our every move.

Once we had got the measure of the atmospherics and I was happy that we were secure, our priority was to engage with the locals to try gain a better understanding of their needs, the area, and the insurgents movements. This is generally done either ad hoc with the ANA and my Intelligence Officer or in a more deliberate fashion establishing a shura where all the local leaders gather and we address them centrally.

Patrolling is hard in Afghanistan. Moving through the poppy fields can be slightly unnerving. If you step on the poppy heads they make a loud popping noise akin to rifle fire and as you emerge from the fields your clothing is stained black with opium resin – I dread the day when I go into the Jocks tents to see them licking their trousers!!!! As you have heard the kit is debilitating heavy, the ground is tough and climate unimaginably hot (it was now 45 degrees at the hottest part of the day). Sometimes we rested up during these times and moved long distances at night to avoid the insurgents prying eyes; although this was not always the case as any pattern setting could be fatal.

The environment does take its toll. On this 6 day operation we lost 7 soldiers; 4 to back injuries, one with ripped ligaments and 2 to the heat. Three of these were sent back to the UK but the others were soon fine. What was heartening to see was the superb nature of the medical services. A helicopter was on hand within 15 minutes to extract my serious casualties, landing no more than 5 m from me!

I should mention a little about where we stayed at night. Sometimes I would select a compound, preferably one that is easy to defend, and we ask the owner if he would let us stay there. We then negotiated a fair price and prepared the defences. So far, I had only had one refusal and in that case we moved on. Only if I had no option would I insist on staying, but this makes us little better than the insurgents who regularly strong-arm the locals into doing their bidding.

A Company Group moving through a poppy field – the poppy field is lush green meaning it's ready for the opium harvest – at this time of year the insurgents were pre-occupied with the harvest ensuring their main source of income was secured. As we were an aviation BG we had the ability to flood an otherwise untouched area with troops – keeping the insurgent on his toes. (MOD – Sgt C Halton)

Op SARAK 1 – First Foot on the Ground – Lieutenant Harry Pearce (26), from Ledbury, 7 Platoon, Bravo Company

Camp ROBERTS, 17 April 09, 2250 hrs

I spent this evening having coffee with other subalterns, after which I split and took a pew in the Fraise Chapel. I've never been a habitual churchgoer nor did I feel particularly religious today but I'm still finding my way, both literally and figuratively to the new surrounds of life in Kandahar. Before this first operation, I thought I'd pinch a few quiet minutes to keep things in perspective. Thoughts of home and the last awesome days spent in Edinburgh seemed only to be interrupted by the whistling rumble of the fast jets from across the desert airfield.

I took a seat alongside Canadian soldiers, none of whom I could recognise by rank or unit. I'd better learn to save embarrassment in the next few months! We did not talk, I figured they were there for the same reason as I and of course, their first language is not mine.

Lt Harry Pearce, 7 Pl Comd, Bravo Coy, and LCpl Joe Taroga.

Dutch Restaurant, 18 April 09, 2040 hrs

In 'Fraise' I couldn't help but think about the impending op, my men's safety, and rather strangely that if I should die, well, I hope it will be quick. Is that cowardice? Why aren't I concerned with those I might leave behind? I should forget home and focus on Maywand Province for the next 5 days – that would be better for everyone.

With the initial op 'canned' I'm not sure how the Jocks feel about the next one, Op SARAK 1. They seem to have lost some of the nervous excitement that bounced off one another last week. Now it has become tense – they just want to get the first one done. The mission holds at its core the intent to disrupt insurgents on target and then understand the 'local dynamics' – quite how, when we land on their crops and enter their homes uninvited with weapons, is something I've yet to learn.

Seven Platoon will be on the BG main effort for this one – to clear and secure compound 342. I'm sure I feel the same as the Jocks; lets do the job right the first time and set the example for the remainder of our time out here. I know they'll perform…watch this space.

Camp Roberts, 20 April 09, 1945 hrs

The platoon responded well to my 2hr set of orders today. They now know they're the main effort and though clearly anxious, seem to be full of a collective confidence – one I must mirror even though I'm sitting here full of concern. I keep reminding myself that we've done all the training and the lads ARE ready. Half of them have done this before and those that haven't will be 'carried' until they find their feet. I should only be worried about myself and not living up to their expectations. Tonight, I'm hitting the sack early – ROC drills 'early doors'.

Camp ROBERTS, 21 April 09, 2315 hrs

Had a heavy lunch and even heavier supper. Might as well, could be my last! A long hot shower, facebook check, battery check and now a quick 30 mins kip before we head to the airhead.

Maywand District, 22 April 09, on and off

We inserted at 0315 hrs, in 'red illum', separate from the remainder of the company. The CH-47 'put down' on a raised bank surrounded by flooded poppy fields about 5ft high.

I led from the ramp, straining through the green/brown haze of my LUCIE goggles hoping I didn't fall. I felt relaxed but with a fear – contradiction I know. It's the reality I guess one can only understand when in those first few minutes on the ground.

This quickly turned to excitement and adrenaline when I realised we were in the correct place and everyone was orientated onto target. I could see it in the other commanders. Head check, comms check, navigation check and we were off – to the job and taking the most obscure route in order to avoid VPs and IEDS.

Once cleared up to the entry point, one ANA without prompt and knowing there were people hiding inside the compound, scaled the gates (alone) and opened the red metal doors from the inside. They surged in as a single 'gaggle'. The locals were squatting, self-segregated, staring back, motionless. It was then I realised – they are terrified of us. They know nothing of our intent, our technology and our ability. I find their intensity unnerving and earlier asked a Jock to move them out of sight of the Jocks.

I kept forgetting today; the attached ANA are on home soil and probably well accustomed to this – I should ask them about their experiences, I should have already done it.

A CH47 Chinook helicopter re-supplying the troops on the ground. We relied heavily on the RAF CH47s which risked a great deal to bring in the vital life support to the BG. (MOD – Sgt C Halton)

The Jocks did well today. They searched for several hours, through the main house, the budding fields, and into what can only be described as a subterranean home. The main finds included; grenades, peroxide, various bits of ammunition as well as wet opium. It has given us some invaluable 'hands-on' experience. The Jocks seemed keen anyway.

When the RMP had finished I took a look. The opium smells unlike anything comparable to everyday life at home. It has a sticky consistency and the look of marmite (with lumps). As it's poppy harvest, they are 'scraping' the heads with scalpels to weep the seeds. The resulting 'sap' gets everywhere. My kit, including rather oddly my headset, is covered in it.

Time to check sentries, confirm the next play with the OC and get some sleep before our resupply.

Maywand District, 23 April 09, on and off

It's like a great British summer at the moment (weather wise) – though today was quite tough for the ECM Jocks. The nights are freezing – quite unexpected. I haven't come prepared at all. Neither have the Jocks. Something I must change for the next one, a warm 'Buffalo' jacket or something, at least for a while.

We tabbed through poppy fields, across desert, through a dry wadi and into another village – all before the sun had risen. En route 2 of the Jocks injured their Achilles tendons, another suffered heat exhaustion and another lost a night sight. Rather selfishly, none in my platoon so I'm slightly relieved but nevertheless not good for the company.

SHOCKER airframes CASEVAC'd the Jocks this morning. The pilots filled the Jocks with confidence when they landed in a clearing no more than 40m sq in order to save our own exposure to the flanks. I'd agree – they're excellent. Unfortunately we got a back full of stones and fine dust that grates on your skin with the weight of the OSPREY.

This afternoon, while clearing the final 3 buildings, one of my ANA was attacked by a 'lion-sized' dog. He unleashed his rusty weapon hitting it in its hind legs. I'm amazed it did anything,

2 CH47s and a CH 53 Super Stallion coming into the HLS on purple smoke to pick up one of the companies. (Lt E Gorrie)

the state it was in – the weapon that is, not the dog. This so angered his commander, the perpetrators rifle was removed and he was subsequently beaten with it. Bit harsh perhaps but he'll probably go for a rock in future. Better for the IO campaign that way. Noted by Jocks.

I asked our medic if she wouldn't mind looking at the owner's ailments, just to pacify them. A dose of something or other was handed across. All was well in the end.

Maywand District, 25 April 09, 2245 hrs

From the 'dead dog village' we crossed incredible expanses of yellow moon surface cut with green strips of fertile irrigation. All this was set to a jagged mountain backdrop, which I'm certain, would be able to attract swathes of tourists, save for the landmines and Taliban.

The Jocks are already settling into routine. It helps that every local we've met is exceptionally friendly – far more than many from home. The Jocks have used some of their famous humour to keep the kids entertained. Rations have been handed out.

Sitting here on the HLS, freezing again, the end feels like a lifetime away. It's going to be a tough ride and contact has yet to hit us but I know the Jocks are full of confidence having experienced the fundamentals. We'll ride on that for as long as we can…

Lance Corporal Gary Richford (28), from Glasgow, 6 Platoon, B Company

My girlfriend has just had a wee boy so at first it was a bit of a shock when I found out I was coming here and I was a bit scared about it. But the closer the time came to coming out, the more excited I got. And now that I'm here I just want to get into my Platoon and get out there. I want to get to know my section and bond with them. I'm hoping to do that today actually, I just need to catch up with my Platoon Sergeant to get myself a bed space and get moved in. I miss my wee boy, my wee star.

Chapter Two

Operation SARAK 3

5–15 May 2009

INTRODUCTION

Following numerous IED strikes along Highway 1 (Afghanistan's national ring road), Route 601 (the road leading to Lashkar Gah and connected at the Durai Junction), and the Nahr E Saraj region, Operation SARAK 3 was designed to thwart such threats to local nationals and ISAF troops. Analysis of the nature of IEDs indicated that many were hidden inside the culverts along these routes. The Battle Group was given the task to dominate the region and enable the Joint Force Engineers to fill numerous culverts along Highway 1 and Route 601. In addition, the Battle Group was to be prepared to conduct further operations in the area following strong leads that may be gathered during the initial period.

The initial plan was to insert Alpha and Bravo Companies through an aviation assault into Objectives CHALK and SLATE respectively, close to the city of Gereshk. Once the companies were established on the ground, the Mortar Platoon in Viking armoured vehicles and the Fire Support Group, mounted in Jackals, would conduct a ground link up. After completion of activity in SLATE and CHALK, the companies would subsequently be moved east towards the Durai Junction and into Objectives QUARTZ and ROCK. As the Battle Group was operating in the Danish area of operation, Vidar Company, a mechanised Danish company, was tasked to the Battle Group. TAC HQ would be located in FOB PRICE, the Headquarters of the Danish Battle Group, but had the ability to deploy in Jackal and WMIK. Finally, the Battle Group was supported by French Mirage jets, American and Canadian helicopters and light guns from 38 Battery, 40 Royal Artillery.

During the operation, the Brigade Reconnaissance Force was conducting its own operation in Objective DINGLE close to the Battle Group. From the intelligence gathered during this operation, the Battle Group received a further task to strike into Objective DINGLE in order to neutralise the IED threat posed by insurgents from that area. As a result, there were 2 distinct phases to Operation SARAK 3. The focus of the first phase, Operation

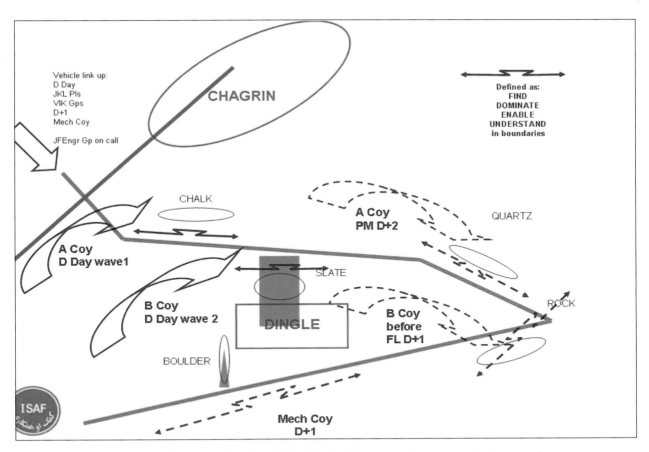

Vehicle link up:
D Day
JKL Pls
VIK Gps
D+1
Mech Coy

JFEngr Gp on call

CHAGRIN

Defined as:
FIND
DOMINATE
ENABLE
UNDERSTAND
in boundaries

CHALK

A Coy
PM D+2

QUARTZ

A Coy
D Day wave1

SLATE

B Coy
D Day wave 2

DINGLE

B Coy
before
FL D+1

ROCK

BOULDER

Mech Coy
D+1

ISAF

The operation schematic for Op SARAK 3. The dotted arrows indicate subsequent aviation novements later in the operation.

SARAK 3A, became the engineer work and the domination of Highway 1, Route 601, and the Durai Junction. The focus of the second phase, Operation SARAK 3B, was the strike into Objective DINGLE.

OPERATION SARAK 3A – EXECUTION

5 May 09 (D Day)

At 0430 hrs the first elements of Alpha Company landed into HLS RANGERS and began the initial stages of controlling traffic, occupying an ANP station and linking up with the Viking Troop and Jackal Group. At 0700 hrs, Bravo Company was likewise established in Objective CHALK. Vidar Company also took up positions in Objective BOULDER. Early in the day, Alpha Company found a number of weapons, ammunition, grenades, anti-personnel mines and other IED material. At 0917 hrs, Bravo Company came under contact from small arms fire (SAF) and RPG close to the village of Yakhchal. 6 Platoon rapidly returned fire and dominated the fight. Shortly after the contact, Bravo Company made a find of 7.5 million Afghanis equal to US$ 150,000 which was assessed to be the sum total of the insurgent tax on the local nationals. Throughout the day, Bravo Company remained in contact and fired a Javelin missile at a suspected insurgent mortar base plate. At 1430 hrs, Sergeant Robertson,

The RSM describes the model at a BG ROC Drill – a ROC Drill is where a unit can rehearse different situations that might arise on the ground, like casualty evacuation, by moving small rocks (denoting sub units) around a model of the area of Operations. (Maj G Shaw)

6 Platoon Sergeant, was injured in the arm from small arms fire and was evacuated to Camp BASTION within an hour. It was believed that insurgents were reinforcing the area from Objective DINGLE. By 1630 hrs, insurgent activity had decreased with one further contact at 1830 hrs; Bravo Company assessed that 3 insurgents had been killed during the day. Despite Bravo Company's engagement, Alpha Company found the atmosphere relatively benign and was able to bring Joint Force Engineers to their location in the early evening. By 1830 hrs, work began on the culverts in Objective CHALK.

6 May 09 (D+1)

In contrast to D Day, 6 May proved to be quiet in both Objective CHALK and SLATE. Alpha Company maintained overwatch in Objective CHALK which allowed the engineers to continue their work on 2 culverts. Bravo Company conducted numerous patrols in Objective SLATE and the Military Stabilisation Support Team (MSST) was able to conduct shuras with local elders. Atmospherics proved to be much more positive than the previous day. Throughout the day, intelligence suggested that insurgents were grouped in Objective DINGLE, however, insurgent action was tempered by overmatch by the Battle Group. Parallel to the activities of the Battle Group, the Brigade Reconnaissance Force inserted to the south of Objective DINGLE and quickly came under contact.

7 May 09 (D+2)

In the early period of the morning, Bravo Company moved to Objective ROCK and conducted a shura with local elders. Although local atmospherics were positive in the area, troops mounted in Jackal indicated a negative reaction further east of the Durai Junction. Local elders and ANP indicated that there was an insurgent stronghold in that area. Joint Force Engineers completed their work in Objective CHALK and Alpha Company inserted into Objective QUARTZ. The Brigade Reconnaissance Force was positioned to the west of Objective DINGLE and continued to be targeted by insurgents. The Vidar Company completed culvert assessments in Objective BOULDER. At 1741 hrs, a suicide bomber detonated a bomb in the vicinity of the Gereshk hospital. A platoon from Vidar Company was tasked to provide security to the hospital. FOB PRICE became the centre of triage for many of the casualties and the Regimental Sergeant Major and other members of the Battle Group assisted the Danish medical staff late into the evening.

8 May 09 (D+3)

Following the suicide bomb the day before, Task Force Helmand imposed a patrol minimize that was not lifted until 0830 hrs. At 0930 hrs, Alpha Company began to patrol Objective QUARTZ and Bravo Company was likewise operating in Objective ROCK. Intelligence from Objective QUARTZ suggested insurgents were observing Alpha Company and also indicated a strong possibility of an imminent attack. Atmospherics in the objective also declined significantly. However, Objective ROCK remained benign throughout the day. At 1830 hrs, Alpha Company was contacted by 2 rounds of indirect fire but did not suffer any casualties.

A ROC drill: The CO (far right) listens to Maj Matt Munro describe Alpha (Grenadier) Company's action on the HLS. (Maj G Shaw)

Members of Bravo
Company lend a
helping hand to a
local national after
he'd ended up in a
ditch. (Lt E Gorrie)

Lt Andy Wallace (A
Coy's IO) talks to
members of the
Afghan National
Police.

A platoon establish themselves in a compound for an overnight stay.

9 May 09 (D+4)

Atmospherics in the area remained reasonably good during the day. Alpha Company began searching its first compound at 0718 hrs. The company spent the remainder of the morning searching compounds and talking to local nationals. Bravo Company moved overnight and at 0518 hrs began searches of compounds and gained an understanding of the area through local nationals. The companies were extracted by Chinook helicopters to BASTION and the Viking Troop and Jackal Group returned to FOB PRICE.

SUMMARY

The response to the Battle Group's activities along Highway 1 and Route 601 was varied. The only manifestation of insurgent threat was seen in Yakchal village which resulted in a robust insurgent reaction through the use of small arms, RPG, and indirect fire on D Day. Prior to the operation, Yakchal area was assessed to be an insurgent command and control node with an emphasis on IED facilitation with a concentration in Objective DINGLE. Brigade Reconnaissance Force probes identified the presence of disciplined and well trained insurgents, including foreign fighters in the western and central area of Objective DINGLE. From this assessment and the completion of all engineering tasks and domination of Highway 1, Route 601, and the Durai Junction, the Battle Group regrouped in BASTION in order to initiate Operation SARAK 3B and strike into Objective DINGLE.

A CH47 drops off another 24 hour re-supply for Alpha (Grenadier) Company.

OPERATION SARAK 3B – EXECUTION

13 May 09 (D Day)

Battle Group Tactical HQ (TAC), mounted in WMIK and Jackal, inserted early in the morning and took up a position in the dasht to the north of Objective DINGLE. Alpha Company and Bravo Company inserted by helicopter and were established in their objectives, RUBY and JADE, by 0330 hrs. The Brigade Reconnaissance Force deployed to the east of the area and Vidar Company secured the southern flank. Afghan National Directorate of Security (NDS) agents interviewed local nationals who were found in Bravo Company's area but revealed little of significance. Both companies completed searches of their objective areas. At 1830 hrs, the Brigade Reconnaissance Force on the eastern flank was contacted by small arms and RPG. Shortly after at 1850 hrs, Alpha and Bravo Company came under fire. By 1930 hrs, the insurgents had broken the contact.

14 – 15 May 09 (D+1 – D+2)

Before first light both companies repositioned in Objective DINGLE. Alpha company searched compounds in the north while Bravo Company moved to the south. Finds of communication equipment and weapons were destroyed with a small amount held for evidence. The mobile elements of the Battle Group, the Viking Troop and TAC, extracted from the area at 2300 hrs. The companies first starting extracting from the area by helicopter at 0515 hrs on 15 May, and all elements of the Battle Group were complete by 0643 hrs.

SUMMARY

The insertion of the Battle Group into Objective DINGLE achieved tactical surprise. The concurrent move of the Brigade Reconnaissance Force along the canal to the east of the target locations coupled with the Danish Mechanized Company move along Highway 1 was assessed to have had the desired affect and dislocated the insurgents. Intelligence sources indicated that the insurgents were not prepared for a strike into their safe area. Although atmospherics during the day were relatively benign, intelligence indicated an insurgent presence who sought to rebalance its forces and engage the Battle Group. The last light attacks on both companies, as well as the Brigade Reconnaissance Force, demonstrated the manifestation of this threat and reinforced the assessment that the insurgent force in the area was well led and a coordinated one.

OPERATION SARAK 3 SUMMARY

The principal achievement of Operation SARAK 3 in terms of intelligence was the increased situational awareness in Nahr E Sarah region, especially in vicinity of Highway 1, Route 601, and the Durai Junction. The operation can be assessed to have created uncertainty in the mind of the insurgent to the ability of coalition forces to reach into insurgent safe areas.

In terms of the experience, Operation SARAK 3 was the first time the Battle Group directly engaged and fought insurgents. For many of the young soldiers, it was the first time that they had fired their weapons and experienced the highs and lows of battle. Operation SARAK 3 was also the first operation in which the Battle Group incurred a significant casualty. Although the injury was critical, it was nonetheless reassuring for all the members of the Battle Group to know that the medical chain worked, and the casualty had been evacuated

Members of Alpha (Grenadier) Company exhausted in the midday heat between ops. (MOD – Sgt C Halton)

to an operating room in less than hour. With the loss of Sergeant Robertson in a key role, Sergeant Buist, formally of the Javelin Platoon, seamlessly took over as 6 Platoon Sergeant.

During the deployment of Operation SARAK 3A, Sergeant Sean Binnie, who was a member of Delta Company and operating as a mentor with the Afghan National Army, was killed in action. During a battle in Musa Qal'ah, Sergeant Binnie led his team to close with the insurgents. Lance Corporal Everett was placed to provide cover for Sergeant Binnie's final advance. Sergeant Binnie went to the compound door and posted a grenade inside. In the gap between posting the grenade and its detonation, an insurgent leaned around the doorway and shot Sergeant Binnie at close range in the upper body. Sergeant Binnie managed to get back into cover around the corner of the compound where he collapsed. He was evacuated to BASTION, but died of his wounds. Sergeant Binnie was the first member of the Battalion to have died on the tour. A veteran of Northern Ireland and Iraq, Sergeant Binnie was highly admired across the Battalion.

Op SARAK 3 – First Contact with the Enemy – Major Al Steele (33), Officer Commanding Bravo Company

Again an aviation assault, again leaving in the dead of night, we were told to probe on the fringes of a known insurgent stronghold in order to try to better understand the area and disrupt his freedom of action. For this mission my Company Group numbered 218 men (and a few women), a huge organisation and well over double the size of what I would expect to have in the UK. To name but a few this included, ANA, engineers, explosive specialists, search specialists, tracked armoured troop carriers, mobile weapons vehicles (Jackals), stabilisation

Maj Al Steele, OC Bravo Company, sending a Sit Rep on the BG HF net. (MOD – Sgt C Halton)

*A model pit in the making – Bravo Company preparing for an orders group from the OC,
Maj Al Steele. (Capt Lowder)*

*Lt Gregor Mill, Bravo Company's
Intelligence Officer, looks at his
map to maintain situational
awareness. Note the scars on the
poppy heads in the foreground –
when the poppies were green like
this, they were scratched to induce
the production of their sap –
opium – which could then be
collected and either sold or turned
into heroin.*

advisors, mortars, military police, medical experts and a very hot sniffer dog called Flash! It
was real challenge to control on the ground! If that weren't enough I had, at times, 2 attack
helicopters and 2 F15s circling menacingly above.

We landed without incident. Within 10 minutes the mobile assets had linked up as
planned. There was no movement in the area at all. This is not necessarily unusual as the
arrival of 6 Chinooks, and 11 armoured vehicles does wonders to encourage people to stay
indoors. We had barely reached the fringes of the landing site before we started to pick up
small readings on our metal detectors. Nothing sinister in itself but the insurgents often
scatter metal shards to mask something more deadly.

I quickly received word that my lead section had found an improvised explosive device

(IED). The company then re-orientated to put themselves out of immediate danger and the helicopter observed from above to look for suspicious activity. As the specialists dealt with the device my platoons and armoured vehicles pushed into depth. The platoons got into a couple of abandoned compounds, put their snipers and heavy weapons onto the roofs and started filling sandbags. Only then did I push the ANA across the 200 metres of open ground to our first objective.

The attack helicopter sighted a pickup truck moving from the area about 600 m away. It was over laden with women and children; something was about to happen. Each man's senses were strained looking into likely areas we might be attacked from.

Nothing happened. The lead section was by now only 50 m from their objective, a large isolated compound. Then, in a split second, calm was replaced by chaos. Insurgent tracer fire was upon us from 3 sides, it was accurate but we were in good positions. The flanking platoons responded in kind with disciplined fire. My biggest fear – civilian casualties – was allayed by the strict fire control from my platoon commanders and their corporals. It was extraordinary how clearly one can sense the initiative, which, despite being ambushed, we still had. There was no panic in the company, just people doing what they have been trained to do.

While the initial firefight was underway the Jackals were sent south on the fringes of the dasht to try and get in behind the enemy to unhinge him. The flanking platoons suppressed

LCpl Scott Mackie's (from Crial) section, B Coy pushes forward.

Sgt Craig Weir from North Yorkshire, 7 Platoon Sergeant, Bravo Company in dead ground.

the positions while the lead platoon got into their compound. The strength of mind required to shift from being under 'contact' (enemy fire) to de-escalating should not be underestimated. The ANA and the lead platoon almost immediately came across a group of women and children cowering in one of the buildings. While the firing continued in the surrounding fields, within the compound the importance of adhering to local sensitivities remained paramount.

I discussed the situation with my stabilisation team, a mix of Danes and Brits led by a female captain. They routinely work in the main district centres with the local Afghan leadership, working alongside the FCO (Foreign and Commonwealth Office) to advise on governance and act as an interface with the military so that our efforts can be fused with Afghan priorities. On this occasion they had been attached to my company to learn about an area we knew precious little about and to ascertain how far the influence of the district centre had extended.

Sporadic firing continued. The rest of my 'tac group' (the key elements of my company headquarters) and I were now in danger of being in the wrong place. It was time to move forward. I dashed halfway across the open ground and sheltered behind a ruined compound only to be chastised by my mortar fire controller, a sergeant of considerable experience, for drawing insurgent fire! Once bitten, twice shy, I pulled the armoured vehicles forward and we walked behind them the rest of the way until we reached the safety of the compound.

The ANA had made short shrift of clearing the compound and my search platoon was able to begin their job. It was not long before they found 7¼ million Afghanis, about £140,000. This was assessed to be drug money destined for the insurgents' hands.

The radio sparked to life again. Another group of civilians had been seen leaving a group of compounds to our southeast and our intelligence also confirmed that the insurgents were reinforcing and trying to out flank us. Up until now we had received most attention from the south and west. With the armoured vehicles already watching this area the ANA were sent back across the ground they had recently come, to gain a foothold in a nearby hamlet.

Just as they were nearing the compound wall they saw a hole appear in what had been an unblemished wall. The hole was a pre-prepared ambush position that had been concealed with a thin layer of mud. The ANA came under contact. Within the blink of an eye there was a large explosion and I thought the worst - that someone had stepped on an IED. Instead, the quick thinking British ANA mentors, a sergeant and subaltern, had rushed the remaining 20 m to the wall, posted a grenade and the engineer section had explosively blown an entry point under the guidance of 5 Platoon Commander. They charged through without casualty but the insurgent had melted away again.

While all this was going on the platoon that had been in contact since the morning on the southwest had managed to give the insurgent a bloody nose but at a cost as I heard the news one of my platoon sergeants has been shot in the elbow. The casualty plan kicked in straight away, the armoured vehicles surged forward to pick him up while an emergency helicopter landing site was established. Within 30 minutes of wounding the casualty was back in the field hospital receiving treatment.

We were now in the hottest part of the day where heat could become an almost bigger threat than the insurgent. Fortunately, his appetite for fighting began to dwindle and the contacts subsided while he regrouped. The Jackals went back down the eastern flank again to try and cut-off any reinforcing or retreating enemy. They were almost immediately contacted at the same time as the Commanding Officer arrived to assess the situation. It is either a brave or foolhardy enemy that takes on 11 heavily armed vehicles. This effectively closed the contact for the day and the company began an orderly extraction a few kilometres into the dasht to establish a desert leaguer for the night.

Op SARAK 3 – First Contact: A Platoon Commanders Perspective – Lieutenant Alex Phillips (26), from Ingham, Norfolk, 5 Platoon, Bravo Company

As I looked at Collins he was rocking back and forwards . . . had I really just ordered my Jocks to fix bayonets . . . I couldn't help but smile. The rounds cracked overhead out of the compound once again, this time narrowly missing the OC and his TAC group.

I looked at Lance Corporal Taroga the section commander and asked him if he was ready. A solid, calm, simple "Aye Boss" was his response.

Wait and on my orders, when I tell you, I want you to assault the position. As I looked in the entrance to the compound to get eyes on the firing point, the ground exploded, dust was kicked up as enemy fire cut across our front.

Lance Corporal Taroga get in there, off he went with his section.

I stood holding my breath waiting for the rounds to start flying.

Silence.

What's going on? Is everything ok? The seconds drag for what seems like hours.

Lt Alex Philips, 5Pl Comd – leading from the front. (MOD – Sgt C Halton)

"POSITION CLEAR!"

What do you mean position clear? Where was the fighting? The exchange of fire? The sound of death?

The simple answer was the enemy had fled.

It wasn't long before the enemy started engaging from further afield and 6 Platoon were locked in a fierce fire fight.

Looking back 5 Platoon have been involved in many more dangerous contacts than our first but like so many things in life, it is the first one that will never be forgotten.

THE TRUTH

Every platoon commander in the Infantry wants to lead his men in battle; why else would he join the Infantry?

When talking about being in contact before one has experienced it there is an envy held by those who have not been in such a position with the question at the back of one's mind: 'Could I do that?'

Those who have experienced it are the only ones who can truly answer the question without a slight pause for self doubt.

The truth is, when that moment comes a hundred thoughts race through your mind, although you remain calm and in control, for a split second you are left stranded while you process what is going on to make a decision.

Will I stand or falter under fire, have I just sent my Jocks to their death; did I make the right decision?

Then the realisation that this is what you have been waiting for, a sense of relief washes over you as you realise you know what to do.

You can't help but smile and get caught up in the moment. The rush is unexplainable and every time it happens that thrill is there all over again. The danger is forgotten and you relish the complete unnatural experience of willingly putting yourself in harms way.

It is difficult for any one to understand and indeed explain. Only once you have experienced it can you relate to others experiences, which will, without doubt vary to your own.

Op SARAK 3 – Change of Pace – Sergeant Danny Buist (35), from Arbroath, 6 Platoon Sergeant, Bravo Company

Bravo Company had a night time insertion by Chinook, 6 Platoon complete along with my FSG section all on one Chinook. Our mission was to push to the flank by first light and be ready to move into a compound. By first light, we had found somewhere that seemed suitable for the task. The compound was about 25 m by 25 m with a $4^1/2$ foot wall around it; the walls were about $^1/2$ a foot thick and provided a good position to give protection to the Platoon.

6 Platoon had secured the area around the compound and was pushing the first section forward; my section was giving support to the flank to allow the other sections to have a clean break in. The compound that was selected had great arcs looking across open ground of about 800 m into a high-vegetated area with compounds running through it.

Once Lieutenant Halliday was happy with the clearance of the compound, he started to move the rest of the platoon in. As my FSG section started to move towards the compound, with Sergeant Robertson and myself at the rear, I heard the distinctive sound of the crack and thump of rounds firing into 6 Platoon's position and ricocheting over our heads.

To our left, enemy gunmen opened up and whilst most of my section had made it into cover with only Sergeant Robertson, Lance Corporal Green and myself were still in open ground. As we took cover, I remember looking up and seeing Private Sovui, on a small hut engaging the gunmen that allowed us to move into the cover of the compound.

I had moved into the compound picking up my FSG section and had taken up fire positions along the compound wall. I spoke to Lance Corporal Simpson who gave me a target indication onto the enemy position. To my surprise I looked over the wall and could see 3 enemy gunmen positioned in the compound 50 m to our front, the enemy were firing over their compound wall aiming at the rooftops where we had positioned our sentries. I reorganised my 3 GPMG gunners to start suppressing the enemy compound, and ordered Corporal Tod, Lance Corporal Green and Lance Corporal Simpson to start engaging with UGLs.

Lieutenant Halliday gave the order to Corporal Bruce to assault the enemy compound. Just as he was about to enter the enemy compound, grenade in hand, pin out, the door opened and an old man appeared dressed in a full white dish dash with a white turban on his head. Corporal Bruce punched in and cleared the compound finding the enemy firing points, but no enemy as they had fled the compound using the rear exit which was out of sight to our sentries.

By late morning we had already spent close to 5 hours in contact with Corporal Bruce taking the brunt of the fighting. The enemy had moved to the compounds to our front 800 m across the open ground using the drainage ditches and rooftops to engage our compounds with accurate fire from PKMs and a scoped weapon.

We used the Engineers with us to blow observation holes in the compound wall. This stopped our sentries from becoming exposed along the top of the walls. We had also placed our sharpshooters on the highest rooftop of the compound along with our MFC, Corporal Mason, to try to pinpoint the enemy firing points.

My Javelin team had spotted an enemy firing point with 2 enemy gunmen on the edge of a compound. The missile fired but failed in flight and landed to the right of the enemy in the open ground, which was a let down as it was the first missile fired.

Ten minutes later, one of the sharpshooters spotted a gunman moving into position on a rooftop approximately 800 m away, he engaged the enemy with one round at 730 m, a great shot. Minutes later another insurgent appeared on a rooftop meters away from the now dead gunman. The sharpshooter again fired and killed him, 2 great shots in a short space of time.

Within 30 minutes the enemy was back. I was standing looking for possible enemy locations with Lance Corporal Simpson when an accurate burst of fire came in our direction. The rounds passed where, seconds before, my head had been. It was only because I had turned to talk to Lance Corporal Simpson that I was not hit, we looked at each other and wee smiles broke across our faces. Another burst of fire came in just above our position this time a longer burst; we could see the tracer hitting the rooftop of the compound.

A Bravo Company Sharpshooter gets his Number 2 to laser range find a target allowing him to make the necessary elevation adjustment to his rifle sight.

Lt Andrew Halliday (right) 7 Pl Comd and Cpl Tam Mason (middle) Bravo Company's Mortar Fire Controller. Lt Halliday was wounded in action (WIA) later in the Op, Cpl Mason was later WIA on Op SPIN ARWA, also in Kandahar province, and died of his wounds. (MOD - Sgt C Halton)

Pte Daniel Durie from Livingstone, Op SPIN ARWA – kit on ready to move. (MOD - Sgt C Halton)

Then we heard it, the words no soldier ever wants to hear, "MAN DOWN". It was shouted twice more, then I saw a figure stumble off the roof and collapse by the only tree in the compound. I moved across to see who was hit and Private Yeaman was first there with his team medics pouch. As I got closer I could see it was Sergeant Robertson lying on his side holding his arm and Private Yeaman was attending to his wound.

The round had struck Sergeant Robertson just above the wrist. Private Yeaman had covered his wound and was asking Sergeant Robertson if he wanted any morphine for his pain. Sergeant Robertson replied that he did not want morphine because he was scared of needles, then we all had a laugh, it was more a laugh of relief, as we knew he would be alright

Sgt Iain Robertson from Bangor, smiling after being wounded and casevaced.

Lieutenant Halliday had already sent the 9 liner back to the Company Main run by the Company 2 I/C and the Company Sergeant Major. A Viking armoured vehicle was sent down from Company Main's location to casevac Sgt Robertson. As he had had no morphine he could walk unassisted to the Viking with me carrying his day sack. He climbed in the back, gave a wave and a thumbs up and a 'see you when you get home mate' and that was it. I was now Platoon Sergeant of a fighting platoon.

I walked back into the compound and sat beside Lieutenant Halliday. We had a quick chat about the events that had happened. He asked if I was happy to take on the Platoon Sergeant role within 6 Platoon, I said, 'yeah more than happy under the circumstances.'

Private David Clark (18), 7 Platoon, Bravo Company joined the Battalion 2 months into the tour

I knew we were going to Afghanistan when we started training which was quite good. My parents didn't want me to go but I reassured them it would be okay. The training at Catterick was more conventional war based, there was no compound clearing. We've done one week's Afghan training at OPTAG, I was apprehensive but I'm up for it like.

Op SARAK I was okay but we didn't get contacted and we wanted to find out what it was like. I had been in the Battalion 5 weeks when I first came under enemy fire. I returned fire immediately, I was a bit angry.

Private John Wynne (18), from Glasgow, 7 Platoon, Bravo Company was in training with Private Clark

I phone home each week and tell my family everything's okay, to keep them happy.

When I came under contact the training kicked in and I knew what to do straight away.

Corporal Duncan Bruce (22), from Stirling, 6 Platoon, Bravo Company

I had my camera out after the first contact – we just looked at each other and laughed. As soon as we can PID someone, we just get the rounds down. Sometimes though if one of our guys is in the open, we have to get the rounds down to cover him so he can get back into cover.

A Sharpshooter, Bravo Company

I got contacted on Op SARAK 3, there were 2 sharpshooters on the roof top, I was on the ground so I got up on the rooftop. A sharpshooter gave me a range and I asked the Platoon Commander if I could fire into the enemy. He said yes, so I took the shot, it took me a while to get my heart rate down and that, I got him through the head. My observer confirmed that for me. Corporal Bruce got contacted from the left, I seen another 2 enemy running about in the fields with AKs, I missed the first shot, the other sharpshooter put me back on again. I got 2 kills. I didn't feel guilty. It's shoot or be shot. It's us or them.

A Sharpshooter, Bravo Company

Basically I came under contact and I fired a couple of warning shots, the other sharpshooter positively identified him for me. The kit that we've got to help us, the Laser Range finders, you just push a button and that's the range. It's a gleaming bit of kit.

Op SARAK 3 – Mass Casualties at FOB PRICE – Private Davy Gow (21), from Dundee, Combat Medical Technician, Mortar Platoon, Charlie Company

For a couple of months the Mortars were based at Camp BASTION from where they had been and were conducting ops in Vikings. After an op we had been tasked to stay at FOB PRICE for a number of days as moving back to Camp BASTION was unfeasible.

During one of the days at FOB PRICE we had some down time, and were chilling out on the internet, when there was an announcement over the tannoy stating that all medical personnel had to report to the Naafi. Upon arriving there I immediately realised that there was something major occurring due to the expression on the doctors face. I was sent straight to the med centre once I told him what qualifications I had.

On arriving at the med centre, I was given a brief from a captain. He informed me that there had been 2 suicide bombings in Geresk, one of which was at the entrance to a hospital and one at an ANP check point, which I later found out had just missed our BRF. It was believed that there was going to be approximately 20 to 30 casualties.

Within a couple of minutes the casualties started arriving by any means possible. Most of them arrived on the back of lorries or trucks, or in the back or cars, one of them even arrived on the front of a motorbike.

My job was to try and keep the casualties alive before they went into the med centre and that they were then seen by the doctor for more advanced treatment. When the casualties started arriving I noticed that most of them had life threatening injuries. The first individual that arrived, had both his legs missing and other injuries that soon followed included chest injuries, missing limbs, shrapnel wounds, as well as shock and severe head injuries. It was at this point I realized that there was going to be a lot more than the initial 20 - 30 casualties that were originally estimated.

At one point, outside the med centre, there was about 5 to 10 casualties waiting to be seen by the doctors as there was no space inside. It was my job, with another 3 medics to try and keep these casualties alive before the doctor could see them. Unfortunately it was apparent that some of them were not going to survive their injuries, and some of them passed away there and then.

While this was going on, the rest of the platoon had been called up to help assist where they could. Some of the Mortar Platoon had been sent to the helicopter pads, to help stretcher the casualties onto the helicopters that were taking them up to Camp BASTION

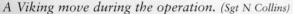

A Viking move during the operation. (Sgt N Collins)

and Kandahar's hospitals. During this time the Jocks were helping to reassure and assess the casualties, making sure that they did not deteriorate.

Private Coulter had a conversation with an injured Afghan Policeman while he was lying dying on a stretcher from his chest injuries. He stated through a translator:

"I hate the Taliban. I have no respect for them. They kill anyone, woman and children, they don't care about the Afghan people, most of them are foreign people. My cousin has just been killed. He just wanted peace. Not this. Send the Taliban to hell……..I have a wife and child. This is no place for them. They are not safe. There are bombings everywhere. You should go home. You will be killed here."

After about 40 minutes after the first casualty arrived, the hospitals were full at Camp BASTION and Kandahar, so we had to send them back to the local hospitals to be treated.

After it all happened, we went down to the med centre for a brief from the doctors just to thank us for the fantastic job that we had done. We learned sadly that most of the serious casualties did not survive due to their catastrophic injuries.

Op SARAK 3 – Life in the Viking – Private Martin Coulter (23), from Dundee, Mortar Platoon

For the first half of the tour the Mortar Platoon had taken to doing most of its travelling to ops in Vikings instead of helicopters. This meant that sometimes we were stuck in the back of them for up 20 hours, only getting out occasionally for a quick stretch of the legs, or for the driver to rest. The best way to describe being stuck in the back of a Viking, was like being in a sauna, except hotter and with no air. This was due to the air con being broken on almost every Viking as the filters were clogged with dust. What little air con units did work usually spewed out dust into the cabin making it almost impossible to breath and dust was continually coming into the cabin through various holes in the Viking.

Dehydration was a constant threat also. The heat in the back of the Vikings with the added effects of wearing body armour and a helmet meant that you had to drink gallons of water. No matter how much you drank, the lads in the back never needed to go to the toilet. We often travelled through areas that had IEDs placed in the past, or were known to have IEDs. With every big bump or bang, the lads in the back would usually look at each other hoping that it was not their last. It was a feeling that I can only assume was similar to that of claustrophobia. It was a feeling that I both hated and dreaded. A feeling that I do not wish to experience again.

Private Andrew Carmichael (24), from Cowdenbeath, Javelin Platoon, Charlie Company,

I'd definitely rather be here than in the Fort (Fort George, Inverness), here with the boys, the 'Dream Factory'. My first contact was with Lance Corporal Bain, in the back of the Jackal, but we'll not go any further on that one eh. We flapped a bit, we got a bit over excited. With the initial contact, I got out the back of the wagon for a pee and the next thing I heard a big whoshing noise and Lance Corporal Bain was standing in the turret, so I got on the GMG (Grenade Machine Gun) and fired 25 rounds and 5 of them hit the target.

Lance Corporal Walter Bain (26), from Saline, Fife, Charlie Company

It was a compound and basically the soldiers popped out and fired an RPG and then we started to engage, we got a bit excited and rounds were going everywhere.

Private Andrew Carmichael

After I'd calmed down, I was fine, I started getting on target through the door. I was buzzing for about half an hour afterwards. It was a good laugh. I had about 6 cigarettes after it.

Lance Corporal Walter Bain

I think what it is, it doesn't matter how much training you've done and how much preparation you've done, once you get contacted its just the adrenaline kicks in. Basically it's nothing like you can experience ever. The adrenaline is just out of this world. It's hard to explain, you've got to keep your head obviously, try and keep yourself calm, unlike us. We've done alright though. We never took any casualties, we all done our job successfully.

Private Andrew Carmichael

It gives you confidence getting your first contact out the way. The young lads especially that have never experienced it before. It's easy enough firing at a wooden target but it's different out here. I think it's going to be a lot better for future tours with this Afghan village being built. I've read quite a bit about it now and I've seen it a few times on the internet. It's a lot of learning on the job. You never really know what job you're going to do until you get here.

Captain Mark 'Stan' Stansfield, 40 Regiment Royal Artillery (The Lowland Gunners)

For the first part of HERRICK 10 I commanded the UK element at FOB PRICE. I remember some of the lads, an advance party if you like, coming in to pave the way for the CO's TAC on the BG's first main Op. In particular Colour Sergeant Easton and Corporal Pratt stood out as being a mixture of industrious soldiers and lovable rogues!

Around this time Sergeant Sean Binnie was killed. At PRICE, we mirrored the vigil that took place in Camp BASTION. I recall our vigil was for 4 guys including 2 from PRICE. It was normal for me as commandant to try to get a soldier from the same unit as those KIA to read their unit's regimental collect. I asked Corporal Pratt if he would mind reading 3 SCOTS collect. He agreed immediately and conducted the task to the assembled ranks of UK, US and Danish personnel with great dignity.

I remember thinking 'well done lad, your friend would've been happy with that'.

Chapter Three

Operation ZAFAR 2

19–23 May 2009

INTRODUCTION

While the Battle Group was deployed on Operation SARAK 3, 2 Afghan National Police check points were destroyed by an insurgent attack in the area of Aynak, Nawa District in Helmand Province. In addition, in May 2009 there was a credible threat to Lashkar Gah, the provincial capital and the city where Task Force Helmand was headquartered. The 3 SCOTS Battle Group was tasked to rebuild 2 check points in the area of Aynak.

Capt Chris Baddeley (Ops Officer), Padre David Anderson and the CO in Camp BASTION before deploying. The Padre carries his 'combat golf iron' with 'ammunition' provided by the CO and Ops officer on his flanks. (Sgt N Collins)

An air photograph annotated for the operation. PYTHON and ADDER were the proposed sites for the new check points.

The Battle Group plan was to escort the engineering equipment in a large convoy led by Alpha Company mounted in armoured Mastiff. The Fire Support Group in Jackal and the Mortar Platoon in Vikings would contribute fire power to the convoy. The convoy would move through Gereshk and then turn south into the dasht following a route running parallel to the Helmand River. Once Alpha Company was in place and a final examination of the build sites by the Joint Force Engineer was complete, Bravo Company would conduct an aviation assault into the area in Chinook helicopters. Construction of both check points would begin on 20 May 09 and estimated to be complete by 22 May 09 with an extraction of all troops by 23 May 09.

EXECUTION

18 May 09 (D-1)

The route to Nawa was affected by 3 critical factors: firstly, the continued threat of IEDs along Highway 1 and Route 601; secondly, concern that a convoy of 50 lumbering vehicles may dramatically disrupt the markets in the city if it passed in the day; thirdly, a significant suicide IED threat to ISAF in the centre of Lashkar Gah. In order to minimise the threat of IED, Alpha Company chose to move through the dasht and along the Helmand River. Also, to reduce a

A typical Camp BASTION view – a Viking ready for deployment at dusk. (Sgt N Collins)

The Viking tracked vehicles, transporting the Mortar Platoon, and the recovery vehicles were located in the dasht ready to support the Battle Group when required. (Sgt N Collins)

Capt Tom Waterman the BG Engineer.

negative impact on the people of Lashkar Gah and to counter the threat of suicide IED, Alpha Company recognised that the convoy would need to be clear of Lashkar Gah prior to first light and so chose to leave BASTION at 2030 hrs.

Alpha Company departed Camp BASTION at 2030 hrs and passed through Gereshk before 2300 hrs. The convoy then moved south off Highway 1 and into the dasht. In less than 60 minutes 3 of the Mastiffs became stuck in the sand and were recovered by the Viking vehicles. Also, one of the Jackals rolled over in the sand. Due to the difficulties of moving through the desert, Alpha Company decided to reroute and move along Highway 1, through the Durai Junction, and then south on Route 601 to Lashkar Gah.

19 May 09 (D Day)

The convoy passed through the Durai Junction at 0530 hrs and moved through Lashkar Gah at 0700 hrs. At 0900 hrs, Alpha Company had secured Objective VIPER, the Fire Support Group had established a protective screen to the West, and the TAC HQ, the Mortar Platoon and the A1 echelon logistic support group prepared a defensive position in Objective MAMBA. At 1030 hrs, the Battle Group Engineers inserted by Chinook and a shura between the Commanding Officer and local elders agreed to build a check point at Objective PYTHON. The second check point that was to be built at Objective ADDER was cancelled as the proposed site was inaccessible to the required engineering equipment and was deemed tactically unsuitable. As a result, Bravo Company was no longer required for the operation and remained in BASTION. At last light, 1922 hrs, the Fire Support Group screen, TAC, the mortar line, and the echelon vehicles were contacted. The Viking Troop and Fire Support Group quickly moved and suppressed the firing point.

20 May 09 – 21 May 09 (D+1 – D+2)

Despite the contact of the previous day the atmospherics in the area remained good, but with some observation of the Battle Group's activities by insurgents. Alpha Company dominated the area around Objective PYTHON and by 1800 hrs, 60% of the check point was complete and the Engineers continued to work throughout the night. At 0100 hrs the check point in Objective PYTHON was complete. A second examination of the proposed second check point in Objective ADDER further confirmed that the site was unsuitable for use by the Afghan National Police. As a result, the stores designated for the second check point were used to enhance the check point in Objective PYTHON.

22 May 09 – 23 May 09 (D + 3 – D + 4)

Upon the completion of the check point, the focus of the operation became the exploitation of Aynak. Alpha Company with officers from the Afghan National Police patrolled south of the check point. At 1122 hrs, 2 Platoon came under contact from an area previously identified as an insurgent position. The company moved south to establish a fire base, the Mastiffs with the company pushed into position to provide additional fire power. At 1147 hrs, a Mastiff driven by Private Sam Morgan and commanded by Colour Sergeant Billy Easton struck an IED. The explosion fractured Private Morgan's right foot and Private Nino, who was manning

The Royal Engineers get to work on re-building the ANP checkpoints. (MOD – Sgt C Halton)

the GPMG in the Mastiff, suffered a dislocated elbow. Both were evacuated from the scene and recovered to BASTION by Chinook. Alpha Company remained in place to secure the area after the contact had ended. A pressure pad IED was identified and destroyed in place. At 2000 hrs, the ANP took over the check point in Objective PYTHON. At 2130 hrs, the convoy of vehicles that originally deployed into Ops Box BELL began its journey back to BASTION. By 0731 hrs on 23 May 09, all members of the Battle Group had recovered to BASTION.

SUMMARY

Operation ZAFAR 2 provided the Afghan National Police with an enhanced check point in Aynak. In turn, the occupation of the check point enabled the Afghan National Police to apply pressure on an advancing insurgent threat. Moreover, it developed an understanding of the area and identified the support of local nationals for the Afghan National Security Forces (ANSF).

Operation ZAFAR 2 was the first operation in which a member of the Battle Group struck an IED. Although Colour Sergeant Easton, Private Morgan and Private Nino were mounted in the armoured Mastiff, the IED strike nonetheless highlighted the lethal capability of an IED and reinforced within all members of the Battle Group the nature of the insurgents tactics and the necessity to conduct the correct drills at all times.

Op ZAFAR 2 – Reflections – Major Matt Munro (36), from Hampshire, Officer Commanding Alpha (Grenadier) Company

Our most recent operation was deep in the green zone adjacent to the River Helmand. We initially based ourselves in a village that is, by Afghan standards, wealthy and prosperous. The locals farm wheat (and not poppy) and were delighted to see us. We were able briefly to bathe in a stream; it was teeming with tiny fish that liked to nibble at our (rotting) feet. I also saw a very skilled kingfisher catching fish that were almost as big as he was.

The insurgents had apparently established a front-line a couple of kilometres to the south; we were there to hold the line. Things soon got busy; we 'tested' and unequivocally found the FLET (Forward Line of Enemy Troops). The lead section of one of my forward platoons surprised a group of Taliban in very close-country; the resultant fire-fight took place at extremely close quarters (25 m). I talked to a (slightly euphoric) Jock afterwards about his experience and he described seeing rounds kicking up the ground around his feet, and perhaps more worryingly, felt air being displaced close to his face as bullets winged past, impact marks on the compound wall behind him confirmed that he had had a close shave. This young soldier had been pinned down by accurate fire in the open. His section commander, (a beast of a man from Fiji) made a conscious decision to risk his own life in order to save him; he sprinted forward into the killing area and dragged his soldier into cover, with total disregard for his own safety he saved his comrades life. He then coolly assessed the threat and coordinated his section's reaction.

As this was going on I was about 30 m away (around a corner, I hasten to add). I flicked my radio to the frequency of the platoon in contact in a bid to learn more about the situation that was developing. Rather naively perhaps, I expected to hear a textbook Brecon-style fire-control order (all British infantry commanders are taught at Brecon; the 'Brecon way' is the only way). The fire control order is used to indicate the direction and range of the threat and to ensure that an appropriate weapon system and rate of fire is employed; like most things in the Army it is formulaic and prescriptive. Anyway, this particular section-commander didn't know that his company commander was eavesdropping and was perhaps excited at his first decent 'contact'. He neglected to issue a 'formal' fire-control order, and his language was ripe to say the least. Within moments we secured the services of an obliging jet; this further encouraged the enemy to take to their heels. We subsequently found the firing point (betrayed by a pile of empty AK bullet cases) but the lack of bodies or blood trails suggested that despite the awesome weight of fire and considerable enthusiasm we had failed to kill any of them.

Shortly afterwards we suffered our first casualties when one of the Mastiffs rolled over a huge explosive device. The driver suffered a really nasty fracture to his ankle and was airlifted from the scene and ultimately to hospital in Birmingham within a day. I am amazed from the size of the crater and the damage to the vehicle that there were no fatalities. Actually, the vehicle in question is armoured and very well protected and a real MOD procurement success story. Later that same afternoon we found a similarly large device that could easily have further spoiled our day.

Although I have described one of the fights that we have had; truth be told we have spent more time drinking tea with Afghans than we have fighting them. The clichéd (but nonetheless valuable) line on counter-insurgency is that it is the 'population that is the prize'.

Success is to be measured in terms of gaining the consent of the neutral local population rather than in Taliban body count. Hence, for example, we go to some trouble to compensate local nationals should we damage their property, we don't normally enter a compound unless we are invited to or if we have good reason to suspect that there may be something suspicious therein. The medic is sometimes summoned forward to treat patients; sadly we have seen several young babies that appeared to be close to death, usually because the mother has been ill and unable to nourish the baby. On one occasion we indented for and received baby formula on our nightly helicopter re-supply. I am not sure where it was sourced from but to the credit of the Quartermaster he was able to get his hands on some. We went to some trouble to deliver it (we diverted our patrol) and the obvious gratitude on the faces of the anxious parents confirmed that that simple act was probably worth more in counter-insurgency terms than a precision munition guided onto a Taliban stronghold.

Op ZAFAR 2 – IED Strike – Captain Samuel Newson (28), from Prestwood, Buckinghamshire, Second in Command, Alpha (Grenadier) Company

Some events burn themselves into the memory so deeply I suspect they will be as vivid in several decades as they were on the day they happened. Some endure because of their consequences, some their novelty and some just because of the intensity of the experience. One such event occurred during Operation ZAFAR 2. It capped what was already an intense moment; members of 2 Platoon were fighting amongst compounds to the front, the ground was close and it was impossible to see in detail where the enemy were or how to get at them. We rolled a Mastiff up the axis to provide some fire support, its elevation and firepower a real boon in the complex terrain.

Had there been less going on, and certainly now we are more experienced, we would have spotted the risk, as it was the Sergeant Major and I twigged just an instant too late. What happened in an instant seemed so much slower, being only fifty feet away we experienced everything in detail but even at such short range the explosion, the boom and the shock wave happened in sequence.

The briefest of flashes, just a sense of heat and light, amidst an instantaneous cloud of dust and debris. The vehicle vanished. The noise a deep solid crump that hung on the air. Last the tremors reverberating through the ground the most subtle but telling indication of the size of the blast. Amongst the cloud some bar armour, a wing and a fuel tank. In my memory vivid and distinct, in reality an unrecognizable blur of movement onto which my subconscious has since etched the detail.

Then quiet, real quiet the contact over the echoes died away and for the briefest of moments silence. Incredulity, anger, frustration, impotence, a hundred emotions, a compressed intense flow of consciousness streaming through the mind, what now?

Clear a route, secure an LS, where's the medic, establish comms, what else? What else? The radio sparks it's the Colour Sergeant he's in the wagon, he's ok, they're all ok, shaken, wounded but no one's dead and no one's going to die, a reprieve, a narrow escape, a moment of relief but then action.

The Mastiff vehicle after the BG's first of many IED strikes.

Op ZAFAR 2 – Vehicle Mounted – Lieutenant Rob Colquhoun (26), from the Isle of Skye, 2 Platoon Commander, Alpha (Grenadier) Company

Monday, 18 May

A hectic morning planning for the op: checking the route and briefing the Jocks. I concern myself with getting us there. We'll be in Mastiffs which are new to me (but very well armoured) and I decide I ought to be in the lead vehicle despite the mine and IED threat in order to chose and prove the route. Without a moments pause I'm at the vehicle park throwing my kit into the vehicle and 'ready' to go.

We set off and I follow the Viking guides to Gereshk before turning off the road and my call sign starts to lead the short cut through the dasht. I'm worried that we have turned off too late as the sand is soft and the incline steep – totally unlike the ground I was briefed to expect. But we had used the correct RV point, guided by the Vikings and checked on GPS, and so ploughed on. In no time a Mastiff is stuck and no sooner is it freed than another is bogged in. We wait patiently as vehicles flounder behind us and after 5 hours I know the route is doomed. We decide to race for Lashkah Gah on tarmac instead.

Tuesday, 19 May

Dawn breaks and we're still miles from Lash. The hairs on the back of my neck begin to stand as I contemplate passing through Helmand's capital in broad daylight with a slow moving convoy 60 vehicles long! I'm thinking Mogadishu in *Black Hawk Down* but actually everything runs smoothly until we run out the far side and the gunners can relax a little.

When we arrive we're watched with interest by a group of boys on the other side of a canal.

Members of Alpha (Grenadier) Company on patrol in the green zone south of Lashkar Gah.

We leave some sweets and as some of them run off to cross the footbridge 20m away one of them plunges in and swims over to get them first! We soon secure the area and use the Mastiffs as weapon platforms to over watch the site of a new ANP check point. The Jocks in one of the Mastiffs are suffering as the air-con has failed and are glad to be able to open the doors.

OP ZAFAR 2 – Personal Account – Private Amphon Supharee (24), from Falkirk, 2 Platoon, Alpha (Grenadier) Company

We were on a compound clearing task moving towards known enemy territory. As we cleared through each compound on foot the Mastiffs followed behind providing rear support if we needed it. The platoon was divided into 2 multiples: Mr Colquhoun and Corporal Welshman were the lead multiple with Sergeant Buchanan, Corporal Dennis Boila and Corporal Koro tasked to provide flanking protection with the multiple I was in.

As our multiple advanced forward along the tree line on the edge of the green zone, Private Johnstone spotted 3 armed men on a roof top ahead of us. As they went firm to try and get better eyes on the gun man, our multiple advanced forward to cut them off. We got to an irrigation ditch in line with the lead call sign and went firm.

Corporal Boila wanted to push forward to get better eyes on with Lance Corporal Forrester and myself. I was carrying the ECM and it was weighing me down. As we reached the corner of a compound wall Corporal Boila heard voices coming from the slope around the corner. Lance Cpl Forrester thought he saw someone ahead and got myself forward to confirm it. As we poked our heads round the corner, 2 gunmen opened up with a burst of automatic fire spraying our position with 7.62mm rounds. The rounds landed inches away from our feet. Our initial reaction was to get into cover round the corner of the wall.

But I was lying on my back, with my heavy day sack weighing me down. I could not move as fast as the others and the rounds were landing all round my feet and head. At this point Corporal Boila came back round the corner, reached forward and physically dragged me into cover. As I was being dragged back I returned fire at the enemy with my feet sticking out as I tried to kick myself back. The rounds were still landing in and around my feet and I suddenly feared being hit. I tried desperately to get up and that's when my adrenaline kicked in, realizing the rest of the multiple could not fire because we were still in the way. We managed to run back to the irrigation ditch where the rest of the multiple was. The whole multiple then engaged, suppressing the enemy at last.

I dumped my day sack and was now more maneuverable and started to suppress too. Corporal Boila then engaged with a 66mm rocket. The gunmen continued to fire on our position so Lance Corporal Forrester decided to fire his 66mm as well. The noise and smoke was amazing and must have had an impact as the 2 gunmen stopped firing and fled South.

Sergeant Buchanan then came on the net asking if anyone had been hit. That's when I got scared and worried so I started to check myself for any bullet holes. I was fine, and grinned when I saw a bullet had grazed one of my boots: a close shave indeed!

The elation of survival was intense but short lived however as suddenly there was a huge explosion and we heard that a Mastiff had struck an IED.

Colour Sergeant Billy Easton (37), from Kennoway, Fife, CQMS Alpha (Grenadier) Company

We were just south-west of Lashkar Gah, we were in a Mastiff. I was resupplying the company at the time. I was tasked to provide fire support for forward elements of the company who were engaged in a fierce contact.

The first thing I felt was like getting a puncture in your car and then someone punching you in the face at the same time. After a couple of seconds I looked and noticed the windscreen was smashed and so I just checked myself over. I was totally upset that I had been caught, or blown up. I thought 'the f******s, they've got me'. My first reaction was to help my comrades out.

The guys behind us said our vehicle went up about 20 feet in the air and came straight back down. It was a big one. We had 2 casualties. Alpha Company had come under fire on my left and I reacted to provide fire support but at the same time didn't realise it was an IED. I told my wife that night when we got back to Lashkar Gah, the phone was quiet for a couple of minutes, then she burst into tears.

CSgt 'Boxer' Easton, CQMS Alpha (Grenadier) Company immediately after he was caught up in the Mastiff IED Strike.

Op ZAFAR 2 – Life in Mastiffs – Private Liam Salter (20), from Perth, 2 Platoon, Alpha (Grenadier) Company

During the 5 or 6 days I spent in a Mastiff on Op ZAFAR 2 in Helmand Province Afghanistan, I realised many things about the pros and cons of being vehicle mounted. Some of the pros are simple things like instead of tabbing the planet with all the kit in the world on your back you can simply attach your kit to the outside of the wagon by using karabiner clips. While doing your sentry duty, you are sitting behind a .50 cal or GMG, making the GPMG that you would normally perform duty behind look like a small toy. Also the added protection of having the armour all around you, gives you a feeling of extra security. While moving you are less concerned with small arms fire and RPG attacks simply because you know the armour can take it, even while you are on sentry these things are easily solved with simple drop down drills. But also there are as many cons as there are pros, such as how much manoeuvrability is lost with being inside such a large vehicle and also the reduced vision from the driver and commander's windows. Also the lack of space within the vehicle makes living extremely difficult with barely enough to move around inside. And if the air conditioning stopped working, which it often did, it makes it unbearable when the outside temperature is over 40 degrees. I'm sure you can imagine what it is like with about 8-10 guys inside with all the radio and ECM equipment inside heating things up.

On the last day of the operation the company was tasked with doing a foot patrol with 2 Mastiffs to the rear to provide fire support, a means of casualty extraction and re-supply if required. One Jock from each platoon was provided to clear vulnerable points, sentries for top cover men and to provide flank protection for the wagons. I was the Jock from 2 Platoon to do this so at around 0700 hrs the company stepped off on their patrol using a main route as an axis and a means for the Mastiffs to travel on, with the company on either side of the track to avoid the IED threat as best as possible. This left the track for me and the other 2 men to clear with one man on top cover to watch the flanks. So the company had covered about 2 km when 2 Platoon (my platoon) came under contact from small arms fire from a range of about 25 – 100m away. The call came over the radio for us to move up to their location to provide fire support or casualty extraction if the worst came to the worst. The Mastiff couldn't have moved more than 100m forwards along the track when something happened. Immediately I was thrown about inside, my ears were ringing and I couldn't see anything apart from a beam of light coming in from the top cover where Private Nino was trapped. It was then I realised what had just happened: we had stuck an IED.

At this point I didn't know what the damage was or if anyone was injured. When the dust started to settle I saw the 'Quartie' (Colour Sergeant Easton) was lying on his side across the area between the front 2 seats. He wasn't moving. I immediately thought the worst and started trying to shout through to him to see if I could get a response. I was relieved to get one but then I noticed Private Sam Morgan the driver had his morphine out. As he injected himself I started to make sure everyone else was ok. Private Nino came inside the wagon having damaged his shoulder by holding on to the gun so he didn't get thrown from the wagon. Once I knew the driver and commander were ok I went out through the top cover hatch and saw someone about 20m for us scanning the ground around the blast through his ACOG sight to ensure there were no secondary devices. When he was happy he ran up to the top cover hatch to make sure everyone was ok. He helped everyone out and I went back inside to help out Sam who had badly damaged his ankle in the blast. The first thing I remember when I got outside was CSM Colville saying to me that I still had 6 months of this to go! I was still in shock, shaking and in total disbelief as to what had happened. When we moved up to the HLS where Sam and Nino were to be extracted, I helped them both on to the chopper. When we all moved back to the blast area I started noticing that there was bar armour, fuel tanks and bits of all sorts of stuff lying over about a 50m radius. I couldn't believe how lucky we had all been. If that had been any other vehicle we would have all been killed. I now have complete faith in the machines and would be happy to do almost anything with them, even without the air con working! It is a day that will stay with me for the rest of my life as well as the comments some of the people said when they saw the blast. Most of us thought we were all dead. I think that I definitely used one of my 9 lives that day.

Op ZAFAR 2 – The Quiet Moments – Captain David Mack (32), from Toronto, Canada, Officer Commanding Mortar Platoon, Charlie Company

There were moments during the tour when one's thoughts were not always on the present but would slip away. They were moments of solitude that tend to occur in the midst of an insertion or an extraction. They sometimes took place when one was in a helicopter, at other times they occurred when riding shotgun in a WMIK or perhaps in the back of armoured vehicle such as a Viking or Mastiff. These moments were not quite the result of boredom and did not necessarily represent a period of daydreaming; rather they occurred when one had little or no control over one's immediate future. Often the hypnotic rhythm of helicopter

Capt Mack OC Mortars, Gnr Barker and Maj Sharpe the BG Battery Commander underneath a cam-net in CO's Tactical HQ. (Sgt N Collins)

blades or the dull roar of a motor engine made conversing with another impossible and allowed an individual a period of focussed concentration. Even though one would neurotically check and recheck GPS coordinates with a map there was really very little one could do and eventually the mind wandered. These were the quiet moments when one fell in upon oneself for a period of introspection and reflection.

More often than not, memories from the past surfaced. Sometimes these memories were distinct, sometimes they were a blur – specific moments in time or vague memories. Various thoughts and images paraded through the mind's eye. Sometimes these pictures were non-descript, images of images, faint memories, while other memories were complete, every minutia of detail recalled, colours, voices, smells. Thoughts of home often merged with memories of friends and family, loved ones, holiday periods – Christmas, Easter, Thanksgiving – school, sometimes even thoughts wondering what old school chums were doing now would emerge alongside the multitude of memories of one's own life history. I can remember remembering canoe trips I made when I was younger along the rivers and lakes and forests of Central and Northern Ontario in my native Canada, or wandering up and down the hills in Wales that ultimately brought me to Afghanistan, as well as the steep climbs up the Semien Mountains of the Ethiopian Highlands. Sometimes the sound of 8 blades striking the water in unison and the movement of 8 rowers travelling along the rails would suddenly appear alongside the feel of a tackle with a victim's jersey caught determinedly in my grip. I can recall travelling through Gereshk and the smells of charcoal mixed with rancid odours of stale sweat and sewage immediately returned me to a previous tour in Iraq, to towns such as Al-Qurna and Ad-Dayr, and more distantly to a time spent conducting relief work at a dump outside of Maputo, long before I had joined the army. Of course, throughout, I would think of my girlfriend who was at her home in Denmark and wonder what she would think if she knew precisely what we were up to and the dangers we were facing.

Sometimes one's thought moved to the immediate future, as the anticipation of what will take place in the upcoming hours raced through the mind. A sudden recital of the orders and the operation's plans would flood my thoughts alongside exact times for events and precise detail of the moment I stepped off the helicopter. Sometimes these thoughts of things to come would become indulgent thoughts of the future, of future operations or even more distant, the months to come, the end of tour and the return to the UK.

Sometimes there was nothing.

Sometimes there was only the feel of the wind whipping against my face and I would simply gaze forward, machine gun to my front and fiddle with my night vision goggles. Sometimes, in the back of a helicopter I would slip off to sleep. And sometimes I would pray, a prayer on behalf of the men I was travelling with, or even a prayer for my own safety.

These were the quiet moments.

Lance Corporal Ryan Gonzales (22), from Dunfermline – FSG 2 Machine Gunner, Charlie Company

It's been not too bad, the first few times out on the ground I thought it was a bit boring, but coming more into the summer time we've seen more fighting. It's close to R&R so the contacts are a bit more worrying. It's been good though. I think for myself and for the other

LCpl Ryan Gonzales from Dunfermline (on the left).

young guys who've not been in the Battalion long, it's been a steep learning curve, particularly being in the senior company. The weight hasn't been too bad. Carrying ECM in the light role doesn't bother me that much, you get used to it. You just put it on your back. After the first couple of times it was alright after that. Now I just put it on my back and go.

When you're in a Jackal and go through towns, you always have your rifle ready because you can't really fire the GMGs because of the damage they could do. I also carry my sig pistol, just in case.

The first time we went through Gereshk I thought everyone was looking at us and I thought it was a bit dodgy. After that I thought it was alright, but after that when 2 suicide bombs went off, you had to be very alert, anyone could pop out, it could be a gunman or it could be an innocent passer by.

To start with I was quite disappointed about how quiet it was when we got here, but now its kicking in its better. My nearest miss was my Jackal getting hit. The small arms aren't too much to worry about, it's more the RPGs and IEDs.

Lance Corporal Robert Ellis (22), from Fife, MT Platoon, Headquarter Company – Mastiff Driver/ Commander

I felt confident when I got here because of my training. I had little apprehension before coming out because I knew I was going to be in a Mastiff. Colour Sergeant Easton walked away from an IED the other day because he was in a Mastiff, it's put a lot of confidence in it.

There's been a lot of night driving which takes it out of you, the boys are chinned by the time they get to the position. Then it's a couple of hours head down and then straight on again. Sometimes there's no break. It's slow because we're clearing the route. As A1 Echelon we're delivering all the rations, stores, water, ammunition and clothing packs.

Chapter Four

Operation OUBA 3

31 May–6 June 2009

INTRODUCTION

Operation OUBA 3 was part of Operation AABI TOORAH DO, a Regional Command (South) operation focused on disruption of insurgent activities and leadership in the Sapwan Kala area of the Upper Sangin Valley. This region was a known safe-haven for insurgent leadership, as well as the production of several types of IED, and an important centre of opium processing.

The Battle Group planned to conduct counter-narcotic raids into the region consisting of 3 separate pulses (raids) between 31 May and 7 June. The first 2 pulses would be aviation assaults with troops inserted in Chinook helicopters and separated by a 72 hour period. Between the first 2 pulses the Battle Group would return to BASTION in order to mask future intentions. After Pulse 2, the Battle Group would extract into a desert box and Pulse 3 would consist of patrols in the area from the desert box.

As a consequence of a 24 hour delay between Pulse 1 and Pulse 2, and a further tasking for the future, Pulse 3 was cancelled. Pulse 1 concentrated in the area of Sar Puzay and Barakzai and Pulse 2 focused on Garmab. During the operation, significant finds of narcotics and processing equipment were made and subsequently destroyed.

EXECUTION – PULSE 1
31 May 09 (D Day)

The operation began with Bravo Company inserting into Ops Box CUTLASS at 2200 hrs. Battle Group TAC also deployed at the same time onto an observation point on top of Brown Rock. During the insertion, the Chinook helicopters were engaged by insurgents and

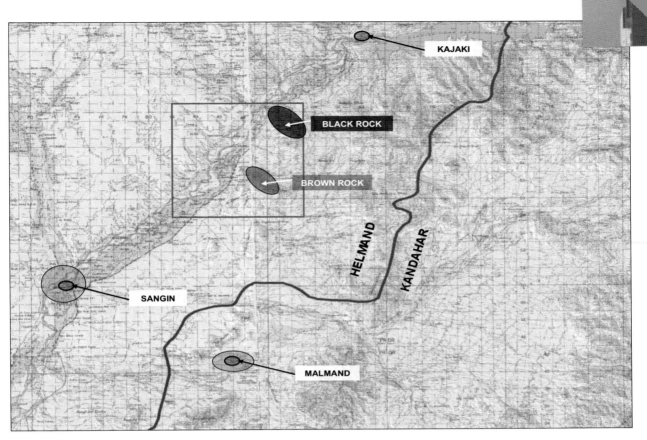

The map shows the Upper Sangin Valley between Sangin and Kajaki. No ISAF troops operate between these 2 positions: the red box indicates the trget area for the Battle Group.

returned fire. At 2230 hrs, Bravo Company came under fire from a compound and used Apache helicopters to provide direct fire and killed a number of insurgents. Alpha Company deployed into the north of the area at 2240 hrs and a reformed Charlie Company arrived in the south at 2343 hrs and adopted a blocking position.

1 June 09 – 2 June 09 (D+1 – D+2)

Shortly after midnight, Alpha Company began searching the compounds in its area of operation. Initially, Alpha Company uncovered 50kg of heroin in a compound. At approximately 0030 hrs, 1 Platoon, known as "the Senior Highland Platoon", discovered a significant narcotic facility that contained large quantities of precursor chemicals (2500kg of sulphur and 120kg of hydrogen peroxide) and also a vast amount of equipment used to process opium. In addition, Alpha Company also found and destroyed 2000kg of wet opium.

At 0645 hrs, Bravo Company was engaged by small arms fire which began a day of accurate fire focused on the Company's locations. Insurgent firing points eventually surrounded the company from the south through the west and the north. By 0900 hrs, 6 Platoon had become pinned down and was unable to move. At 0946 hrs, Lance Corporal Taylor, attached from the Royal Engineers, sustained a gunshot wound to his upper arm. At the point of wounding, Private Turner provided first aid until the Regimental Medical Officer

Troops line up in the chalks at 'little Heathrow', Camp BASTION awaiting insertion by CH 47. (MOD – Cpl R Freer)

Maj Matt Munro, Officer Commanding Alpha (Grenadier) Company, with his fire support. Alpha Coy were inserted into a forward LUP in daylight and reinserted onto target after dark. (MOD – Cpl R Freer)

4 CH 47 Chinooks approach the Helicopter Landing Site – HLS – at the end of Pulse 2, Op OUBA 3.

(RMO), Captain Ryan Wood, was able to tend to Lance Corporal Taylor. As Bravo Company's situation became increasingly difficult, Apache helicopters were used to observe and engage insurgent positions. Upon receipt of Bravo Company's casualty report, Battle Group Main Headquarters immediately tasked the casualty evacuation Chinook helicopter. It arrived in location at 1030 hrs, however, as the Chinook attempted to land, insurgents engaged the helicopter and an RPG narrowly missed the core of the helicopter. An American Blackhawk medical helicopter was subsequently tasked to extract the casualty. Despite Bravo Company's ongoing battle, the Blackhawk successfully extracted the casualty at 1200 hrs. Throughout the morning, Alpha Company experienced harassing sniper fire and Charlie Company was also engaged by bursts of small arms.

At 1600 hrs, Alpha Company identified the compound of the sniper and struck with GMLRS. Following this engagement, Alpha Company was ordered into the green zone to facilitate the extraction of Bravo Company. Once Alpha Company was in position, Bravo Company extracted. Both companies subsequently moved to the east and established defensive positions prior to a final move out of the area after last light. Alpha, Bravo, and Charlie Company all moved north during the night and Battle Group TAC was extracted by Chinook at 2300 hrs. All troops had returned to BASTION by 0700 hrs.

SUMMARY

The insurgent response to the Battle Group's presence was rapid and robust with insurgents showing an ability to react quickly and employing accurate small arms, RPG, and indirect fire. Insurgent response to the insertion was immediate and intelligence assessed the engagement to support the withdrawal of key leaders from the target area. In addition, coordinated single round and accurate bursts of fire demonstrated the technical capability and proficiency of the insurgent fighters in the area. The large finds and the resilience of the fighters confirmed early assessments that the area was an insurgent command and control node with a strong emphasis on narcotic processing.

EXECUTION – PULSE 2

5 June 09 (D + 5)

Pulse 2 was planned to be a short operation to take place over a 12 hour period at night. The Battle Group inserted in 2 waves into the target area. Bravo Company deployed at 2135 hrs and Alpha Company, TAC, and the Mortar Platoon deployed at 2320 hrs. Early into the searches, B Company discovered a massive drugs laboratory which was destroyed.

6 June 09 (D + 6)

At 0011 hrs, a second drugs lab containing 1000 kg of opium was located. All material and drugs were destroyed. Alpha Company also made a small find of drug related equipment which was also destroyed. Prior to first light, the Battle Group moved east to the mortar line and began to extract at 0445 hrs. During the extraction of the third wave, troops came under contact from indirect fire. The Apache helicopter that was providing support to the extraction fired a number of warning shots at an insurgent position. All members of the Battle Group were in Kandahar Airfield at 0910 hrs.

25kg of the opium being destroyed – drugs and opium finds were usually destroyed by fire or explosives. (MOD – Cpl R Freer)

Relief – The inside of a CH 47 Chinook after Op OUBA 3 on the way back to Kandahar.

SUMMARY

Pulse 2 comprised synchronized targeted strikes against suspected narcotics facilities within the course of a single night. Unlike Pulse 1, only one contact occurred which was an opportunistic indirect fire on the extraction point of the helicopter landing site. Our intelligence suggested that indirect fire and ambushes were being prepared for the morning, the tempered reaction indicated that the insurgents were more cautious following the events of Pulse 1.

SUMMARY – Operation OUBA 3

The most immediate measurable achievement of Operation OUBA 3 was the destruction of a number of insurgent narcotic processing factories and a significant amount of narcotic equipment in the Upper Sangin Valley; approximately 15% of the narcotic processing capability of the Upper Sangin Valley. The destruction of the equipment and narcotics impacted insurgent funding streams and an insurgent perception of security in the region. Operation OUBA 3 demonstrated the vulnerability of the insurgent and the effective reach of ANSF and ISAF.

Operation OUBA 3 provided the Battle Group with important development experiences. The key narcotic finds from both pulses are listed below.

Wet Opium (Kg)	5513.00
Morphine (Kg)	220.00
Crystal Heroin (Kg)	50.00
Brown Heroin (Kg)	5.00
White Heroin (Kg)	55.00
Hashish (Kg)	148.00
Ammonium Chloride (Kg)	5805.00
Sodium Chloride (Kg)	200.00
Poppy Seed (Kg)	150.00
Sulphur (Kg)	2500.00
Opium Presses	20

Op OUBA 3 – NARCOTICS IN AFGHANISTAN

Context of Afghanistan Narcotics issue / Cultivation / RC(S) policy

The cultivation of opium poppy is an issue of critical importance for Regional Command (South) and Afghanistan as a whole. It feeds the Taliban insurgency, fuels corruption and destroys the good name of the Afghan population. Currently, southern Afghanistan continues to cultivate over 90% of Afghanistan's opium; in 2009 opium cultivation decreased by 22%, from 157,000 hectares (ha) in 2008 to 123,000 ha today yet southern Afghanistan was estimated to have produced over 7,000 metric tons of opium. This will generate almost $450m for illicit means, based on a figure of $61.74 per kg of wet opium. Such funding will continue to define and bolster a narco-insurgent nexus that adversely affect the promotion of GIRoA legitimacy and impedes the implementation of the Afghan National Development Strategy and the success of ISAF's Counter Insurgency (COIN) efforts within the RC(S) AO. However, the United Nations Office on Drugs and Crime (UNODC) Opium Survey of Afghanistan, September 2009, surmises that the bottom is starting to fall out of the Afghan opium market. It states that for the second year in a row, cultivation, production, work-force, prices, revenues, exports and its GDP share are all down, while the number of poppy-free provinces and drug seizures continue to rise. In Helmand alone, cultivation declined by a third, to less than 70,000 ha. This dramatic turn-around in Helmand has been attributed directly to an effective mix of sticks and carrots: governor leadership, a more aggressive counter narcotic offensive, terms of trade more favourable to legal crops and the (related) successful introduction of food zones to promote licit farming. RBG(S) has been directly involved in aspects of this policy, most notably on Op OUBA 3 in June.

It is readily recognised that controlling drugs in Afghanistan will not solve all of the country's problems, however, the country's problems can not be solved without controlling drugs. As exposed in numerous publications, there are several major contributing factors to this problem. The first is poor security conditions, caused not only by the insurgency but also by criminal activity. The second is destruction of the infrastructure and institutions needed for legal and high-value agriculture. Typically, farmers do not have access to high quality inputs or technical support, and they lack access to markets and customers. The third factor is widespread institutional corruption, which allows drug mafias to operate with relative impunity. Of particular note are the central Helmand areas synonymous with poppy growth and where all parties concerned have a vested interest and the Insurgency has considerable intent and capability. The GIRoA and ISAF are actively involved in combating all 3 of these aspects to the issue, predominantly through political and civic initiatives. During its time as RBG(S), 3 SCOTS, has been directly involved in combating the first and the third of these. Until relatively recently, it was commonly held that the insurgency had mainly benefitted from taxation, however, it has become increasingly apparent that the insurgents are directly involved in protecting all aspects of the narco-trade (including cultivation, processing, trafficking and lines of communication) through the use of kinetic effect, an aspect directly experienced during by RBG(S) during Op HERRICK 10. It should be emphasised that this is not an insurgency fuelled solely by narcotics; if the flow of funds derived from the narco-industry is stemmed, there is evidence that insurgents will continue to derive finance from

The inside of a drug manufacturing plant.

other sources (e.g. the taxing of wheat), nevertheless, the impact on insurgent capabilities would undoubtedly be significant.

Warlords / Narco Barons / Corruption

Despite the progress, opium remains a major source of income in one of the world's poorest and most unstable countries. In Afghanistan, many farmers grow opium out of subsistence, depending on advance loans provided by traders as a down payment for the subsequent drug harvest. This entraps farmers in to a form of debt bondage, forcing them to continue to cultivate opium poppy in order to subsist. On the other side of the spectrum, criminals, insurgents and corrupt officials are involved in the narcotics trade through the common pursuit of greed and power. As the UNODC point out this has happened elsewhere in the world; in Colombia drug trafficking by the Revolutionary Armed Forces of Columbia (FARC) and the National Liberation Army (ELN)) started as a means to a political end a way of funding an ideologically motivated *guerrilla* movement. Afghanistan is approaching this point. After years of collusion with criminal gangs and corrupt officials, some insurgents are now opportunistically moving up the chain: not just taxing supply, but getting involved in producing, processing, stocking and exporting drugs.

As a result there are a multitude of vested interests in the narcotics industry. In response to ISAF and GIRoA counter narcotic policy, insurgents conduct an aggressive information campaign in order to portray counter narcotic operations as a threat to local national's livelihood, question GIRoA rule of law and the legitimacy of counter narcotic operations as well as alternative livelihood programmes. The desired effect of this is to increase insurgent support and distance the populace from GIRoA and ISAF endeavours, its results though are mixed. RBG(S) experience has demonstrated that this policy, despite being actively employed by the insurgents does not always gain purchase. Op OUBA 3 in June, a BG raid targeting narcotics processing facilities in the Upper Sangin Valley, an area in which ISAF and GIRoA has no permanent presence, was very well received by local nationals in the area, expressed by local nationals both on the ground at the time and subsequently at shuras held in Sangin district centre. Local nationals stated that they wished for more operations of this type to take place. In addition the operation proved a catalyst for disagreement and confrontation between local nationals and insurgents over the location of narco factories in the Upper Sangin Valley with local nationals confronting factory owners and demanding that they move away. Although the insurgents refuted these demands, they nevertheless demonstrate the success in terms of perception that GIRoA policy is having. Further, additional demands made by insurgents on the local national population to replace the revenue lost through counter narcotic operations increases the growing wedge between the insurgents and the local national's population. Although this may have a short term negative impact on the LN population, the potential positive political ramifications are significant.

Assessed impact of RBG(S) operations

In the first half of 2009, military operations in RC(S) have destroyed over 90 tons of precursor chemicals, 450t of seeds, 50t of opium, 7t of morphine, 1.5t of heroin, 19t of cannabis resin and 27 labs. Of this, since taking over the role of RBG(S), the Battle Group has been directly responsible for the destruction of over 6t of opium (equating to $370872.18 based on the UNODC calculation of Jan 09), 220kg of morphine, 1.838t of hashish, 750kg of brown heroin, 150kg poppy seeds, 110kg Marijuana seeds, 443lts of Acetic Anhydride as well as a number of further precursor chemicals and production related equipment.

In the case of Op OUBA 3, the most immediately measurable achievement was the destruction of a number of insurgent narcotics processing facilities and a significant amount of narcotics materiel in the Upper Sangin Valley. It was assessed that this large scale destruction of insurgent materiel equated to approximately 15% of the Upper Sangin Valley narcotic processing capability, inflicting significant impacts upon both insurgent funding streams and, perhaps as importantly, on insurgent perception of security in the Upper Sangin Valley. The risks of drug trafficking are undoubtedly increasing, enhancing the wedge between the insurgencies which remains intertwined with the trade in public perception and the local national population. The UNODC survey of September 2009 shows that farmers are increasingly wary of retaliation, trading has become more discreet, and stocks are now buried underground.

In addition, the friction between local nationals and insurgents that emerges as a result of operations targeting the narco-insurgent nexus, although in the short term may be painful,

A drug manufacturing plant destroyed during Operation OUBA 3.

nevertheless accentuates the political/tribal opportunities for GIRoA to reach out to important but politically disaffected individuals and diminish insurgent shadow governance in rural areas. Operations such as OUBA 3 demonstrate the vulnerability of the insurgents and narcotic producers as well as the effective reach and capability of ANSF and ISAF. Nor should these operations be seen in isolation; operations such as Op MAR ZAY, Oct 2009, targeting insurgent weapons facilitation aim to amplify this effect on the insurgency.

Op OUBA 3 - Sangin Calling – Major Al Steele (33), Officer Commanding Bravo Company

We had about 5 days back in camp to sort ourselves out before redeploying. This time we were heading to the Upper Sangin Valley; a place of incredible natural beauty. Dissected by the Helmand river the valley has a wide expanse of thick green zone on the eastern bank that gives way to steep sided barren mountains. On the western bank the dasht starts almost immediately with imposing sand cliffs that rise out of the river. Once an area where the Russian military elite would take a break it was now home to a number of key insurgent leaders as well as being the opium production hub of the province and therefore Afghanistan.

Perhaps more so than any operation to date, there was an acute sense of trepidation as we sat on the helicopter in the dark. Our task was to search a number of suspected narcotic labs and insurgent command centres and shut them down. It was about 5 minutes before

Soldiers look on as a Guided Multi Launch Rocket System strike hits its target.

landing when the enemy fire began zipping either side of the Chinook. Immediately the pilot began to take evasive action, weaving all over the sky while the door gunners "returned the compliment". I remember not being overly concerned, after all there nothing I could do to change the situation so there seemed little point in worrying. What did concern me was that any chance of surprise had now gone and when we landed we would be up against it. Sure enough as the Chinooks put down and the ramps lowered we were greeted by red tracer fire lighting up the sky all around us. Fortunately, the insurgents had not managed to mount a coordinated attack, which allowed us to make sense of the unavoidable confusion and disorientation of a night landing site.

Knowing that we had attack helicopter overhead for a couple of hours we pushed straight on in the hope that we could locate the enemy groupings and put the Apache to work. We managed to get about 50 m before we were pinned down on 3 sides, one of my platoons stuck crossing open ground; with quick thinking and a couple of grenades they where able to extract themselves to the relative safety of a compound.

Over the next couple of hours we edged forward until reaching the relative safety of our initial objectives. Time was the real enemy now, I had planned for each platoon to deal with one of these 3 isolated buildings before pulling back in to a more balanced position by first light. As dawn approached we had found some modest hauls of heroin and drug making equipment in the 2 flanking positions and it would now take time to document and destroy them. The choice became whether to leave these and perhaps not find anything else for the rest of the day or risk having the company spread out whilst dealing with the finds properly. I chose the latter, a decision that would see the company pinned down for the next 11 hours.

Thanks to some good work by the Jocks and the helicopters overhead there had been a slight let up in insurgent activity in those final 2 hours before sun up. However, as it became light the Taliban's response was immediate. Ironically, the daylight afforded us less of an advantage. The terrain was extremely close with countless places the enemy could approach and fire from whilst remaining undetected. Our overhead assets were of less use as the enemy kept his movement under the cover of trees. Most of all, we were working in an area he knew well and that was wholly alien to ourselves. For our part, we were in 3 easily defendable compounds so it could have quite happily been stalemate were it not for the requirement to keep pushing on to other suspected drugs labs.

This became the story of the rest of the day, us trying to break out of compounds while the insurgents tried to hold us in place while they rallied more troops and equipment. 6 Platoon to my north tried several times to move east and west in a bid to get back to our location. Each time they were pinned in the open by heavy and accurate fire. 5 Platoon to my south had better luck and were able to move between several compounds. The final platoon and my headquarters were stuck in the middle in contact from 3 sides and it wasn't long before we took our first casualty. Mercifully, only a wound to the upper arm but now we faced the problem of how to get him out in an area where the enemy was adept at targeting helicopters. The first tried hard to get in but limped away with 26 bullet holes, the second had more luck and managed to make it back to the field hospital, albeit on one engine. We were lucky.

The exchanges of fire continued all morning, with periodic successes from my snipers, taking advantage of occasional rare mistakes by the insurgent. We were slowly wearing them down. At times it was hard to avoid the temptation to call in artillery, which would have quickly ended matters but there were still plenty of civilians cowering in their compounds and the risk would have been too high. We did however manage to drop a few smoke rounds to provoke a reaction, allowing us to silence a few more positions. By lunchtime the company had been fighting for almost 7 hours and the heat was beginning to take its toll. In every platoon there were individual acts of bravery as we tried to get the upper hand. Our intelligence indicated that they were pausing to bring in reinforcements of ammunition and fighters and take out their fallen. Given that we had achieved all that we had set out to do, it seemed that a good time to extract to the comparative safety of the rest of the Battle Group who were sitting astride the main Sangin road. A Coy were pushed forward to cover the move but we still had 500 m of largely open ground to get through first and our foe enemy hadn't finished with us yet. 7 Platoon led the way and were contacted at close quarters from 2 positions. The lead section reacted instinctively assaulting the first position with such aggression that it was silenced once and for all. The second position was swiftly dealt with by the Apache gunship hovering above. The feeling of relief after moving through A Company was incredible.

We managed an hours sleep in the dasht before we were off again, moving a few kilometres off to where we would be picked up by helicopter. Last to leave, a few of us moved up onto the high ground to guard against rocket attacks. We were still in range and as soon as the Battle Group started lifting it wouldn't take long before the insurgents tried to target us. Sure enough, a couple of motorbikes approached after A Company had gone. One was seen with a radio and there was little doubt he was relaying our position. I asked the attack helicopters to look into areas in dead ground to us and they sighted a group of insurgents moving with weapons in cover. They were quickly dealt with giving us just enough breathing space to be picked up and get safely back to Camp BASTION.

It was only 2 days before we were off again so there little time to repack and start planning the next phase of the operation. This time we would attempt to be in and out during the night. As we landed this time it seemed as though we had caught the enemy completely by surprise and by the time they had had a chance to respond we were safely on the move. When we got to our target compound it was full of nothing more than a scared and startled family who weren't prepared to tell us anything about drug labs. It was as we left that someone proudly told me that the drugs were made next door! 5 Platoon quickly moved around and stumbled on the lab. The side door was still swinging as they got into the compound; someone had had a lucky escape. In their wake they left 8 vast cauldrons of steaming thick brown opium. As the search continued we found more and more; white (processed) heroin, bags upon bags of morphine rocks, drums of chemicals used in the processing, the list goes on. It was a massive find. Keen to get on the move we had only an hour to rig the compound with explosives. We could have simply hit the building with artillery but I was concerned about the locals still left in the adjacent compound. Instead the company's engineers set-up some altogether more subtle explosives, or so I thought! The resulting fireball was massive and could still be seen as we reached our HLS in the dasht!

Although 2 kms away we were still far from safe. In direct line of the green zone we were

Drugs and opium finds were almost always accompanied by ammunition, money and weapons finds. (MOD – Cpl R Freer)

Another insurgent drug manufacturing plant is sent up in smoke by 1 Troop, 25 Sqn, 38 Regt, Royal Engineers as Bravo Company ex-filtrate the target area.

Around 40 soldiers, fully laden, could be crammed into a CH47. (MOD – Cpl R Freer)

The return flight back to camp at the end of Op OUBA3. (MOD – Cpl R Freer)

last to leave again. We had just blown up what was estimated to be a fifth of the areas heroin production and it was unlikely the insurgent was going to just let us wander off. With A Company already back in Kandahar the CO was next to go. Just as his helicopter lifted there was a whoosh above our heads as a rocket narrowly missed the aircraft and exploded into the mountainside 100 m away from where one of my platoons was sat. With a brilliant bit of fieldcraft one of my sharpshooters spotted a position 2 ½ kilometres away, unfortunately out of our range. It was a nervous 30 minutes that followed as we waited for the helicopters to return. Eventually we managed to bring the attack helicopter into the area and the position was neutralised. Within a few hours we were back in the safety of Kandahar Airfield sipping an espresso in the French Café: bizarre!

WO2 (CSM) Paul Dargavel (39) from Dalgety Bay, Fife, Bravo Company

What's the hardest thing about the tour?
Day to day we're generally quite busy – I think getting things done is a lot harder in Camp Roberts because you haven't got an office with a phone, and you either spend your day trying to find people or waiting on somebody. I find that quite nauseating to the fact that a task that would normally take me 15 minutes back in Fort George takes me about 3 hours by the time I track somebody down.

What has been the best thing about being out here?
I think having the full deck of cards. Being able to do your job, I think we're lucky with the job that we've got at the minute. A Battle Group that has no restrictions in the way of kit. We've got all the kit, we've got more kit than any other unit because of our role. We've got so many aviation assets, we've got the full shooting match with what you would wish to have. This job is generally better supported because you're away from Helmand and you're under Regional Command (South), it's fortunate we've landed where we have.

Being out on the ground the time passes quickly, but I think coming in, planning an op, passing on the plans and briefing up the guys, getting the company ready G4 (logic) wise as well, and then obviously going on the ground, just sort of eats into the time as well. The OCs get thrashed. It's a good pace though. You've got to handle the pace. A lot of the Jocks don't see what happens behind the scenes.

Are you impressed with the Jocks?
Yes, totally. When we went to Iraq the Jocks did well, and as a Platoon Sergeant I couldn't ask for more from the guys. You always get guys of mixed ability and you'll always get people who'll come here and they'll be a dark horse at the beginning but they'll burst through and they'll take it in their stride. It's not just our Jocks, I think it's the Jock's nature, a 'canny Jock' – they just seem to get on with it, and they adapt quicker than what I've seen other people and again they've come through and they've come up trumps. Yep, they have their faults like anybody, but at the end of the day they know how to do their job and they do it well, and I wouldn't ask for anybody else.

Have you had near misses yourself?

Yes. The op in Sangin where we were pinned down and I had to deal with the casualty and the incoming fire on the helicopter. At that moment, we were pinned and obviously when we're on the ground, our lifeline is the air, because that's how we'll get our water and rations out, if anyone has an accident or a wounding, that's how we get them out, and that's how eventually they get us out. So that minute when the helicopter couldn't land, then you've got that realisation of isolation. 'What's going on here then, he can't get down, we can't get to him' and I need to get rid of him (the casualty) because he's wounded. We need to look at the drawing board and think again.

The MERT call sign that came in initially took over 30 rounds and there were 3 RPGs fired as well. It was quite a hairy moment and it shows you a bit of luck, and that the Chinooks are quite robust, it didn't go down. One of the rounds was a couple of inches away from one of the hydraulic shafts. That was quite hairy. More hairy for the air crew than us.

Before you came to Afghanistan, did you ever think you would be doing an assault with 12 Chinooks?

No. I didn't foresee us doing that with the Americans, Canadians, it was amazing. It was a key operation.

Can you think of any ridiculous situations you have been in?

I think lying on the deck on OUBA 3, getting incoming from the snipers, the 2IC was digging in with his teeth and I was laughing at him and saying, 'What are you up to son?'. We were laughing and he was looking at us wondering what we were laughing at. Those moments, you take away. It sort of helps situations to have that humour when things are bad. We lost 2 ANA soldiers that were attached to us, you can't focus too much on this, the fight's over for them which is unfortunate, but you need to get them away, you have not to dwell on it at the time, and you have to crack on. We have to use light humour to get through those times.

The Jocks crack me up, they're phenomenal, the stuff they come out with, just phenomenal comments. The one liners the Jocks come out with, you could probably create a book itself of their one liners.

One of the highlights for me was when we were going on an op down in Kandahar, the guys that rocked up turned out to be Canadian Black Watch which they told us within about a minute of meeting them. We got a good photograph with them with their Hackles. That was one of the major highlights actually meeting them, after hearing about them for years, since basic training. They still wear the old style TOS (highland headress), they call it a TAM. They were cock-a-hoop meeting us as well.

Corporal Alexander Wells (24) from Inverness, 6 Platoon, B Company, from Inverness

It's been alright so far, it's been an experience, a few hairy bits, but we just get through it as a platoon, it's not that bad. When we were in Sangin last week, my section was quite unlucky, we were point section all the time, we got caught in the open about 4 times, pinned down by fire. The first time we finished clearing one of the compounds and as my section entered the field, that's when we got pinned down from a firing point. I thought 'What the heck am I doing here.'

It took us a good 5 minutes to identify the firing point to get fire down, my point man passed a target indication to where it was and I managed to get the rest of the section onto the compound where they were firing on us from. I took the LASM off my back and managed to fire it and got the firing point on top of the roof where the gunmen where. It gave us a break to draw back to the bundline, where we continued the engagement and broke contact again.

Delta fire team were on the left of us, they were on a compound wall covering the move, and my Charlie fire team, we were walking up the track. Just as we got about 50m from a compound wall the Taliban started shooting down the track at us so again that was another near miss. I ended up with my Delta fire team stuck on a compound wall and because I was the point man, I was off to a river bank about a good 10m away from the rest of the section. So my fire team had to come over and put a fire base for me to extract and it was a case of getting the Delta fire team from the compound. It was pretty hard, we couldn't get comms on the PRR to see if they were okay, it took quite a while for us to establish were they were.

We were stuck in that compound for most of the day. It was pretty hard as quite a lot of the Jocks in the section had to get the courage to cross the open ground again. We were point section most of the day so it was a case of right we'll go into this compound. There was about 70m of open ground and it was just building up the courage of saying 'right we need to go now' then sure as has it 20m out in the open we were getting contacted again and pinned down. You knew it was coming.

When I fired the LASM and I seen it hit the target I let out a wee cheer myself, it was just like a relief. That's one less firing point to worry about. It was my first time firing it as well so I didn't really know what to expect, I just read the instructions.

Private Bob McTurk (22), from Fife, 5 Platoon, Bravo Company

It opens your eyes when you come out here. When you come under contact it helps if you laugh, if you dunna laugh you're gonna cry. I never thought you'd be able to fire lying in the prone position looking through your SUSAT with all the kit we have to carry on your back but I've proved it. In the heat of the moment when you come under contact you don't get a chance to take off your daysack, you just get down and start to fire. We've got a lot of smaller guys who are stronger than the bigger guys.

The assets that support us are amazing. It gives you a lot of confidence – Apaches, Pedros, B1 Bomber... you hear the jets but you can't see them. I've seen the Javelin fired a few times and the GMLRS.

Private Donnie Campbell (30), from Oban, 6 Platoon Bravo Company
31 May 2009: (Op in Sangin Valley Phase 1; 36 hrs)

We are to be ready to go at 1830 hrs for transport down to the airhead and wheels up at 1930 hrs. Everything was done, my kit was all squared away ready to go. We left BASTION at 1930 hrs and fly out to a desert leager about 3-4 kms from the objective. The flight took about 45 minutes, at one point I thought the Chinook was going to crash but it was just the pilot doing some evasive flying. We took off again from the leager at about 2245 hrs and were out the back of the choppers and formed up in a 'NATO T' 5 minutes later. The choppers leave then 'bosh' we get contacted, we move to an embankment and try to identify the firing point with no luck, so my section push forward to see if we can get eyes on. We only got about 15m when they open up again. I hit the deck that hard that I snapped one of the bi-pod legs off my rifle. There was a ditch behind me about 3 m away so I crawled in to it to give myself a bit of cover. I got a chance to look around through my night sight but couldn't see anyone, then it came over the net that the fire had been onto 7 Platoon's position. The call went in to the Apaches overhead and we hear rounds from the 30mm cannon hit the deck followed a second later by the sound of the gun firing.

We stayed in that area for a while, watching the flanks so that 7 Platoon could go and break in to the compounds. When we moved up to the compounds later on we found that 7 Platoon found some raw opium. We headed off towards another compound, our objective. Just as it was starting to get light, we spotted a bloke in front of us in a white dish dash and approached him. He disappeared however. We found another 10 'fighting aged males' and women and children. The groups were segregated and the men were questioned. The men claimed to be farmers. The compound was searched and we found a load of raw opium, about 15lbs of weed and 2 opium presses, not a bad haul. The engineers rigged the presses with some explosives and destroyed the drugs. We then joined the rest of the platoon and set off back to the other compounds of interest.

We were lead section so we set off first, we had to cross some open ground as we set off and must have only got about 150m when we got contacted to our front. As myself and most of 1 section were out in the open, there wasn't much we could do but hit the deck. The lads then started putting some rounds down. I was thinking we're stuffed out here in the open with no cover and within easy reach. I could hear the rounds flying past my head and the ping of them hitting the deck and ricocheting over me. It's funny but I wasn't that scared, I was probably preoccupied with trying to slip my arm out of my bergan so I could get some fire down more easily. I heard Wellsy say he was going to fire the LASM which at this point I thought was a great idea. Now Wellsy was further forward than me and in just as much shit as I was if not more, but he still managed to set up the LASM, get on one knee and fire it. It was a great shot and right onto the firing point.

It was time to get out of there, and the rest of the lads who by this time had got into a base line behind some cover to our rear, put down some covering fire so we could peel back into cover. As the boys started peeling back towards me I got up on to a knee ready to move and put some rounds down. When the last man to my front was past me I was up and off like a shot, it's amazing how light your kit becomes when you're being shot at.

We bounded back towards compound 21 and the boss decided we could move back to it, but first we would have to clear round it. So again 1 Section took the lead, we headed off in our fire teams with Keatsy taking the left, Durie, Crooks and myself on the right. Keatsy headed along the outside wall of the compound toward a building to the rear. We headed off down a path towards some buildings to the right of Keatsy's position. As we approached the building which was now about 20m to our front, we got contacted from the building. The rounds bounced up the path towards us like something out of a movie. Wellsy and Durie dived right towards a large pond, I dived left against a bank at the side of the path, then realised it was not the best place to be, so I made a dive across the path to the pond side. The insurgents would fire anytime we tried to move, so yet again we were pinned down and unable to return fire as we were in a pond and we had no eyes on each other never mind the enemy. Wellsy was stuck in a position that offered little cover, so we had to get him out of there. Hart got some rounds down with the GPMG so Durie could get to Wellsy, then Screwy turned up and between him and Hart they managed to suppress the enemy so we could extract to a better fire position.

We then heard that Keatsy's fire team are stuck in a compound and have one ANA casualty. Keatsy patched him up and the engineer blew a hole in the wall, the lads fell back to compound 21 to join back up with us. We moved back into compound 21 and the boss told Wellsy to put us in fire positions outside the rear of the compound were we stayed for the rest of the day. We got fired on several times. 'B' spotted an armed man digging a murder hole so took him out with the L96. The Apaches came in and then we heard that 7 Platoon had taken a casualty. One of the engineers took a round in the arm. The 9 Liner was sent and the PEDRO came in to casevac him back to BASTION. The chopper was fired at repeatedly but the pilot stayed put until the casualty was on board, which is pretty ballsy if you ask me.

The insurgents tried to airbust RPGs over us as well but were falling about 100m short of us. When we moved off from compound 21 to go and meet up with 7 Platoon we had to cross the same open ground we got contacted on in the morning. I've got to say I was not looking forward to it, you've just to get on with it though and crack on. We made it across no bother this time, but as we moved towards 7 Platoon's position we were contacted again. This time though, no one was out in the open. We got rounds down onto the firing point and the Apache overhead put a burst onto it. Duncy Bruce hit it with a LASM just to make sure.

We moved into the compound 7 Platoon were in and chilled out for about 15 minutes. Just enough time to get some water down us and have a smoke before being told we had to push through and take compound 10. Of course the minute we left the compound the rounds starting flying again, we legged it to a wooded area across from compound 10 and let 7 Platoon deal with the insurgents who had been firing at us. We had a little soak period then pushed out of cover towards compound 10. I was the fourth man and was just about to move off when we got contacted (again) from what we thought was the east. So Durie made a run for the compound wall, it was only when we seen rounds hitting the wall above Durie's head we realised it was coming from the west. I moved out as far as I could without exposing myself and shouted to Wellsy that there was plenty of space where I was for the boys to run into.

5 and 7 Platoon were to our rear and started putting down covering fire so the boys could leg it into cover. The decision was made to use the Apache to fire on the position so we could move. It worked a treat and the company got out safe and sound. As the last of the lads got in, we got IDF'd, it landed just outside the compound. From here the OC planned to move us out to a desert leager. We moved off towards A Company's position, pushed through them and into a FUP in some dead ground in the desert. A Company then pushed past us at the desert leager about 2.5 kms into the desert. We heard C Company getting into contact just as we moved off. We reached the leager position, had some scoff and got our heads down. It was about 2200 hrs and we had been fighting since we landed the night before so everyone was bollocksed. The Chinooks picked us up about 0600 hrs on the 2 June and flew us back to BASTION. Tired but still in one piece.

Op OUBA 3 – Insertion – Captain David Mack (32), from Toronto, Canada, Officer Commanding Mortar Platoon, Charlie Company

It's some time before midnight. We're on the flight line waiting to board the helicopter. TAC is on the first wave this time – TAC is normally always on the last wave, the companies have got to get on the ground first to maintain surprise. The helicopters arrive, there is somebody with a glow stick, we follow him on to the helicopter. TAC is going to a hill top to get eyes on the area. I strap myself in my seat. I keep my rucksack on, the helo is full and I can't place it on the floor as there are Jocks everywhere. It is tight and cramped in the helo, my arm is pinned by the weight of the rucksack and my body armour and I already feel my arm numbing. How long is this flight? 45 minutes, I reply to myself. The sound of the propellers is loud, the cabin is warm, it's dark and even if I wanted to speak with someone the troops are too focused for idle chit-chat. I slowly doze off.

BANG! Suddenly, flares explode from the helicopter. For an instant I see everyone in the cabin. I can feel my heart pumping. RAT-TAT-TAT. The guns open up. I look out the window and see streams of red tracer pouring from the helicopters flying parallel to us; a barrage of hot lead looking for targets. I am told later that we routed through the Musa Qal'ah Wadi, a hot bed for insurgents who are happy take a shot at helicopters. I pray, Hail Mary, Hail Mary – I'm not even Catholic but I'm certain I saw it in *A Bridge Too Far* – Hail Mary, Hail Mary. How does it go? Hail Mary, the Lord is with thee – yeah, that's it – Hail Mary, The Lord is with thee, blessed art thou amongst women, blessed is the fruit of thy womb Jesus, pray for us sinners now and in the hour of our death. RAT-TAT-TAT. Hail Mary. Forget it. Lord God, take care of these men. Though I walk through the valley of the shadow of death, I will fear no evil. Please

God, take care of these fine young men. I need a smoke. I can't smoke, I'm in a helicopter. I won't be able to smoke even on the ground and I'll have to wait until sunrise. Dear God, dear God, dear God. I doze off again.

We're turning in the air as the helicopter comes into land. We're dropping in altitude as we approach the ground. The helicopter touches down and the rear ramp opens up. The RSM and his party step off checking the ground. The remainder of TAC follow him. We squat in a line. The helicopter lifts off and dust, sand, and rocks spray us from the downdraft of the propellers. The helicopters are away and the companies are safe on the ground. Comms are established through our radios, each of my men check in with me. It's dark and I look up and see the stars. There is a warm breeze moving along the valley. All quiet.

Captain Ryan Wood 'The Doc' (28), from Camberley, Royal Army Medical Corps

For me as a doctor coming out here and doing the job I'm doing at the really pointed end of the fighting here is just phenomenal. I'll never be able to get this sort of level of trauma experience anywhere in the UK, but it's more than that. It's being out on the ground with the Jocks that makes the big difference. For me its seeing how these young 18 year old lads cope in the most horrendous situations; carrying a phenomenal amount of weight, carrying mental burdens really, carrying the worries and fears they all have going on as young men not knowing what they're going to meet, and then seeing how they've dealt with that and moved on and grown up. And the phrase 'boys to men' is very 'twee' but we're watching it happen out here and they're doing an amazing job. And just to be a part of that as a doctor has been a privilege.

I'd got to meet the Jocks in Kenya and I'd got to see how they coped in the heat, and also away from home, and in reasonably arduous conditions but my memory of Kenya was that it was a lot easier than it has been here. And although it was good training because the heat was very similar, it doesn't fully prepare you for here. Being very honest before seeing the first op, I had a real worry that the Jocks weren't up to the task, physically and mentally. Four months down the line, I have no worries whatsoever. They've turned into tough little buggers, they've turned into tough guys who can really do this job amazingly well. Everyday I'm so impressed, I'm impressed by how they deal with the day to day stresses of being out on the ground, their humour, the stories they tell, every now and again tempers will boil over but that's human and it's an important part of being out here. The way they banter with one another is phenomenal, it's all really good for them.

My big regret is that I can only do half of this tour. I wish I was able to finish the tour with the Battle Group, I feel that I've been through an awful lot with them, I've learnt a hell of a lot both from the medics around me, in particularly my med Sergeant, Sergeant Paul Cooper, who has taught me so much over the months I've known him, about soldiering, but a bit about life as well. Again at the risk of sounding cheesy, I've really learnt an awful lot. What I'm going to miss, and my big fear is that I'm going to miss the times when I feel I could have helped the Jocks in the future. God forbid if we are involved in any other big incidents, anymore injuries, I'll be sat at home reading about them in the paper knowing that if things had of been different, I'd still be out here. And I do feel that all of my medics and I have a lot to offer these guys when they get injured, we're very well trained and that training kicks in very fast and we can help them out a lot, and we can buy them the time they need to get them back to the real heroes who work in the hospitals who save their lives.

The medics are Combat Medical Technicians and I think more and more the emphasis is on that first part, combat. These guys are doing exactly the same on the ground as the Jocks, they are on the same patrols, they are carrying the same weight, they're carrying their rifles and at times they are having to fire their rifles to defend themselves and their patients who are the Jocks around them. And then with all those stresses going on, they're also having to treat their patients. There's nothing easy about that and they're really pulling out all the stops. And some of my young medics have dealt with some horrific things that consultants in the UK have never seen, and they're dealing with it on their own and really

Alpha (Grenadier) Company disembark their CH47 into a holding area before last light prior to their find by insertion to the target area. (MOD – Cpl R Freer)

very well and I'm so desperately impressed with them. They should be good, I've taught them!

To give you an idea of what we do, I'll talk about one particular case. It was a very difficult op. It was phase 1 of Op OUBA 3 which was a 24 hr raid into kind of the mid part of the upper Sangin Valley between Sangin and Kajaki. And it was Tiger Country. We were in contact from 10 minutes before we landed, we were contacted in the air, and we were in contact for 20 hrs after that, which was a long time and it was really hard work. And at one point an Engineer got shot whilst he was on sentry, he got shot in the arm. It quickly became apparent that a lot of damage had been done, so I worked quite hard to initially stabilise and control his bleeding and then get him comfortable. And that for me as a doctor, the additional skills I bring to the table, is the pain control and pain management I can give. So I immediately looked to control his pain with some of the drugs I carry with me, and get him settled and make sure the bleeding was controlled. Once I'd done that it was a priority to get him out urgently but we were still in contact. We had 3 snipers all around us in 3 directions and the only place we could use to get a helicopter down was 'hot'. There were rockets coming onto it, RPGs coming onto it every half hour, there were small arms rounds and the helicopters had to fly in. Originally the British MERT, which is the Chinook, flew in and it got shot up. It received 40 – 50 rounds and an RPG launched at it, it got very close

Bravo Coy extraction just after first light.

to the landing site and I think the pilots did an heroic job to get it as close as they did, but it had to retreat.

So I've got a casualty with me who is now starting to deteriorate, the bleeding is becoming very difficult to control, he's deteriorating in himself, and I was asked on the radio, can we hold this guy, because the choppers are getting shot up. And I had to make what was a reasonably difficult decision, and I had to say no, I need a chopper now. So I had to risk another pilots life effectively and the crew to get this guy out. And they're difficult decisions to make, but in some ways they're very easy, because the clinical picture makes the decision for you. If I couldn't control that bleeding, which was becoming more difficult to do, he could have easily died.

One of the American Black Hawks flew in, it landed on, and we watched out from near the landing site, and again with rounds coming down around our feet, the helicopter was shot whilst it was on the landing site. I gave a handover, which I always do, to the medic on board, and normally they run out to meet you. But to give you an idea of exactly what this landing zone was like, he wasn't leaving his chopper. So we had to run all the way up there, give the handover to the medic and then they flew off, and that guy got back and he's done very well. That was a really long day. A really difficult time. But they're the sort of casualties we get. We just buy them a bit of time, that's all we're able to do on the ground, get them back to the hospitals where the guys really do some amazing stuff.

We'd been in sustained contact for a few days on one op, and at one point the OC came up to me and said, 'Are you alright doc' and I thought to myself, 'Yeah I am alright, but thanks for asking'.

Corporal Sean Martin (31), from Stoke-on-Trent, 14 Signal Regiment, Corps of Royal Signals

The most vivid memory I have of this tour is stepping off the Chinook with the CO's TAC onto the high ground, over looking the Upper Sangin Valley. Looking down through my NVG at all the tracer and RPG fire between the various contacts and also directed at the helicopters. It was unreal.

Sergeant Eddie Nichol (37), from Dundee, 3 Platoon (Minden), Alpha (Grenadier) Company

Just coming back from R&R I spoke to a lot of civilians who are absolutely criticising the government and saying that they're terrible, we've not got the kit, we've not got the equipment. But they don't understand the whole picture, and how many Americans are here supporting the effort and how high their casualty rates are.

The kit we have is a vast improvement to the past, however it could be even better. The kit we've got is fine but it's far too heavy and far too bulky. The radio batteries don't last long enough so I'm carrying at least 5 heavy batteries with a huge radio to last 24 hrs.

Chapter Five

Operation TORA ARWA 1

10 June–15 June 2009

INTRODUCTION

Operation TORA ARWA 1 was part of a Task Force Kandahar operation focussed on disrupting insurgent capabilities prior to the Afghan National Elections and also to prepare the region for US expansion in to Kandahar Province. The Battle Group was tasked to conduct Operation TORA ARWA 1 in the area of Nalgham, Zhari District. Intelligence reports had noted this area as an important insurgent command and control centre as well as a centre for IED production; ISAF commanders had labelled the area "the Heart of Darkness".

The Battle Group planned to conduct an aviation assault into Objective CHARGER prior to first light on 10 June. Alpha Company would initially secure Objective GATLING, the Afghan National Army Company attached to the Battle Group would similarly secure Objective MUSKET, and Bravo Company would secure Objective CARBINE. Battle Group TAC and the Mortar Platoon would be established on the Canadian Patrol Base Ghundey Ghar. Once the objectives had been secured, the companies were then tasked to establish patrol bases in the objectives and conduct disruption patrols within boundaries. On 12 June, the Battle Group would conduct a second aviation assault into Objectives CANNON and RIFLE. The Battle Group were scheduled to extract on 15 June.

EXECUTION – PULSE 1
10 June 09 (D Day)

Alpha Company landed on its objectives at 0240 hrs followed shortly afterwards by the Afghan National Army Company and B Company an hour later. The UAV soak that had begun several hours prior to H-Hour indicated that the pattern of life in the area was normal and

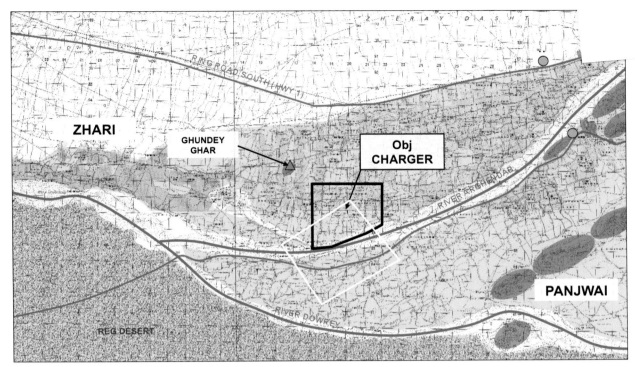

The map of the operation area, targeting the green zone north of the River Arghendab.

The operation schematic, showing the Company objectives.

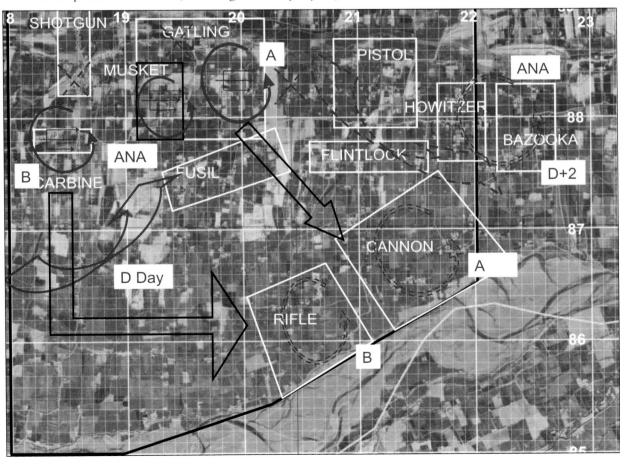

a number of local nationals were working in the field threshing wheat that night. At 0430 hrs TAC and the Mortar Platoon landed in the Canadian hilltop patrol base at Ghundey Ghar; in the air, the Battle Group had use of UK Harriers and Apache helicopters.

Early in the morning, intelligence suggested that the insurgents were aware that the Battle Group had arrived in the area but they were uncertain of its location. By 0500 hrs, the 2 companies had shaken out and begun the process of searching and securing compounds and Alpha Company had a made a significant find of an AK 47, anti-personnel mines, 880 rounds of 7.62mm ammunition, 140 rounds of 9mm ammunition, two 9mm pistols, mortar fuzes, 115kg of wet opium and a set of Canadian combat clothing.

At roughly 0630 hrs Bravo Company had noticed quite a bit of activity as local nationals were leaving the area, a key combat indicator that suggested an imminent attack. At 0652 hrs, Bravo Company was subsequently engaged by 15 insurgents firing small arms fire and RPGs from no more than 500m away. Throughout the remainder of the day, Bravo Company was in and out of contact and used all the weapons at their disposal including Javelin missiles and 81mm mortars. Alpha Company continued with its own patrol until it was similarly contacted in the afternoon. The companies remained in contact throughout the afternoon until roughly 1800 hrs. All 3 companies occupied compounds during the evening, although Bravo Company also set an interdiction patrol at 2300 hrs.

CO's TAC Group – Maj Jeremy Sharpe RA (BC), Capt Chris Baddeley (Ops Officer), WO1 (RSM) McDougal, Lt Col Stephen Cartwright (CO), Capt Dougie Bartholmew (JTAC) (MOD – Sgt C Halton)

An 81mm high explosive round leaving the barrel, Mortar Platoon, Charlie Company (Pte G Johnson)

11 June 09 (D Day+1)

The day started with the companies continuing to search and secure compounds. Following the resupply early that morning, Alpha Company reported that almost half of its rations had not arrived – it was assessed that they had fallen out of the cargo nets underslung from the helicopter, during the flight from Kandahar. During the morning, the radios intercepted a moderate level of communication by the insurgents and conspicuous movements. At 0755 hrs, Alpha Company was contacted by small arms and indirect fire from multiple firing points. Mortar fire missions were immediately called to support the company.

By 0900 hrs, the Afghan National Army Company had reported that it had cleared numerous compounds and Bravo Company had found a small amount of ammunition.

Moving east (with 2 platoons 'up') towards its primary objectives, Alpha Company was contacted by accurate and sustained small arms, RPG and rocket fire. A section from 2 Platoon was pinned down by accurate rifle fire. Private Robert McLaren manoeuvred forward to improve his position and relieve pressure on his comrades. Tragically, at 1004 hrs an IED exploded and killed Private McLaren and injured another soldier, Private Mark Connolly; both casualties were evacuated from the site and extracted by helicopter at 1118 hrs.

The remainder of the day consisted of sporadic engagements against Alpha Company and the Afghan National Army Company while Bravo Company made numerous finds.

12 June 09 (D Day + 2)

As a result of the intense activities of the previous 2 days, the original plan to relocate the companies by aviation into Objectives RIFLE and CANNON was cancelled. Rather, the companies continued to conduct compound searches. Bravo Company was now south of Objective CARBINE and was moving east towards Objective RIFLE; Alpha Company had moved out of Objective GATLING and into Objective FUSIL. The day was punctuated by numerous engagements and some finds of marijuana (170kg) and opium (3kg), weapons, ammunition and radio equipment. At 1505 hrs, Bravo Company became involved in a protracted contact that lasted for 2 hours. Contacts ceased with the last light and a resupply for the Battle Group took place at 2042 hrs.

13 June 09 (D Day + 3)

At 0307 hrs, the Afghan National Army Company conducted an aviation assault into Objective BAZOOKA and held firm in compounds until first light. At 0421 hrs as Bravo Company patrolled east into Objective RIFLE, an IED exploded in a compound and killed 2 soldiers from the Afghan National Army. The force of the explosion broke the arms of the interpreter and threw Lieutenant Andrew Halliday, 6 Platoon Commander, across the compound's courtyard. Although initially he appeared to be unhurt, Lieutenant Halliday subsequently returned to the UK from injuries sustained by the explosion. Following the IED explosion the company took particular caution and was rewarded by finding 5 suspected IEDs.

During this period, Alpha Company patrolled into Objective CANNON and conducted a shura with local nationals who indicated that insurgents were not in the village but were very close.

14 June – 15 June 09 (D Day + 4 – D Day + 5)

Following the casualties of the previous day and a number of IED finds in the area, Bravo Company established a cordon and at 0852 hrs was engaged. During this contact, a soldier from the Afghan National Army stepped on an IED that severed one leg and caused catastrophic bleeding to his other leg. He was quickly evacuated and was immediately in surgery upon his arrival in Kandahar Airfield. Late that evening at 1759 hrs, the Afghan National Army Company was contacted by indirect fire. Corporal James Couper from the Reconnaissance Platoon and an Afghan soldier were both injured and were evacuated at 1930 hrs. In addition, Bravo Company was also contacted by small arms fire and indirect fire. Extraction began at 0219 hrs on the morning of the 15 June 09 and all troops were complete in Kandahar at 0330 hrs.

SUMMARY

Operating in rugged terrain, blistering heat and under intense weight from body armour and other equipment, the Battle Group successfully completed an arduous 6 day operation in the heart of insurgent territory in Kandahar Province. In all, the unit found numerous weapons

Members of the 3 SCOTS Battle Group remember Pte McLaren. (MOD – Sgt C Halton)

Padre David Anderson, the 3 SCOTS Battle Group Padre taking the service at Pte McLaren's vigil held in Camp Roberts. (MOD – Sgt C Halton)

including AK 47s and pistols, anti-personnel mines, 1176 rounds of 7.62mm ammunition, 150 rounds of 9mm ammunition, explosives as well as 118kg wet opium, 190kg of marijuana and 110kg of marijuana seeds. In the words of Major Matt Munro, "Op TORA ARWA 1 was an enormous success. We emphatically achieved our mission of disrupting the insurgents, we secured the area and killed large numbers of insurgents and found and denied large quantities of his equipment and material."

Nonetheless, despite the remarkable feats of arms of individual soldiers and countless acts of bravery the Battle Group sustained numerous casualties including the death of Private Robert McLaren and 2 Afghan warriors. Morale amongst the troops was buoyant; however, the intensity of the days of Operation TORA ARWA 1 and the Battle Group's tragic losses, were felt by all members of the Battle Group.

Op TORA ARWA – Into the Heart of Darkness – Major Al Steele (33), Officer Commanding Bravo Company

As we sat back in the safety of Kandahar the Canadian Brigadier General, commander of the province, explained that the area that we had just spent 5 days was known as the 'Heart of Darkness'. Prior to the operation I'm not sure if we would have believed him. Whilst it was a Battle Group affair the companies were geographically well separated. Again we would be flying into a heavily agricultural green zone although this time the crop was predominantly grapes. The vines spread for kilometres running from east to west making movement north south at best heavily canalised.

Maj Al Steele (on the radio) and his Signals Det commander, Cpl Kev Dowdles (MOD – Sgt C Halton)

A Fire Support Group moving through the green zone – note the poppy field in the foreground post harvest. (MOD – Sgt C Halton)

We landed without problem and steadily made our way to our initial objectives. We had been sent in to try and disrupt a highly effective insurgent grouping that had been regularly targeting convoys moving along the main highway through Helmand and Kandahar provinces. Not knowing the enemy dispositions I placed 2 platoons as flank protection north and south and by first light they were concealed in position while the rest of the company began their clearance of a small village.

It emerged much later that we had landed in between a force of insurgents and Ghunday Ghar, a prominent feature in the area upon which a small grouping of Canadians and Afghan National Army (ANA) were based. It was also where Battle Group HQ and our mortar platoon had landed. Instead of being able to attack Ghunday Ghar the company became the focus of the insurgents' attention. The contact began as 6 Platoon pushed through their objective and out to the eastern flank. They quickly repulsed the attack while my Fire Support Group (FSG), until that point concealed, opened up. With the insurgents now fixed in the middle of the grape vines we called in the mortars for the first time since arriving in theatre. Between their accurate fire and the snipers we were able to inflict heavy casualties. This was later confirmed by the local nationals we spoke to further south who had seen groups of injured fighters and their dead being moved out of the area. It was the last time in the operation that they took us on head to head.

The next 2 days were spent patrolling south, having changed our original plan to keep pressure on the insurgents. There seemed a strange mix of individuals in each of the villages we came to. Most were scared and submissive, some warned us of that they had seen insurgents digging in IEDs. Others were more outgoing and even cocky. Their carefully manicured hands and the deference shown to 2 individuals was at odds with their surroundings and we were reasonably confident that they were significant figures within the local insurgency. However, without any evidence there was little that we could do.

By the end of the third day tensions were running high. During both nights we had marched several kilometres to break through the IED screens that had been laid to fix us in position. 7 Platoon had done a fantastic job finding several devices, allowing the company to get into position by morning unscathed. Alpha Company had suffered one soldier, Private Robert McLaren, tragically killed by an IED whilst fighting off to our flank. We had had a few minor skirmishes but nothing on the scale of the first day. At one point 5 Platoon were attacked whilst in the middle of a set of orders. Their response was immediate as they set off in pursuit of the small insurgent group having the presence of mind to use flash bangs and not grenades as they cleared through a house, having seen women and children in it earlier in the day. That night 7 Platoon led the advance again finding another 2 IEDs en route.

Nevertheless, by first light we were set to clear into another village believed to contain a safe house for use by insurgents in the area. 7 Platoon were slowed up as they found yet more IEDs. My focus on this was abruptly interrupted by the sound of a massive explosion on the other flank of the village where 6 Platoon were moving. I cannot describe how sickening a moment this was as I saw a mushroom cloud of thick grey dust stretching 50m into the air. There would certainly be casualties it was just a question of how many.

Mixed emotions took hold as I reached 6 Platoon. All the Jocks that I had left Scotland with were safe but of the 2 ANA warriors that had been with them, one was now missing both of his legs and the other was missing altogether. Despite being deaf in the one ear the platoon commander was miraculously alive, standing next to the crater that had once been the floor of the compound. He and the Jocks around him were covered from head to toe in a thick grey dust and getting on with the task of securing the area. The other platoon commanders maintained incredible composure while all this was going on at a time where we all wondered if the next step that we took might be our last.

Gradually we were able to secure and clear a couple of compounds and gain a foothold. Unfortunately, news travels fast and the insurgents knew they had us fixed as we conducted a detailed clearance of the area and recovered the dead bodies. The second ANA soldier was found intact but dead about 40m away in a different compound, such was the force of the explosion. We consolidated overnight with all of the company making a fantastic effort to rally. The next morning we set about clearing the other IEDs that 7 Platoon had found. 5 Platoon were first to leave, putting in an outer cordon for 7 Platoon to move in the explosive specialists.

Soon after leaving the relative security of the compounds the enemy opened up on us. It takes a disciplined soldier to remain fixed to a cleared track when rounds are landing all around. The instinctive reaction is to run for cover but to have done so in such a heavily IED'd area could have been disastrous. 5 Platoon held the ground and 7 Platoon got into a position from where they could support. Just as we were gaining the upper hand there was another explosion, another IED and another ANA casualty. Thankfully, this time he was alive although in a very poor state; the medics doing a fantastic job until the evacuation helicopter arrived.

Fighting continued and as the insurgents began to reinforce their positions we consolidated ours. With our extraction confirmed for the small hours of that night we had to give them a bloody nose less they try to target the aircraft. Sporadic contacts continued into the night, sometimes at less than 70m as the insurgent probed our perimeter. Fortunately, due to the robust response of some of the platoons these tailed off and we were able to extract unhindered.

Looking back, the 'heart of darkness' seems no less fitting a description of the area and made us all acutely aware that it isn't just Helmand where the fighting is fierce.

OP TORA ARWA 1 – Personal Account – Captain Euan Quin (30), from Bath, 38 Battery, 40 Regiment, Royal Artillery, attached to Bravo Company

On breaking into our first compound it did not take the insurgents long to begin engaging us. As my FST element of Company TAC established itself on the rooftop the crack of small arms fire could be heard as our FSG was engaged from the vineyards to the South. I turned to my MFC A , Sergeant Porter, and he quickly laid the mortars onto the target. Lance Bombardier Craig Biggins established communications on the TACSAT and began feeding in sitreps to the BC to help build up the battle picture to ensure our response was both robust and proportional in equal measure. Once we received "airspace clear" the order was given to fire and we waited for the rounds to land, our first High Explosive (HE) rounds of the tour. After a few adjustments the mortar rounds began falling effectively onto the firing points. This forced the insurgents to move across open ground and they were quickly picked off by the remainder of the Company. Running engagements occurred throughout the next few days, with intense fighting by day and then the quiet, anxious night moves in order to outfox the insurgent and keep him guessing as to our next move. On the third day of the operation my MFC B, Corporal Tam Mason, sighted an insurgent emplacing an IED and expertly called in a mortar mission onto him. He told me his heart was in his mouth as these were the first rounds he had fired in anger but this was replaced with a sense of excitement and relief when the initial rounds landed right on target and after giving the insurgent a high rate of fire, the threat was neutralised. Later on that day B Company had been pinned down in a compound for 40 minutes under effective small arms, RPG and sniper fire from a compound 300m to our West. Bombardier Richard McAuley and Gunner Toby Mewett had located the firing point and were able to provide a mensurated grid for the target. Having gained clearance to engage from my Company Commander I requested a precision munition to engage and was allocated a Canadian M777 Troop equipped with the Excaliber GPS guided 155mm HE round. Only 2 of these rounds had ever been fired in support of operations in Afghanistan. The hard work and exercises we had conducted before we deployed onto the ground was paying off and the fire orders were passed exactly as they had been practiced in Kandahar. As we were waiting for the dust to settle, the crack of the .338 sniper rifles combined with a Javelin being launched into the compound confirmed the fate of the insurgents still intent on fighting on. Out of the 5 insurgents who had engaged us, 3 were now dead and 2 had fled north and into the arcs of our FSG. The jubilation and pride at this engagement was sensed in the looks on the faces of all the members of my FST. We had done exactly what we had practised in training, this time in the harsh environment of Southern Afghanistan.

Op TORA ARWA 1 – Personal Account – Lance Corporal Gary Richford (28), from Glasgow, 6 Platoon, Bravo Company

I was standing about 2 metres in front of the ANA soldier that was just killed by an IED, I got thrown off the wall, I've got whiplash. Total shock, sort of numb, just checked to see if I had all my bits and pieces. I was quite amazed that I was still alive. And I was even more amazed to see that none of our guys got killed. Unfortunately for the ANA boys they weren't so lucky. Initially I did'na realise I'd been hurt, we extracted back, got the casualties back to the HLS, got them out first and after about half an hour I started to feel the pain myself. So eventually I got casevaced.

For B Company this op was sort of run of the mill, contacts in the morning and late in the afternoon and stuff. It was quite harsh to hear about the Alpha (Grenadier) Company boy, so after that everyone was sort of more aware and stuff.

Op TORA ARWA 1 – First Contact – 10 June 2009 – Captain Harry Gladstone (26), from Dumfries, Machine Gun Platoon Commander, Charlie Company, from Dumfries

The ground to our front was bare for about 200m before changing into a grape field. The grapes grow on walls about 5 feet high. I placed snipers and machine gunners on my flanks and kept a Javelin missile ready in the centre of the position.

We discussed how bored we were going to be for the next 5 days, and even started predicting what would happen in the next few days. Corporal Tod predicted absolutely nothing would happen. I said that we would have no enemy action for 2 days then we would start to find a few IEDs. I also said it was likely that we would have a contact on the last day. I could not have been more wrong. After about an hour in position, we were attacked from about 300 m. The enemy was using a grape wall as a covered position from which to fire at us. Three accurate RPGs landed very close to our position. Corporal Tod fired an under slung grenade which missed the enemy. Corporal Reynolds then sent him adjustments and his second grenade scored a direct hit on the enemy position. There must have been other positions because the enemy fire continued. My 2 GPMG gunners on either flank engaged.

Once we could hear our own rounds going towards the enemy we all felt a lot happier. I reported the position to my OC who replied angrily "check if they really are 100Kms away!" Feeling stupid I rechecked and gave him the correct enemy position. In my haste I had misread the map. The OC was able to relay this position to the mortars via his Mortar Fire Controller. After 2 salvos, the rounds were on target. At one point another RPG landed on our position at the same time as friendly mortars were landing. A stone was kicked up into Corporal Tod's Face leaving a large mark. This made me think we were under fire from our own mortars in a blue on blue, and I called a check fire. I soon realised I had been mistaken and allowed the mortars to continue.

A sniper accompaned by a Machine Gunner. Snipers were very good at spotting movement and identifying insurgents. The x25 Schmit and Bender Sight combined with the new .338 calibre sniper rifle was a deadly combination. Information could then be used by Machine Gunners to bring down heavy weights of fire if needed. (MOD – Sgt C Halton)

The Mortars finally brought an end to the enemy firing. They made a whistling noise as they went over our heads giving us time to take cover. Earth and debris were thrown high into the air with each round. The noise was deafening but lifted everybody's spirits. At last the rounds were complete and silence was restored to the area. I considered moving, but could not see any position better than the one we were already in. I moved around the troops to find out if there were any weak spot in our defences. I was concerned that the attacks would resume from our flanks, so I moved my machine gunners to cover the flanks. On the advice of the Platoon Sergeant, Sergeant Robertson, I was able to spread out our soldiers so that they were not concentrated in one area. The OC moved another platoon down to cover my most vulnerable flank. Meanwhile the remainder of the company resumed its search of the village to the north.

After a period of 20 minutes a small group of men moved towards us. We were all very nervous and we searched and questioned them thoroughly. It became clear that they wanted to continue to farm their fields. This is normally a good sign and indicates that insurgents have left the area. They were angry about the fields which had been burnt by the impact of the

RPGs near us. We tried to explain that the fire had been started by the Taliban RPGs. They asked for permission to try and put it out. They had put out half of the fire when we heard the crack of rounds above our heads. The enemy had attacked again, this time from much closer and by using a different grape wall for cover. The farmers ran away from us and hid in a building nearby.

I was able to send up an enemy position much faster this time. The range was described as danger close which means that we were in danger from our own mortars. The Fire Support Team commander came on the radio in a clear and calm voice and explained exactly what was going to happen. He planned to start the mortar rounds behind the enemy and then creep them slowly closer using our observations to make adjustments. I gave my assessment that the risk was worth taking because we had such good cover. He asked "explain what kind of cover you are in?" I replied that we were in a dry drainage ditch about 4 feet deep with hard dried mud on either side. With this information it was agreed that we would proceed to mortar the enemy.

Again we heard the whistling sound of mortar rounds going over our heads. This was our cue to duck and get in cover. The rounds were so close that we could feel the pressure change caused by the explosions. The enemy withdrew and left us alone for 2 hours. In the quiet that ensued we were able to eat some lunch and try and rest in the small areas of shade as the temperature rose up to 40 degrees Celsius. Sergeant Robertson arranged for a re supply of ammunition from 7 Platoon who were on our western flank.

Around about midday the enemy attacked again. They were using a small hut at a range of 600m which had small slits as firing points. The snipers to my east noticed movement through the grape field which had been used previously. This turned out to be a small group of insurgents trying to out flank us. The fire from the hut was starting to get accurate and was kicking up mud around our sniper. He tried to suppress the slits with .338 rounds but failed. The situation was getting critical so Corporal Tod fired a Javelin missile into the grape hut flattening it. The missile had a strong psychological effect on the enemy and they did not bother us again.

We returned to the remainder of the company at dusk. We had spent a full day in the sun on edge and fighting for long periods. The OC was keen to find out what happened and make an assessment of what kind of enemy we were facing. The snipers were very useful in this process because they had been observing enemy movement throughout the day. They reported that some of the insurgents were moving in the open without using cover with their weapons in full view. Others were more disciplined and crawled into position with concealed weapons. We were glad to get some rest at last.

Op TORA ARWA 1 – Personal Account – Lieutenant Robert Colquhoun (26), from the Isle of Skye, 2 Platoon Commander, Alpha (Grenadier) Company

For me, deploying to Afghanistan was both exciting and terrifying at the same time: a chance to do what I had trained to do, to lead my men in combat, and an adventure into the unknown. Although I had considered the awful possibilities, I certainly didn't go to Afghanistan expecting to lose one of my soldiers. I hoped it would never happen and allowed myself to be distracted by the excitement of it all.

Having found a significant weapons and drugs cache on the first morning the Jocks of 2 Platoon knew the enemy would make an appearance and when they did a little later, we relished the opportunity to engage them with everything at our disposal. Snipers reported successes with their precision weapons and riflemen sprayed 'suppressive' rounds with satisfaction but far less effect. The buzz and excitement of being shot at and missed is one of the most thrilling I have ever experienced and the smiles and laughter belied the mortal danger every one of us was in. As things quietened down after dusk, we were given orders to conduct a night march to gain surprise before clearing through the compounds that had been used as firing points against us at dawn.

We set off buoyant; confident in our abilities and enjoying the challenge. There wasn't a

Lt Rob Colquhoun – 2 Pl Comd, in the heat of the midday sun. (MOD – Sgt C Halton)

123

Pte David Todd from Kirkaldy, A Coy finds someone to talk to at last.

sign of nerves or tiredness despite the few hours of sleep on a hard mud floor. Everyone was alert, focused and up for the task ahead and the prospect of finding and killing the insurgents was too great an incentive to hold back.

As we swept into the first compounds we were soon contacted from those beyond. Bursts of automatic fire raced across the intervening ground and although we were safe behind the mud brick walls, the Jocks were keen to get on to the roofs to expose themselves and have a crack. We were soon tasked to close with the enemy and clear through the firing points and I could not contain my excitement as I briefed the guys on the plan.

2 Platoon went forward using a low wall as cover while 1 Platoon was engaged by RPGs and AK47s to our front. The morale boosting crack of 1 Platoon's sniper rifles overhead gave us courage as we knew the enemy could only expose themselves at their peril. We doubled over and picked up the pace, weighed down by the kit on our backs, blinded by the sweat running into our eyes, but rejoicing in the thrill of the attack. My first section crossed some open ground and I sent the second to secure our flank on the right. Everything was going to plan. Like a hundred attacks I'd done before on the hills of Wales.

And then suddenly, all was not going to plan. The lead section had been pinned down in the middle of crossing the open ground by accurate fire and was desperately trying to take cover behind fist-sized clods of earth. I watched as Junior NCOs struggled to locate the enemy, return fire and move their guys forward under that withering fire. To regain the initiative, I called my reserve section to follow me and led the way forward down an irrigation ditch that was so overgrown it was like cutting my way through a jungle.

Suffering from claustrophobia and palpitations of fear I slashed at the vegetation with my rifle butt, with enemy fighters at the end of the low wall to my left. Every time I poked my head up to see whether I could link up with the lead section I'd hear them say "Boss, another 10m along, then climb out of the ditch and run like ****" which didn't seem all that tempting an option as the open ground was ripped up by another burst of automatic fire. I continued pushing forward, knowing that at any moment I could come face to face with death at a range of less than 5m. I began to wish I'd fixed my bayonet before pushing forward into this jungle.

With 2 sections in contact from 5 different firing points, the enemy started firing Chinese rockets at us. We ducked down deeper into the ditch and those still in the field prayed for the ground to swallow them up as the most terrifying fireworks display I've ever been the

Lt Rob Colquhoun and 2 Platoon, Alpha Coy.

target of winged metal all around us. Suddenly, there was a huge explosion to the South and a massive dust cloud rising from the area I knew 2 Section to be in. There was no way that that explosion could have been anything but what it was and yet as I looked around at my Jocks' faces, all suddenly looking in at me, imploring me, willing me to tell them it was not so, I prayed with all my might that they were right. Time stood still, as the dust cloud rose and I desperately cried out for information. Little seemed to penetrate through the surreal feeling of shock, but I knew with growing dread it had been an IED. After 30 seconds that felt like an hour, the radio crackled into life with the terrifying announcement we had all feared: 'Man Down!' Soon it was confirmed, Private Robert McLaren was dead and Private Mark Connolly was injured and needed extracting.

The efforts of my platoon, to see those 2 casualties to the waiting helicopter, were exemplary. Despite the noise, confusion, grim horror and continued enemy fire they did everything required of them and more. When I spoke to them immediately after they had completed the extraction they seemed like men possessed. Shocked certainly, terrified perhaps, but determined to continue. Before my very eyes, and in the space of only that morning, these young Jocks had become men who had seen more in a moment than many would want to see in a lifetime. It no longer seemed such an exciting adventure to be at war.

As the op continued there was no let up from the enemy and we had to put our mourning on hold as we continued to pursue the enemy wherever he was found. It was one of the most difficult things I've ever had to do to stand in front of them that night and urge them to keep going, but it was all we could have done. There is a grim simplicity to a soldier's life where the entire focus hones in on getting the job done and surviving to see the morn. With young McLaren's heroism and bravery in the forefront of their minds they were fully aware of the sacrifice that he had made for his friends. And it hardened us all to ensuring his life was not given in vain. Whether it was taking turns on stag to trade fire with the enemy sharpshooters or moving to clear the enemy from abandoned compounds and tree lines, the Jocks never once lost sight of the task in hand. The skill and resilience with which they plied their trade, under the most testing of conditions, filled me with pride and admiration. These are ordinary young men doing extraordinary things on a daily basis many miles from home. It has been my honour to lead them and, as one of my Jocks put it, 'share the battlefield' with men like Private Robert McLaren.

Op TORA ARWA 1 – Sergeant Gary Buchanan (31), from Arbroath, 2 Platoon Sergeant, Alpha (Grenadier Company)

On the second day the contacts were more sustained and we were delivered with a huge blow when the Private McLaren was struck by an IED. The Platoon was in shock to begin with but despite the horror they gathered themselves and cracked on with the operation ahead. Both I and the Platoon Commander have the upmost respect for them, as they showed professionalism and courage to carry on. It certainly gave some of the younger Jocks and JNCOs a very steep learning curve but they dealt with it superbly. You have to grow up fast living out here.

Alpha (Grenadier) Company settle down inside a compound before dusk – Pte Rab McLaren, the first fatality of the tour within the 3 SCOTS BG, was killed earlier that day.

Op TORA ARWA 1 – Interview – Corporal Paul MacLeod (28), from Brechin, Signals Detachment Commander, Alpha (Grenadier) Company

My Dad was in the RAF so he's very proud of me. On Op TORA ARWA I was on the roof and a sniper was taking pot shots at me and the OC. I was alright while I was up there, it was when I got down off the roof, I thought to myself 'that was a bit close'. It sank in then. I haven't told my Dad yet.

Op TORA ARWA 1 – Personal Account – Corporal Shelley Pardoe (31), from Hereford, Signals Detachment Second in Command, 209 Signals Squadron, Royal Signals, attached to Alpha (Grenadier) Company

I look at the poor guys sat on the floor in the middle of the heli. Feel sorry for them, it must be uncomfortable with their bergan still on their back. Some in stress positions trying to balance their heavy GPMG with its muzzle to the floor. I try to get those last 30 minutes shut eye. I say a few words to the man upstairs, 'Please keep us safe'.

'Two minutes' is passed down the heli. The lads in the middle are helped up by the guys on the seats to a kneeling position. With more often than not a bump and we've landed. Time to go go go! Tonight though there was such a hold up. Normally I'm chasing after the OC making sure I don't lose sight of him in the dust. I see what the hold up is when I hop off the back, knee deep in thorn bushes. The field had large irrigation ditches to scrabble up and down.

I'm darting after the 2IC. Painfully pulling up on a knee next to him. I move the knee, ouch, more thorns. I curse myself for forgetting my knee pad, of all the times. Mental note 'remember knee pad'. I throw off my day sack, fire up the comms. Ping up my 'umbrella' and let KAF know we've all landed on the HLS complete.

I'm not apprehensive anymore, I look around and see the lads spread out in defence. Take in the atmospherics, quiet, night, anyone? I'm at ease. Here we are on the ground. It's still dark, the stars are shining brightly and the sky is so clear you can see the clouds of the milky way. The platoons head off towards their objectives under the cover of darkness. Later we follow on with the reserve platoon. We find a position off the perimeter of the objectives and go firm.

On day 2 I remember going with the Company Sergeant Major to provide comms down at the HLS. We lost Private McLaren that day, and had also taken a casualty, who was devastated and really unable to know what to think, his arms bandaged, he let a plea of 'Sir' out. The Company Sergeant Major put his arms around him and said 'You'll be alright son'. My heart sank. The heli was in bound and we moved to a cleared area behind a wall.

Op TORA ARWA – Personal Account – Corporal Dennis Boila (30), from Fiji, 2 Platoon, Alpha (Grenadier) Company

The main highlight for me was 2 Platoon's contact on the first day. Private McLaren was next to me returning fire during this contact; very professional and calm under fire despite being new to the Platoon. 2 Platoon used two 66mm Rockets and hundreds of rounds of 5.56mm until the enemy fled and an A10 Tankbuster flew low overhead in a show of force. After the contact we went forward to investigate the firing point and found one of the Taliban's flip flops which he had left in his hurry to escape!

Op TORA ARWA 1 – Personal Account – A 'sharpshooter' Minden Platoon, Alpha (Grenadier) Company

We were patrolling back into the compound when we took incoming fire from the Taliban. We immediately moved to a compound to get a better position to see the enemy. We had already been in contact earlier in the day and were confident that we could defeat them pretty quickly. I was trying to get up onto the compound wall to get a good fire position. The sniper rifle gets used a lot out here so it's important that the sharpshooters get in a good position.

I didn't realise what had happened initially. A round hit my rifle. When I got up onto the roof one of my mates who had seen it happen pointed it out to me. I couldn't really believe it, but we were still in the middle of a fire fight so I didn't have much time to take a look. It's about a 2 inch hole, and we managed to get the round out which will make a pretty good souvenir. I certainly used up one of my nine lives today.

Lance Corporal Wullie McCarthy (23), from Dunfermline, Charlie Company

Being an infantry soldier is a demanding and often exciting job; to see the enemy through your sights is an amazing feeling, knowing you're about to engage and kill the militia who are putting everyone's life in danger.

Op TORA ARWA 1 – Interview – Private Christopher Craig (18) from Lochgelly, 2 Platoon, Alpha (Grenadier) Company

What did you think when you first came under contact?

It was scary. On Op TORA ARWA we were in a compound, we were pushing forward to compound 301 because we were getting fired at from there the day before. So there was a grape hut to the right and 2 Section was going to push up on the roof of the grape hut, 3 Section we pushed up along an irrigation ditch to the south and we got half way along the irrigation ditch and come under heavy contact and then we hit the deck. And then I looked behind me, Scottie McFadden was running, so I had to get up and we got to the corner of the compound and formed up there. Mr Colquhoun and 1 Section were in an irrigation ditch behind ours, they pushed along there. They were coming under contact too. So they were pinned down in the irrigation ditch.

Me and Rab the Fijian got pushed forward to get eyes on the entrance to compound 301. We had eyes on the grape hut. We came under contact. There was no roof on the grape hut so 2 Section they pushed forward into the bund line. Rab McLaren was there and he went back into the grape hut. Private Mark Connolly also went back, he was the LMG gunner, he

tried to get on high ground in front of the doorway of the grape hut, then I seen the blast. We were 30 m away and knew someone had been killed. We then heard over the net that there was a casualty, they couldn't confirm how bad because of the dust. Private Connolly knew Rab McLaren was KIA. Then we heard over the net KIA. We came under heavy contact, IDF, mortars, 12 Chinese rockets fired at us, very accurate. A Black Hawk came in and picked up Connolly and Rab. It was quite horrible the way the Taliban done it, as soon as they saw the blast they then dropped loads of mortars on us and Chinese rockets. Just relentless.

The boss told us to switch to Channel 9, and said look boys we need to push on. We just lost one of the guys and we need to keep a straight heed on, need to focus. We pushed into compound 301, we cleared the compound, checked the rooms, pushed on the roof, we did half way rotations on the sentry, then it was my turn to go on stag, so I went onto the roof. I just popped my heed up and got one foot up on the roof, and got contacted. I ran up to the GPMG and asked the sniper where he was and he pointed to a compound. So I put a burst of about 50 rounds into the compound, and then we never heard nothing from them all day. The sniper said the enemy was at the corner of the compound in the long grass, so I rattled the long grass and never heard nothing. Then we pushed back into the compound for that night.

The next day we moved on and come to a compound and set up on the roof. I was on the roof and it was pretty quiet all day, a couple of contacts that evening. We seen enemy out in the open, they opened up on us so the MFC dropped about 30 mortars on them and then we dropped 10 artillery shells on them. There was still movement, then the casevac plan

A US Black Hawk conducting casualty evacuation lands on an HLS marked by purple smoke.
(MOD – Sgt C Halton)

Members of 2 Platoon watch over the secured HLS as the CH47 re-supply flies overhead. The BG used RAF and US CH47s throughout the tour and Canadian CH47s on a couple of operations. (Sgt N Collins)

came in and I was rattling away on the GPMG, fired about 300 rounds at them. I think we killed 2 enemy. The snipers shot someone and then we bugged out.

I'm now much more aware, I'm a bit more on the edge, loud noises sort of freak me out.

Have there been any 'lighter' moments during your time out here?
We were moving at night and there was this river and there were loads of rocks, and the guy in front of me tripped up and fell flat on his face right in the middle of the river. I was in stitches, he couldn't get up because of the weight of his kit.

What about your 'field admin'?
We share an electric razor in the field, one per fire team. It's because of the weight of the kit, we can't take too much comfort kit with us.

The new ration packs aren't bad, the 'boilies' (boiled sweets) are much better, vegetable korma and that. Porridge you just add water to, you get jam, much better.

Op TORA ARWA 1 – Personal Account – Sergeant Kevin Stobbs (28), from Newcastle, 38 Battery 40 Regiment Royal Artillery

On Op TORA ARWA we were in a compound, it was 20m by 20m and we took between 10 and 12 rounds of IDF that were landing about 10m away. A couple of the lads got blown off the roof, 'Coops' got shrapnel in his backside. We were all in the same compound. I was just trying to get eyes on because we had M777 Canadian 155 guns and I was trying to get sitreps to get them laid on. We wanted to get eyes on to PID (positively identify) the firing position and bring either fast air or any artillery on to that position, to destroy the enemy and stop the indirect fire coming into us.

One of the funny moments was after Corporal Couper had got hit in the backside, I was on the wall and he was lying underneath me and giggling. I thought he'd been pumped full of morphine but he assured us that he hadn't. He was just sat there laughing with his combats ripped to shreds.

Op TORA ARWA 1 – Interview – Corporal James Couper (23), from Livingstone, Section Commander Recce Platoon, Charlie (Fire Support) Company

Were you prepared for Afghanistan after training in Kenya?

Not completely – it's a different type of heat and climate in Kenya than over here. If we'd had the kind of kit and equipment we had over here in Kenya then it would have been perfect, by the simple fact we'd have been carrying the kit and equipment and getting used to it. I'd only had Osprey to tell you the truth on once prior to coming here.

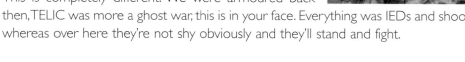

How does this tour compare to TELIC?

This is completely different. We were armoured back then, TELIC was more a ghost war, this is in your face. Everything was IEDs and shoot and scoot, whereas over here they're not shy obviously and they'll stand and fight.

The last day of Op TORA ARWA Cpl Couper was injured and casevac'd.

We were accompanying and providing protection for the FSG who were attached to the Afghan National Army Company. The first round landed outside our compound. I remember the second one coming in and I just remember saying to Corporal Pow 'F***ing hell' and I remember lying there, and laughing because he had his bergan up against him where he was lying trying to protect himself. I remember thinking I wish I had my bergan which was in the centre of the compound. I remember him saying to me 'F***ing hell, here we go.' I knew when the second one landed we were pinned. The third one landed close. I knew we were being observed so I jumped up onto the roof with a set of laser range finders.

Corporal Bruce was on the roof of the compound when the first explosion went off, he saw some smoke to the North West. When I jumped up I heard a thud. I wouldn't have made it off the roof in time other than jumping and it was pretty high, about 12 foot high so I didn't want to jump, not with all my kit on. So I thought well what's my chances, I remember seeing on the roof all the metal jugs, pots and pans – everything you can imagine all on the roof. I knew if a mortar landed on the roof then every single bit of that was coming through me so I was trying to push and kick as much off as I could.

I remember still trying to kick it off and then I just heard the mortar coming over my head. So at that point I flung myself towards the wall and I just remember looking underneath my belly at the time of the blast and I couldn't breathe at that point (I was later told it had landed within a few metres of me). My helmet had blown off my head and I remember seeing everything I'd kicked off the roof coming back over the top of me. My helmet had got blown off into my lap and I remember getting up and looking at my hands and giving myself a quick tap over. At the time of the explosion I was panicking because I couldn't breathe. I checked my hands and they were still there and my feet, still there. I remember at the time of the blast I was screaming 'I had been hit, I'd been hit, I'd been hit'. I remember getting up and feeling something running down my arm, I then stood up and ran off the roof and fell flat on my face. I don't think I realised I was on the roof.

I could feel wet on my arm and the boys said for me to roll onto my belly. At that point they cut my trousers off me and I looked down at my legs and they were just pure red. I picked myself up and grabbed my rifle and ran towards the medics who patched me up. At that point I was fine, I never felt any pain, and the adrenalin was there. I had got shrapnel in my backside. I remember running again to get into a different compound and then realised I was the only person in that compound. I ran back and grabbed Private Johnstone with his LMG and told him to cover the alleyway and then I ran in and physically touched everybody in the section to make sure everyone was alright, and then ran to find Powy.

I then heard another mortar go off and I thought 'f***', and then another one went off and then I remember lying back and I got my wallet out and I looked at my daughters in my wallet, and I thought at this point I couldn't be bothered running anymore and I just lay there, but I was still shouting on Powy. But I don't think he heard me because nobody answered me and I thought well at that point I thought he had been killed. And then the third one came in and I just remember saying right I've got to go and find him again. At that point I was scared, I was thinking this is me, as they were landing at my feet 20 m away. I remember running into the centre compound to find him and then I seen him. I've never felt so much relief in all my life. I seen everybody and at that point Ken White grabbed me and flung me into the room and said "right you're not getting out of that room". At that point an ANA soldier came in with shrapnel injuries and so he got patched up. Everybody was scanning their arcs and just waiting to see what was happening. At that point it was starting to get dark and the 9 Liners had been sent up. I was really worried because I was leaving and everybody else was still there, and I didn't know whether they were still going to get attacked. So I was more scared and worried about them than anything else. We were just having a laugh about getting billed for my trousers. I've heard my Section has been in loads of contacts since. I really miss them.

Op TORA ARWA 1 – Interview – Private Callum Scott (19), from Dunbar, Reconnaissance Platoon, Charlie (Fire Support) Company

My nearest miss was getting IDF'd when a mortar landed nearby (Corporal Couper incident). We were searching a compound about an hour before last light and we started getting hit hard with IDFs and mortars coming in. But happy that we all came back alive. We were very lucky. It was difficult trying to locate the observer and get a firing point as well – there were lots of women and children about, and farmers wandering about in fields, so it was quite hard looking for the observer.

Op TORA ARWA 1 – Personal Account – Private Graham Johnson (22), from Inverness, Mortar Platoon, Charlie Company

Our defining operation as a Mortar Platoon was in Kandahar Province, commencing 10 June. Arriving by Chinook at dawn, within a Canadian Patrol Base we sited near the top of a hill, approx 50-75m high and 250-350m in radius. Shortly after establishing our line (5 barrels) we set about lugging our under-slung ammo up the hill to our position. I have never worked as hard on the tour as I did on this Op and at this moment. Carrying 5 ammunition greenies to give my detachment something to run with until we could get a wagon or quad to ferry the remaining ammunition from the drop point to the mortar line. Half way up the third journey (I just wanted to lose my helmet/armour and rifle to do this at this point) the call

The Day of Reckoning – The Mortar Platoon in action. The mortars provided the majority of the BG's fire support during TORA ARWA. (Pte G Johnson)

Pte Graham Johnson hands a High Explosive round to the Number 2 during a fire mission.

came through from one of the companies for fire. From then on, for a couple of days we were called upon to support the ground troops, firing with first round accuracy - sometimes at our maximum range. The satisfaction at having helped your own forces is immense.

Having used ammunition throughout the day we received overnight re-supplies. On the first of such re-supplies we formed a line and passed each "greenie" from the tailgate between us away from the chopper. Once this was done, I thought I was beckoned to follow onto the Chinook in file presumably to lift a bag of radio batteries or similar from the floor and file off - as we had done on re-supplies on other ops. Alas, I was not following one of my colleagues but a couple of the Canadian soldiers who were being lifted out that night - I had in fact been the front mortarman in the line. Upon arriving in the recess of the Chinook I quickly realised the error I had made but was it too late? Spinning around I saw the ramp clunk closed and heard the unmistakable sound of the engines building power, the pilot wanting to lift off ASAP. Frantic waving at the door gunner conveyed my wanting to get off, and he lowered the ramp enough for me to jump as it took off.

Op TORA ARWA – Interview – Private Alan Brown (24) from Dundee, Javelin Platoon, Charlie (Fire Support) Company

The time goes quickly when you're out on the ground. You lose track of days and time, you're constantly on the move and thinking about what you're doing next. When you're stuck in camp it's more commanders' time, so for the Jocks it's more low level chill out when you're not doing anything. I'd rather be out constantly for 6 months, that sounds weird but when you're on the ground you shimph, but when you're not on the ground you shimph. So I don't know whether that's a Jock mentality or I just think out there it's what you get paid to do. It's funny, like you see in the videos, we always think it's 'Aly' when we get shot at so, it's part of the life.

Op TORA ARWA was pretty hairy when we became a mini FSG under Mr Gladstone and we were attached to 6 Platoon, Bravo Company, Mr Halliday's platoon. Five days, it was quite intense. We were dropped in and from 7 in the morning until about half 8 at night, we were in contact. It's hard to explain, it's a buzz and you think you're lucky you're in the Army because you've got this advantage. I've got this outtake on life you know, it's just something I like doing, you'd be surprised, everybody dislikes the depot, but you'd be surprised how much the skills and drills come into play. Your training just kicks in and that's it really.

I'm usually carrying Javelin kit and an SA80 but the last op I had a GPMG and that's when the Taliban hit us quite strongly. I was quite lucky to have a GPMG because it's nice fire power and you're able to pin back the Taliban and it's obviously a better capability. Once you've pinned them back far enough the snipers or Javelin come into play and then you're able to eliminate the enemy threat. Sometimes they get quite close so it is good to have a personal weapon or a shot gun. It's good, plus you've got mortars, fast air and artillery, you've got

Pte Brown during Op TORA ARWA 1.

everything so you can't complain really. We're totally a better fighting force than them but people I think back home underestimate the Taliban because I've been in quite a lot of contacts and only on the past 2 ops I've actually really seen the Taliban. I've been shot at but I never actually saw the Taliban until about a month ago.

I was engaged in a firefight. Private Hunter was on stag and everyone else was chilling or monging it, and it was a couple of hours into being on the ground and an RPG came flying over our heads. It was quite close so everybody got into stand to. We got up and the enemy was only 500m away from us, you could see them, you could see them actually in the bund line cutting about. The sniper commander done quite exceptional actually, got me and Corporal Green up on the GPMGs and he had his sniper rifle and we were just laying down rounds, pinning down enemy and I actually seen one of them peeling up a bund line and I brought my weapon system up and I just fired. People say is it weird shooting to kill another man, is it for queen and country, but you've got to understand it's just for the boy next to you because every one of them are my pals and I think to myself well its either him or one of my friends. And it's just a weird thought.

Over here they are wanting to take you on because they genuinely believe that they're fighting for a cause and there's no fear with them. You do get the contacts here as well as the IEDs and they're willing to fight to the bitter end. They detest us. We're here for a good cause because Britain is at war with terrorism. I don't mind being here. People have got to remember 9/11 and 7/7. I like it here, this is what the Army's all about. Like when I joined up, Iraq was just kicking off and I never thought anything about Afghanistan, but this is what it's all about, this is soldiering on the front line.

Chapter Six

Operation PANCHAI PALANG 1
(PANTHER'S CLAW)

19 June – 24 June 2009

INTRODUCTION

Operation PANCHAI PALANG was an operation planned by Task Force Helmand and focussed on the area of Babaji, Helmand. The intent was to secure the area of Babaji and thereby isolate the Chah – E Anjir Triangle (CAT). Task Force Helmand's plan was to conduct reconnaissance and shaping operations by the Brigade Reconnaissance Force. Task Force Helmand was then to deploy the RBG(S) to secure the Luy Mandeh wadi and establish a control point along the canal. Once the wadi was secure, The Welsh Guards Battle Group

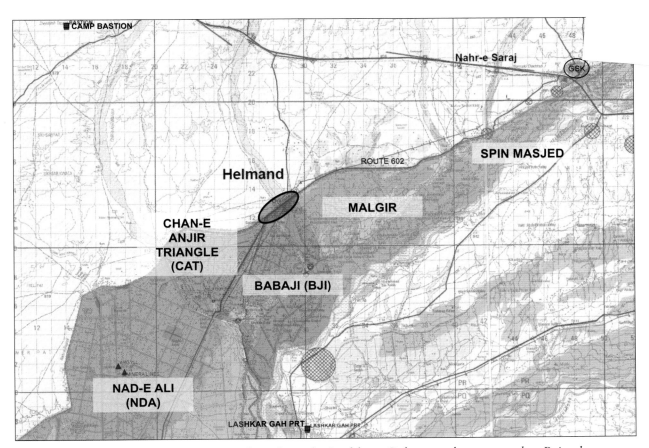

An overview map of Central Helmand. Lashkar Gah was home to the Brigade Headquarters. Camp BASTION is the main UK operating base and the red oval was the target area for the Battle Group.

would then deploy from the south along the Shamalan Canal with the intent of taking command of the area. In addition, the Light Dragoons Battle Group would simultaneously press west from Gereshk and link up with the Welsh Guards. The operation's name PANCHAI PALANG is a Pashtu translation for panther's claw that was derived from 19 Light Brigade's emblem, the panther.

The Battle Group's plan was to insert by aviation into the Luy Mandeh wadi in one wave of 350 soldiers and seize Objectives WHISTLER and ZERMATT; Alpha Company was to secure ZERMATT, the Luy Mandeh wadi bazaar, and Bravo Company to secure WHISTLER, west of the wadi along the Nahr-E Burgha Canal. Also, a convoy of Jackals, Vikings, Mastiffs and engineering stores would deploy from BASTION and move south from Highway 1 along the Luy Mandeh wadi; in the vanguard would be Task Force Thor, an American Counter – IED unit. Once the Battle Group had secured the wadi crossing, the engineers would begin the work of building a secure base to the west of the crossing and also establish a control point along the canal which would take the shape of hesco bastion chicanes and barbed wire. The Battle Group was to remain in place until the 24th June, at which point Bravo Company would remain and Alpha Company would return to BASTION and prepare for R & R.

Left: The CO (right) receiving a back brief from Maj Matt Munro (left) and Maj Al Steele (middle) during the planning phase of Op PANCHAI PALANG (Panther's Claw). (Maj G Shaw)

Vehicles lining up by the gate in Camp BASTION, ready to clear the way for the Jackal group and Echelon at the start of Op PANCHAI PALANG. (MOD – Sgt C Halton)

EXECUTION

19 June 09 (D–1)

The aviation assault was executed according to plan and landed south of the wadi at 2330 hrs. In total, 12 Chinook helicopters from the US Combat Aviation Brigade and the UK Joint Helicopter Force, 4 US Apache helicopters, one KC-130 Spectre Gunship and 2 US Blackhawk helicopters were deployed to support the Battle Group's insertion. At 2340 hrs, the 64 vehicle convoy departed BASTION.

20 June 09 (D Day)

The hours between landing on the objectives and first light saw little insurgent activity allowing the Battle Group to effectively isolate the area of the wadi crossing and the bazaar. While Alpha and Bravo Companies were securing their objectives, Charlie Company and the remainder of the vehicle convoy moved along the Luy Mandeh wadi and linked up with Bravo Company at 0900 hrs. Intelligence assessment suggested that insurgents were anticipating a ground assault from the north down the Luy Mandeh wadi and had placed IEDs in the vicinity of the bazaar and wadi crossing. These assessments were corroborated with a significant number of IED finds in these areas during the course of the operation. Of particular note was an almost complete lack of local nationals in the area which indicated that civilians had anticipated an operation and had left out of fear of the ensuing fight.

Engagements with insurgents started at 0700 hrs. Following first light, insurgents were able to identify Battle Group dispositions and proceeded to mount harassing attacks of small arms fire and RPG from multiple firing points, demonstrating a good tactical understanding of the ground. At 1230 hrs, Alpha Company reported an IED contact which resulted in one soldier from the Afghan National Army killed; Bravo Company's secure location was subsequently named FOB WAHID after the soldier. At 1310 hrs, one of the vehicles carrying engineering supplies rolled over and 3 soldiers from the Battle Group were injured. An American Blackhawk medical helicopter evacuated the body of the ANA soldier and the 3 British casualties.

Contacts and engagements with insurgents carried on throughout the day. Despite the harassing fire, the engineers got to work building defensive positions in FOB WAHID and establishing the control point along the crossing. Bravo Company established a platoon rotation consisting of base security, patrols around FOB WAHID and the security of a platoon house seized to the south earlier in the day. Captain David "Harry" Hood, the Regimental Careers Management Officer and veteran of Northern Ireland, Kosovo, Iraq, and a previous tour of Afghanistan, was given command of 6 Platoon following the injury of Lieutenant Andrew Halliday on Operation TORA ARWA, and he took charge of overseeing the defences around FOB WAHID. Alpha Company similarly maintained security of Objective ZERMATT while also conducting patrols in the area. Charlie Company secured Objective ASPEN and split its force to escort the armoured flat bed lorries back to BASTION in order to collect further engineering stores. Battle Group TAC and the Mortar Platoon were located with Bravo Company in FOB WAHID.

21 June 09 (D+1)

The second day of the operation was equally as vigorous and busy as D Day with contacts and harassing attacks by insurgents. The companies used platoon level weapons and mortars to defend themselves. Charlie Company departed BASTION with engineering stores at 0700 hrs. Alpha Company was manning 3 blocking positions around the bazaar and first came under contact at 0700 hrs and Bravo Company continued with patrols in the area to gain some depth and maintain offensive action. At 1045 hrs, a UAV positively identified 3 insurgents

Some of the Jackals and Echelon making their way down a wadi to link up with the rest of the Battle Group who had inserted by CH47. (MOD – Sgt C Halton)

approaching an Alpha Company position. The UAV fired one missile killing the insurgents. By the end of the day, half of Charlie Company had once again returned to BASTION to collect engineering stores.

22 June 09 (D+2)

Maintaining vigilance throughout the night, Bravo Company identified possible insurgents at 0330 hrs and fired 5 warning shots. Shortly after, the company identified a pressure pad IED which was denied at 0403 hrs. At 0430 hrs, elements of Charlie Company mounted in Jackals moved west to Objective VERBIER to occupy, secure and establish a block along the Shamalan Canal.

Insurgents continued to engage the Battle Group throughout the day and Alpha Company was first contacted at 0655 hrs. Bravo Company came under attack from small arms and RPG at FOB WAHID at 0900 hrs. At the time, intelligence suggested that insurgents were grouping for a significant attack against the Battle Group. At 1030 hrs, Charlie Company found 2 improvised claymore mines, 5 pressure pad IEDs and a quantity of conventional and military blocks of explosive in the area of VERBIER.

A Jackal vehicle with 50 cal. The Jackal is a huge improvement on the old WMIK which was an armoured Landrover. (MOD – Sgt C Halton)

Royal Engineers putting up razor wire to secure the Lu Mandeh gap - the first phase of Op PANCHAI PALANG. (MOD – Sgt C Halton)

The day proved to be one of intense fighting that required substantial indirect fire to support the Battle Group. At approximately 0850 hrs, Bravo Company came under accurate indirect fire landing roughly 50m north of its headquarters. Radar was able to identify a firing point, and the mortar line fired 3 rounds onto the target area; no further attacks came from that area. At 1625 hrs, Exactor missiles were fired onto a target in Alpha Company's area. At 1900 hrs, Charlie Company used a 500lb bomb to destroy a target that had harassed the company throughout the day. Also, at about 1920 hrs, a group of perhaps 15-20 insurgents were identified infiltrating towards Alpha Company's position from the south. A fierce firefight ensued. Over a period of about an hour Alpha Company fought a fierce defensive battle at close range. A barrage of enemy mortars dropped as close as 120m from the forward 1 Platoon positions finally dispersed the enemy.

Despite the attacks upon the company locations, the Royal Engineers continued the construction of the control point along the Luy Mandeh wadi crossing. Due to the length of the crossing (400m), and the requirement to use a combination of barbed wire and Hesco Bastion the control point was eventually nicknamed "Hadrian's Wall".

23 June 09 (D+3)

Early in the morning, Bravo Company began a company patrol into the south west of Objective WHISTLER and LECHT with the Viking Troop providing intimate support. At 0735 hrs,

A Royal Engineer Corporal ground commanding. (MOD – Sgt C Halton)

FOB WAHID once again came under attack from indirect fire. Radar was again able to identify the firing point and the mortar line fired 3 rounds. At 1054 hrs, Commander Task Force Helmand, Brigadier Radford, arrived at Bravo Company's location to inspect the construction. By 1155 hrs, Bravo Company had returned to Objective WHISTLER. The remainder of the day was quiet and the engineers were able to complete the construction of "Hadrian's Wall" by 1530 hrs.

24 Jun 09 (D+4)

At 0405 hrs, Charlie Company, the Viking Troop, and the support vehicles commanded by Captain Robb, the Mechanised Transport Officer, extracted from the Luy Mandeh Wadi. The lead Jackal, commanded by WO2 Parker, struck a pressure pad IED at 0539 hrs: fortunately, no injuries were sustained and the Jackal was recovered to BASTION. At 0630 hrs, Alpha Company and TAC extracted by helicopter and returned to BASTION in order to return to the United Kingdom for R & R.

Bravo Company remained in place and occupied a compound in Objective VERBIER while also remaining in FOB WAHID. The company also retained command of one section of mortars as well as 4 Jackals manned by members of the Fire Support Group. With the departure of half the Battle Group, the company repelled a number of attacks by insurgents throughout the day.

25 June 09 – 04 July 09 (D+5 – D+14)

Bravo Company remained in and around FOB WAHID for the following 10 days. Throughout that period, the company sustained numerous attacks from insurgents and aggressively patrolled the region. Also during this period the Welsh Guards slowly pressed north along the Shamalan Canal and suffered significant casualties, including 2 fatalities. In the early morning of 3 July, the advance party from the Welsh Guards was finally able to link up with Bravo Company and had taken command of the area that evening. Bravo Company extracted from the area at 0520 hrs and the mobile elements had returned to BASTION by 0630 hrs.

Part of the extraction from Op PANCHAI PALANG.

SUMMARY

The success of the initial phase of Operation PANCHAI PALANG was documented in British media. Tactical surprise was achieved and the insurgents in the area were defeated. Intelligence estimates made at the time suggested that the Battle Group had encountered approximately 100 insurgents. Insurgents tended to operate in small groups of 2 or 3 during the day, although at night they grouped together to mount more concerted attacks. The Battle Group estimated that during the operation 48 insurgents had been killed with another 20 more either killed or wounded. These numbers of insurgents encountered corroborated previous assessments that Babaji was a major centre of insurgent activity.

In the larger picture, the seizure of the Luy Mandeh wadi enabled Task Force Helmand to complete the clear and hold of Babaji. Although the Battle Group would return to the area a number of times, the initial gains made at the end of June and beginning of July shaped the ongoing operations conducted in the area and defined the achievements of Operation HERRICK 10.

Op PANCHAI PALANG 1 – Forward Operating Base WAHID – Major Al Steele (33), Officer Commanding Bravo Company

It was the biggest aviation assault that anyone in Afghanistan had attempted since 2001. We were to be the first action of the main event of the summer, Op PANCHAI PALANG (Panthers Claw). The Battle Group was to land in force behind an insurgent defensive line that had been laced with IEDs to establish a foothold. A couple of days later the Welsh Guards would begin their advance from the south east to link up with us. With these blocks in place the Light Dragoons were to then advance from the north east clearing any remaining enemy out of the area.

We landed in the gloom expecting to be in contact but apart from an attack helicopter engagement off to A Company's flank, all was quiet. 7 Platoon made good progress onto our target, a compound that we would transform into a new forward operating base over the next 2 weeks. We were butted up against a canal with dasht to the north of that and with green zone to the south.

For the first few days the whole Battle Group remained on the ground. The priority for

Pte William Yeaman from Perth, of Bravo Company "Hard targeting" – the way to cross open ground during contact by the enemy is to make one's self as hard a target as possible.
(MOD – Sgt C Halton)

the company was to turn our compound into a forward operating base (FOB) whilst at the same time clearing the immediate area of insurgents. With the former we had the help of an engineering troop who worked day and night to build sanger positions and reinforce walls. One of my platoon commanders built crenulations to give us more firing positions and we all filled sandbags, over 4000! Every sleeping bay was dug in and sandbagged in case we were mortared. In fact by the time that we had finished all that was missing were barrels of oil on the ramparts! Early in the operation A Company sustained an ANA soldier KIA whilst completing the difficult job of clearing a sprawling Bazaar close to our FOB. In his memory we named the compound FOB WAHID.

As the rest of the Battle Group prepared to leave we had all seen 4 days of heavy fighting as the insurgent was gradually pushed back from our positions. B Company was to remain in place for a further 10 days as the Welsh Guards pushed towards our position from the south west. The next priority was to establish a platoon patrol base (PB) so that we could dominate the area the Battle Group had vacated. We quickly settled into a routine of one platoon on guard in FOB WAHID, one platoon in the PB and the other conducting patrols. Every third day I reduced the manning on guard and the FOB to an absolute minimum so that the Company could mount larger operations. Often this meant that our attachments, from military policeman to artillery specialists, were manning the sangers as the company set out at around 2 am. There was little respite for the Jocks, if they weren't patrolling or sleeping they were improving the defences.

I was fortunate to have been left a hugely capable group that over and above my 3 platoons included 9 Jackal vehicles, an ANA platoon, a mortar section, mortar locating radar, a small UAV with a camera fixed to it and 'downlink' screens that allowed me to tap into the footage that other aircraft circling above could see.

We were mortared only twice but each time the radar was able to quickly identify the firing point and we returned fire. The UAV was of particular use as we were able to 'fly' the area looking for targets. It was also useful when in contact as we were able to maintain aerial observation of the enemy groupings as they tried to out flank us or extract. Sometimes this meant striking them there and then with armed UAVs, sometimes we would follow them back to a compound to cue up a subsequent company operation. Perhaps the most potent tactic we used was to combine Jackal vehicles with infantry. My platoons would push forward clearing the ground while the Jackals remained at the rear until we came into contact. At that point the Jackals would push forward and fire over our heads.

The patrolling was relentless, it had to be to keep the insurgent on the back foot. We knew as soon as we took the pressure off he would have the space to start laying IEDs. I managed to get out on almost all of these with my TAC party and was able to see first hand the tenacity of the Jocks and platoon commanders as they time and time again responded to close contacts. For the first few days we received regular and accurate sniper fire from our north east, 600m across the dry wadi that we had landed in. So accurate was the fire that the wall behind the sanger was now pitted with strike marks. I tasked 5 Platoon to mount an ambush patrol to try to catch the perpetrators who were becoming increasing brazen. In position by 0400 hrs the ambush was triggered at 0800 hrs as one of the sections saw 2 insurgents moving into position at close quarters. In the ensuing fight they managed

An Afghan settlement in Babaji – moving through areas like this took hours.

to kill one and our armed UAV was able to track another fleeing the area and stop him in his tracks.

As the FOB neared completion the platoons were tasked with improving the facilities for the Welsh Guards handover. This saw the Jock's ingenuity at its best with a diving board, refrigerator (dug into the river) and various furniture all being constructed. The river itself was a huge bonus after a hot patrol and the Babaji swimming club was formed, complete with an armed life guard! Some of the Jocks turned their hand to fishing and our rations were soon bolstered by crab and carp.

All the while the Welsh Guards were inching closer. We were gutted as we heard frequent updates of their casualties including the shattering news that their CO had been killed. We couldn't help but think we might have pushed some of the insurgents their way. There was too much to do to dwell on this. Numerous IEDs still had to be cleared to the north of our position and we still had plenty of defences to put in to control crossings on the canal. I also started sending mobile patrols further and further away from the FOB to try and look for the locals that had once been living in the area; it was of course for them that we were here. As the days drew on it was heartening to see more and more people come to the FOB to talk to us. Although generally pleased that we were in the area they were vociferous in their dislike for the ANP and made it clear that they would certainly side with the insurgents if we were replaced by them.

Eventually it was time to handover to the Welsh Guards who looked exhausted but in good spirits from the 7 days hard fighting they had had trying to link up with us. I knew both the Company Commander and Company Sergeant Major from previous jobs and we had just enough time to catch up before patrolling out into the night to our helicopter pick up a few kilometres away.

Op PANCHAI PALANG – Reflections – Major Matt Munro (36), from Hampshire, Officer Commanding Alpha (Grenadier) Company

Planning time was compressed; the turnaround after Op TORA ARWA was tight. This particular op was significant because it would be our last before we headed home for some well earned R&R. Truth be told, we were all exhausted. The preceding weeks were a blur of planning and operations and like any other, Op PANCHAI PALANG demanded a very intensive cycle of briefings, meetings and planning sessions right up to the time of deployment.

As we boarded the aircraft I was told that an officer I knew in the Welsh Guards had been killed earlier that day. I didn't know him very well but had seen him in Lashkar Gah only a few weeks before (he had talked lovingly about his family). On this occasion I was simply too tired to worry about dying. We deployed in the dead of night; to a man my command team was acutely sleep deprived; I slept throughout the 60 minute flight from Kandahar.

Crossing an irrigation ditch, a vulnerable activity but also a chance to cool off. (MOD – *Sgt C Halton)*

The plan for the company was to aviation assault into the heart of Babaji, walk a little over a kilometre and then prior to first light seize the Taliban bazaar on the NEB canal. This is more or less how it turned out. We were targeted on the landing sight by enemy fire, gratifyingly however, an Apache attack helicopter killed the insurgent machine gun team on a nearby rooftop and thereafter we were unmolested. Our move to the bazaar was not without its difficulties. The ground was wet and was criss-crossed by streams and drainage ditches; there was little or no ambient light. Canalised by the water features, we ended up a little further north than I would have liked. Crossing a water obstacle is a precarious and slow business at the best of times; more so on this occasion when a Jock slipped off the log he balanced on and fell bleeding into the river below. Hesitatingly, therefore, we made our objective just as the sun began to rise. The bazaar was empty of insurgents; we think that they knew that we were coming.

We surrounded the bazaar. The platoons threw up road blocks and established defensive strong points. The bazaar was judged to be critical to the financial sustainment of the Taliban's activities and just as tellingly had probably been perceived by the Taliban as a safe-haven. It was now ours.

As predicted, the Taliban had laid and armed multiple IEDs. Wahid, a warrior of the Afghan National Army was killed when he stepped on a pressure-pad device. His broken body was hurled through the air; bits of his equipment, bloodied and torn, were strewn over a wide area. His wounds were catastrophic and despite the best efforts of Lance Corporal Quinn and Private Dye he soon died. The IEDs were everywhere; over the next few days as we consolidated our position 13 devices were found and denied by controlled explosion. Time and again the enemy tried to re-infiltrate the area and dislodge us from his ground, he was not successful. Attacks from the north, east and south were all repelled with both vigour and control. The vigilance of the troops allowed us to identify the enemy's approach routes early and through the precise co-ordination of assets we brought effective fires to bear.

A sniper pair manned an Observation Post on a flat roof in the Bazaar, this pair remained exposed over a period of 72 hours, killing dozens of insurgents. On the first evening, an enemy sharpshooter armed with a Draganov sniper rifle identified the position and engaged it 12 times; rounds hit the roof itself, the sandbag wall to the front and passed close over their heads. Between the insurgent's shots, despite the considerable danger, a sniper exposed himself in order to personally observe the insurgent firing point, which he eventually located on the roof of a compound 850m away. He killed the enemy sniper. The following day the snipers destroyed a heavy machine gun post whilst under sustained, deadly fire from it.

Later that day as dusk fell, the sniper pair observed the enemy massing in compounds to the south for an attack on 1 Platoon's (relatively isolated) position. The snipers reported the movement and killed 6 enemy gunmen. A further 14 fighters were seen hiding in a tree line within 150m of 1 Platoon. Lieutenant Colquhoun, Officer Commanding 2 Platoon, indefatigable and typically brave, called in and adjusted mortar fire and directed machine-gun fire onto the insurgent grouping. Throughout, the occupants of the rooftop position, Colquhoun and the snipers were undeterred by the rounds that thumped into the sandbags around them. After the enemy were fought off Corporal Boila led a clearance patrol across the company's front. After an initial nerve-wracking search revealed nothing untoward he was

A Sniper pair crossing another obstacle – The green zone was littered with irrigation ditches and compound walls, making the going very difficult and slow. (MOD – Sgt C Halton)

alerted to a heat source in the next field. Leaving his cover men at a safe distance he chose to advance alone towards the heat source to reduce the risk to his men and single handed, he cleared the threat area and secured the open flank. This courage was typical of Boila, a lion-hearted Fijian whose Jocks would follow him anywhere.

The Jocks were awesome. By this stage of the tour they were combat-hardened. Lean and tanned (the result of weeks spent roughing it in the field), our battlefield experience was such that we all instinctively now knew the difference between incoming and outgoing rounds (not as easy as it sounds), we could judge how close incoming rounds were and we were relatively blasé about how close to our own forward positions we dare call in our own mortar and artillery fire. These things instilled a quiet confidence in the young Jocks (who perhaps now held eye contact a little longer and stood a little straighter). As we reached the

Cpl Michael McLaughlin QGM from Kinross, C Coy, showing his compassionate side.
(MOD – Sgt C Halton)

mid-point of our tour there was a real confidence, not the swagger of bravado but the quiet measured assurance of young men who had been thoroughly tested and had not been found wanting.

With all this excitement it was with huge relief that the company stepped off the helicopters in BASTION. Like any other operation there was a palpable excitement and sense of euphoria. For the most part I put this down to a sense of a job well done and the anticipation of a good wash, scoff and the chance of uninterrupted sleep. However, there was no doubt that we were also relieved to be back in safely. Most of us had several tales of near misses; perhaps a sniper's bullet, a close-shave with a pressure-pad (that would have initiated an improvised explosive device) or maybe a burst of machine-gun fire that was fortunately a little high. Our thoughts were finally free to dwell on thoughts of home and loved ones.

Op PANCHAI PALANG 1 – Personal Account – Lance Corporal Aaron Graham (22), from Fife, 1 (Senior Highland) Platoon, Alpha (Grenadier) Company

Probably the highlight of the tour was the main operation for HERRICK 10, PANCHAI PALANG, an operation in Babaji. Our job was to clear the bazaar and give Bravo Company freedom to build a patrol base. Probably one of the heaviest contacts that we have been in as well. Which is good, seeing myself as a commander and a lot of my young private soldiers, they came out of their shells a bit and they just reacted.

Op PANCHAI PALANG 1 – Personal Account – Private Willie Brown (23), from Fife, 2 Platoon, Alpha (Grenadier) Company

There were still plenty of insurgents who didn't want us to be there and we were awoken every morning to the crack and thump of firing points engaging us from all around. Every time I heard this I thought "time to have some fun", but the enemy were only visible to the snipers on their roof top, not to us at ground level. With contacts going on all day and the sniper kills mounting, we all wondered when we were going to get our chance to see the enemy. Shortly before last light of Day 3, the familiar crack and thump of incoming rounds could be heard once more, but this time the GPMGs on the sentry position were firing in return. The GPMG link wasn't lasting long, and the enemy were making a determined attack, so the Jocks in the sections down the bottom of the bazaar took it on themselves to form a baseline and take the fight to the enemy. With everything firing – rifles, UGL and LMG – we raised hell. For a long time we were unable to stop the advance, but eventually the enemy attack started to falter and finally after mortars were dropped on them too they fell back defeated. It was pitch black by then and we went to bed buzzing with excitement after an evening few of us will ever forget.

Op PANCHAI PALANG 1 – The IED threat – Lance Corporal Jim Forrester (20), from Methil, 2 Platoon, Alpha (Grenadier) Company

We reached our FUP and formed up ready to move into the bazaar at first light. These were nervous moments as we knew that the bazaar was littered with IEDs. On H-Hour the order

A Viking roles through the Luy Mandeh Bazaar – The Royal Engineer Search Team cleared approximately 20 IEDs from the Bazaar. Instrumental in this was also the Ammunition Technical Officer (ATO). (MOD – Sgt C Halton)

A journalist accompanying the Royal Engineer Search Team takes cover during a patrol.
(MOD – Sgt Halton)

to move was given and with a clearance team leading we pushed towards our objective. Whilst building up our defensive positions, one of the Jocks, Private Christopher Byrne noticed disturbed earth on the route we had just crossed. After being brought to the attention of an attached engineer it was confirmed as a Pressure Plate IED connected to 15kgs of homemade explosives (HME). In typical Jock fashion we all had a laugh and joke at how close we had come to serious injury or even death. Later whilst speaking to The Ammunition Technical Officer (ATO), Captain Dan Shepherd of the Explosive Ordnance Disposal (EOD) Group, Royal Logistics Corps, we were informed that the battery pack that powered the IED had run flat. This was the sole reason the device had failed to detonate. Looking back now we realise how lucky we are to be alive.

We got firmly into routine whilst beating back the Taliban who were trying desperately to regain control of their bazaar. However they were over-matched with the snipers and awesome assets we had at our disposal and out-skilled by the Jocks. Whilst we were soaking up the pressure from the Taliban, the Royal Engineer Search Team cleared the area of IEDs which allowed other Engineers to start building permanent hesco defences in and around the bazaar. Our section's area was the last to be completed. With the hesco frame already in place, all that was required now was the truck to fill it with earth. When the truck was within 10m of the lads chilling out, a massive explosion tore through the air. The shockwave blew Privates Black and Craggs into a nearby building. At the time of the blast there was fear and confusion. My initial thought was that Private Black had triggered an IED, but I couldn't understand how as we had been there for 3 days by then. I had just squared Blacky away with water and rations, when he left the room. Seconds later there was a large explosion which shook the building. I knew it was close because the room went dark with all the dust and debris. I ran out of the room expecting to be met by casualties. I found Blacky lying on top of Craggs groaning and disorientated. As the air cleared I realised that the weight of the truck had set off a deeply laid IED just metres away from our position. I proceeded to clear my way up to the truck to find the driver a little shaken, but without any serious injury. The armour on the truck which surrounds the driver, known as "the coffin", had saved his life.

Over the course of the operation, the company group had found 22 IEDS of which 2 detonated. An ANA soldier was killed by one of them, despite the best efforts of the medics trying to save him. The other 15 were disposed of by Captain Dan Shepherd, who undoubtedly through his knowledge, experience, professionalism and courage saved the lives of many soldiers.

WO2 (CSM) Andy Lambert (34), from Newcastle-Upon-Tyne, Charlie Company

Were you able to close in on the insurgents?
It's slow because they place the IEDs in places that you want to go. You can't launch assaults as much as you would want. I was an instructor at Brecon teaching section attacks, platoon attacks, it's not as easy as that because they're smart, they know which way you're going to come, they look at the ground as much as we look at the ground, they place IEDs

155

The Royal Engineers complete the obstacle across the Nahr-E Burgha Canal. (MOD – Sgt C Halton)

everywhere. The best thing to do is keep your distance, win the fire fight, once you've pushed them out and then go forward, just keep pushing them on the back foot and holding the ground as you go along. It's not like a conventional war, like the Falklands, where you could assault positions. There are times when positions do get assaulted but it seems to be few and far between with the IED threat. The only thing that we've really got that can nullify that is good drills with our equipment. The Jocks have got it down to a tee now, very professional. They take their time, very diligent, they've found a lot of IEDs through good drills, saving lives.

We're not going to start engaging the insurgents until the local nationals have left the area. The Taliban sometimes wait till they've gone until they open up, or they'll open up when they're in between you which is obviously quite hard for us, because we value life more than they do.

Op PANCHAI PALANG – Interview – Private Alan Brown (24), from Dundee, Javelin Platoon, Charlie Company

My grandfather is totally proud, he's ex forces himself, he was in the Navy. He's totally over the moon, apparently he goes to all the reunions and he always talks about me and shows people photos of me. I know my mum is proud, and obviously she worries, every mother worries but I try and phone them as often as I can and I don't want to tell them everything. I just like to tell them I'm doing alright and what the weathers like.

Operation PANCHAI PALANG 2

10–15 July 2009

INTRODUCTION

Bravo Company spent a total of 2 weeks on Operation PANCHAI PALANG and operated from the area of FOB WAHID. Having returned to Kandahar Airfield on 4 July 09, the company had initially been warned to conduct an operation in Kandahar province. However, during Operation PANCHAI PALANG, the Light Dragoons Battle Group was having difficulty as it was pressing west into Babaji from Gereshk. Bravo Company was tasked to establish a block along the Babaji Road in support of the Light Dragoons Battle Group; the intent of the block was to prevent insurgents from reinforcing areas cleared by the Light Dragoons Battle Group.

Bravo Company intended to conduct an aviation assault into the area and establish a block in Ops Box DAHL. The company would dominate Ops Box DAHL through relentless framework patrols based from Objective MULL and a focus on local national engagement.

EXECUTION

10 July 09 (D Day)

The company landed on HLS ACHILLES at 0300 hrs and immediately split into 2 half companies securing Objective EIGG and Objective MULL respectively. The landing was unopposed although armed insurgents were identified by UAV. In Objective EIGG, a variety of ordnance was found alongside opium processing equipment. In Objective MULL, the troops had

Pte Buchland, Royal Army Vetinary Corps and his charge "Benji". Together they could search for and find drugs and explosives including fire arms and ammunition. (MOD – Sgt C Halton)

positive engagement with the local nationals. At 2200 hrs, a standing patrol was established in the south west of Ops Box DAHL to overwatch Route MARS and disrupt any night time insurgent activity.

11 July 09 (D+1)

At 0400 hrs, 5 Platoon was out on patrol to clear a number of compounds along the Babaji road returning at 1200 hrs. Later, at 1600 hrs a platoon size patrol deployed to the north from Objective MULL and conducted a shura before returning to the company location. During the shura, local nationals revealed that the majority of residents in the area had fled. Also, the shura confirmed that insurgents had previously dominated the area and that insurgents were actively placing IEDs along the Babaji road.

12 July 09 (D+2)

At 0330 hrs, the company deployed south to conduct searches of the compounds in the area. The Fire Support Group, commanded by Captain Gladstone, provided flank protection to the north. At 0800 hrs, lead elements of the Light Dragoons Battle Group, mounted in Scimitars, arrived in Ops Box DAHL to establish positions for the remainder of the Battle Group.

13 July – 15 July 09 (D+3 – D+5)

The company provided a screen to the north of the area as the Light Dragoons Battle Group continued to clear along the Babaji road. A single find of a PKM was made and a shura was conducted. The following day, the company was split in two and tasked to hold ground while the remainder of the Light Dragoons Battle Group pressed further west. Local national engagement over the course of the 2 days continued to be positive. By 0320 hrs on 15 July, Bravo Company had fully extracted from the area in 2 waves of 5 Chinook helicopters.

SUMMARY

The deployment of Bravo Company on Operation PANCHAI PALANG 2 facilitated the manoeuvre of the Light Dragoons Battle Group as it pressed along the Babaji Road. The momentum gained during this period would later enable the Light Dragoons Battle Group success on clearing and securing its objectives in Spin Masjed and Babaji. Bravo Company returned to BASTION in order to return to the UK on R & R.

Op PANCHAI PALANG 2 – Change of Axis (Op PANTHERS CLAW - Phase 2) – Major Al Steele (33), Officer Commanding Bravo Company

When we got back to Kandahar the Battle Group Headquarters was, as usual, well advanced with the planning for the company's final 2 short operations in Kandahar province prior to R&R. Unusually however, I felt a great deal of unease. The Light Dragoons were now on the move and taking heavy casualties and I felt it would be in Helmand and Babaji where we

Cpl Jamie Rock from Perth, Mortar Pl, C Coy making a Scottish side salad. (MOD – Sgt C Halton)

should return. The CO was of the same mind and other planned operations were cancelled. This meant that we had only 3 days to complete our preparations. Despite being so close to R & R I was greatly impressed by the Jocks who, almost to a man, wanted to get back on the ground to help the British effort.

We were to drop in ahead of the Brigade advance to block and screen insurgent movement while they cleared the area behind us in detail. With surprise on our side we were able to make our way unhindered to our objectives. The company moved into a compound that was able to control the main routes ahead of the advancing Battle Group. The occupants looked after us particularly well allowing us to buy several chickens to eat. They even taught some of the Jocks how to milk a cow, although they were a little bemused when one individual decided to try quenching his thirst directly from the udder! Like the operation before we patrolled continuously, but despite finding some IED making equipment and drugs the area seemed to be free of insurgents. We were however able to feed the rest of the Brigade timely information about their movements, IED emplacements and general local dynamics. By day 4 the company was exhausted; now at the height of the summer the heat and terrain had taken their toll. With one full day to go the CO of the Light Dragoons arrived at 9 in the evening ahead of his Battle Group's move into the village to our rear the next day.

SSgt Simon O'Connor AGC (RMP) from Bangor, Co Down, demonstrating to some local children how to use a camera – interaction like this happened all the time and was vital in gaining the trust of the local nationals. (MOD – Sgt C Halton)

My orders were to push 5 kilometres further south to establish another block. Although giving me until lunch time to get there I was keen to move under the cover of darkness and out of the punishing sun. We had 2 hours to receive our rations, take down our defences and issues orders. After a 16 hour patrol that day, a night without sleep, was less than palatable.

We left at 1 am and again, with their obscenely heavy kit, the Jocks came up trumps with 7 Platoon getting us into position for first light; even the Dragoons' CO hadn't held out much hope of us getting there by then. Throughout the day, with local patrols and a 2 hour shura, it was clear that insurgents had already fled the area. During the latter there was a painful hour long discussion on which roofs I had put my sentries and would I mind moving them, so it was clear security wasn't an issue! We handed over to a scimitar troop in the evening and extracted at first light.

Corporal Shane Mackness (22), from Leicester, 173 Provost Company, Royal Military Police

How do you feel about working so closely with the infantry and going everywhere they go?
I'm actually glad I'm doing it, we were eager to come out and get stuck in and do the job. I believe most of the company feel the same, they're raring to go and they love being on the front line.

On every op we've gathered some kind of evidence. We've gathered 7.75 million Afghani dollars, we've recovered weapons, explosives, notebooks, and a lot of drugs.

There are 5 Military Police attached to the Battle Group. I'm attached to Bravo Company and we've worked with the same boys every time. The Jocks are a good bunch of lads, I thought it was going to be harder working with them because they're infanteers and we're RMP. But they've actually welcomed us and it's good to see.

I've had a few near misses, a few rounds ping around us. It didn't really bother me at first but when you come back in and you're sat down, that's when you think about that and think 'oh that was close'. You've just got to get on with it.

Lieutenant Gregor Mill (26), from Glasgow, full time reservist – Bravo Company

I had no idea what to expect, it being my first tour, and I've found it unbelievable how close and similar it is to training. Quite a lot of the time on the ground you're just sitting there going these are the exact same drills. I've been through Brecon and it's very similar. I was put through the Regular Brecon Platoon Commanders course to enable me to be a reserve platoon commander. It was definitely an excellent experience, 10 weeks long including a jungle phase in Belize which was awesome.

When I'm based in camp I'm working with the Intelligence Cell here, so there's a team of people just trying to gather intelligence and prepare and get all the Jocks as best prepared as they can for going out on the ground. And when I'm out on the ground I'm working with the Jocks trying to gather as much information as possible, then send it back up to Battle Group HQ.

You'd be surprised how much the Jocks really engage and take part in what they can do. Before we came out I had to teach them a bit of pashtu so they know the basic language. What's more so they can stop people at a distance and do the long range searches which

Lts Gregor Mill and Mike Goodall on the 'thunder box'. (MOD – Sgt C Halton)

helps them tactically. But lots of them want to take it on and learnt a few of the niceties, hello, thank you, that sort of thing. And you see them trying to engage the locals when they can.

You can see short term goals here but I think that the end state is definitely long term, but we're getting there and you can see within the locals how they are seeing coalition forces differently now from how they were originally. They can be very welcoming when they see coalition forces and we often get to go in and have chats and have tea with them which is good. If there's lots of 'fighters' coming with weapons to your home you're obviously going to be a bit apprehensive to start with, but lots of the time because we've been trying to learn the language and do as much as we can, and our interpreters are excellent, after 5 or 10 mins of engaging in conversation we're very easily able to put the message across and we generally see them on side after that.

I think meeting the locals has been a high point of the tour, at first you're told how they have a totally different culture from ours, but mainly from speaking to interpreters, you can see a lot of similarities in our cultures and religions.

Pte Buchland and Benji, Royal Army Vetinery Corps at the end of the operation. (Maj G Shaw)

Operation PANCHAI PALANG 3

20–27 July 2009

INTRODUCTION

By the middle of July, the Welsh Guards Battle Group was in full control of the area of the Luy Mandeh wadi and along the Shamalan Canal. The Light Dragoons Battle Group had made significant gains in Spin Masjed along the Babaji Road. The 3 SCOTS Battle Group was given the mission to secure Objective BLACK in the vicinity of Loy Adera. Securing this area in turn would allow the Light Dragoons Battle Group to subsequently clear the remainder of Babaji, Malgir, and Spin Masjid. Once this final clearance had taken place Operation PANCHAI PALANG would conclude and Task Force Helmand would transition to Operation CHASMI PALANG. Operation CHASMI PALANG in turn would focus on the 'hold' of the region and permit a secure link between Lashkar Gah and Gereshk.

The Battle Group planned to conduct a one company aviation assault into the area of the Loy Adera cemetery with a subsequent armoured link-up. Once Alpha Company was secure on the ground, Charlie Company, 2nd Battalion, The Royal Welsh, would move along Route MARS and secure Objective PEAT; Charlie Company, was an armoured infantry company mounted in Warrior armoured vehicles. Once Objective PEAT was secure, Assaye Troop, a Scimitar mounted troop from the Light Dragoons Battle Group, would hold the area and allow Charlie Company to clear Objectives GAS, OIL, and COAL. Upon the clearance of these objectives and the clearance of Route Mars of IEDs, the Light Dragoons Battle Group would then take control of the area and bring a conclusion to Operation PANCHAI PALANG.

EXECUTION

19 July 09 – 20 July 09 (D–1 – D Day)

At 2320 hrs, Charlie Company, 2 R WELSH and the logistic support vehicles departed BASTION in order to rendezvous with Assaye Troop in FOB PRICE.

At 0244 hrs the following day, Alpha Company and Battle Group TAC deployed from BASTION in 5 Chinook helicopters and escorted by 2 Apache helicopters arriving south of the target location at 0300 hrs. With no sign of the insurgents in the area, Alpha Company regrouped and began its task. At 0410 hrs, the vehicle convoy, led by Charlie Company, left FOB PRICE to link up with Task Force Thor; the convoy subsequently separated into 2 groups, with Charlie Company and Assaye Troop in the vanguard and Task Force Thor escorting the logistic support vehicles.

Early in the morning, 2 and 3 Platoons conducted a series of searches of compounds after

Scheme of Manoeuvre

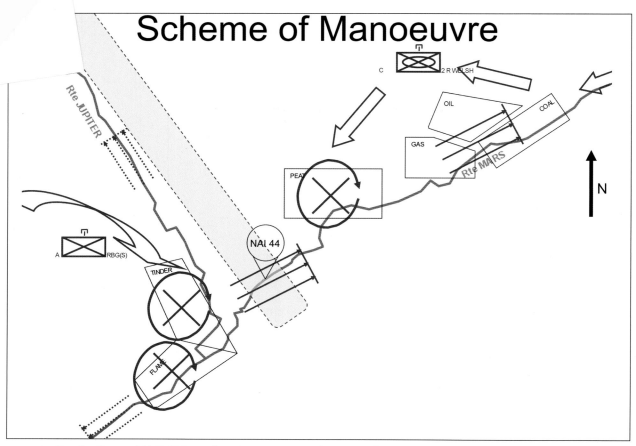

Battle Group TAC HQ and A Coy Air Assault into Babaji, with an armoured link up from the North East.

first light and secured Objective PORSCHE while 1 Platoon remained with Battle Group TAC. At 0750 hrs, Task Force Thor and the logistic support vehicles began its move down Route MARS. By 0800 hrs, Charlie Company and Assaye Troop bypassed Objectives GAS, OIL, and COAL in order to clear and secure Objective PEAT. By midday, Alpha Company had conducted shuras with local nationals who proved to be very welcoming to ISAF forces. Charlie Company secured Objective PEAT at 1530 hrs at which the company withdrew to the north of the objective. Brigadier Radford, Task Force Helmand Commander, arrived during the evening and stayed with Battle Group TAC. Patrols were conducted throughout the night across the area.

21 July 09 (D+1)

Alpha Company continued to dominate Objective FERRARI through patrols in the area. In the morning, Assaye Troop took control of Objective PEAT and adopted a position of overwatch which allowed Charlie Company to clear Route MARS through Objectives GAS, OIL, and COAL. Royal Engineers, attached to the Battle Group, also began to build a defensive position around Alpha Company's central location. In addition, the Fire Support Group mounted in Jackals, commanded by Captain Jon Kerr, deployed to FOB PRICE to rendezvous with Task Force Thor. Task Force Thor subsequently guided the Fire Support Group into the area.

22 July 09 (D+2)

Before first light, the Fire Support Group relieved elements of Alpha Company. Alpha Company subsequently conducted a company level patrol parallel to Route MARS. After first light, the Battle Group's logistic support vehicles moved from its position in the Light Dragoons Battle Group's area into Objective PORSCHE. Assaye Troop took responsibility of Objectives GAS, OIL, and COAL and Charlie Company began the clearance of Route JUPITER. During the day, Commander ISAF Afghanistan, General Stanley McChrystal, visited with the Battle Group and conducted a shura. Assaye Troop spent the majority of the day maintaining a positive influence in the area by engaging with local nationals and providing medical care.

23 July 09 – 24 July 09 (D+3)

Charlie Company continued to move north proving Route JUPITER and finished the day poised to link up with the Welsh Guards in FOB WAHID. Alpha Company conducted patrols in Objectives ASTON, FERRARI, and JAGUAR. In addition, Assaye Troop conducted a shura with 40 local nationals who informed the troop that a wedding was to take place in Objective PEAT. Assaye Troop agreed to respect the wishes of the local nationals and to stand off from the area for the next 2 days. The following day, elements of the Light Dragoons Battle Group came into the area to conduct a reconnaissance in preparation to hold the area once the Battle Group had departed. Assaye Troop conducted another health clinic treating 5 local nationals.

Lt Col Ed Flute and the CO attend a shura – shuras, similar to council meetings, were a way of identifying the local nationals' needs and also a way of showing them our commitment and trust. (MOD – Sgt C Halton)

Two Jackals – The one on the left is mounted with a 40mm Grenade Machine Gun. When static, the Jackals made excellent sentry positions to provide airwatch in support of the dismounted troops. (MOD – Sgt C Halton)

Lunch after the shura – Afghans take pride in their hospitality. (MOD – Sgt C Halton)

25 July 09 (D+5)

Early in the morning, 2 Platoon deployed to the south and the Fire Support Group conducted a reconnaissance of an Afghan National Election potential polling centre. At 0700 hrs, the lead Jackal from the Fire Support Group struck an IED. The force of the explosion turned the Jackal 180 degrees causing 3 casualties; Bombardier Hopson was thrown from the Jackal, the driver, Private Kidd, had his foot trapped under the driver's door but was fully conscious, and Private Stewart was in shock. Lance Corporal Scally, the combat medical technician, with Lance Corporal Palmer applied tourniquets to both of Bombardier Hopson's legs and attempted to perform chest compressions. Corporal Herd attended to Private Kidd and administered morphine.

Recovery assets and Assaye Troop were immediately dispatched to support the Fire Support Group. Scimitars and Vikings mounted with 2 combat medical technicians moved to assist the casualties. At 0721 hrs, Staff Sergeant Hall from the Royal Tank Regiment, who was commanding a Viking, reported an IED strike. Corporal David Hindson, one of the combat medical technicians, began to triage casualties. Sergeant Church, also a Viking commander, had injured his left leg and a splint had been applied, however, the real concern was of possible abdominal injuries and internal bleeding. Trooper Kay, the other combat medical technician, and Craftsman Lee were both injured. The casualties were brought to a central emergency helicopter landing site.

When the emergency medical helicopter arrived, Private Kidd was still trapped under the Jackal and the medical crew attempted to lift the Jackal. By this time, the recovery assets had arrived and all the casualties were evacuated to BASTION, but tragically Bombardier Hopson was pronounced dead on arrival. Despite the tragedy, the troops endeavoured to exploit the IED strikes and recover the stricken vehicles.

26 July – 27 July 09 (D+6 – D+7)

Alpha Company remained in Objective BLACK conducting patrols in Objective ASTON. Assaye Troop continued to hold Objectives PEAT, GAS, OIL, and COAL. Bravo Company, the Light Dragoons Battle Group, arrived at 1700 hrs in order to take command of Objective BLACK. The Battle Group focus then changed to its own extraction. The logistic support vehicles and the Fire Support Group extracted from the area and arrived in BASTION at 1800 hrs. Alpha Company extracted from the area at 0330 hrs. However, one of the Battle Group's mortar lines, under command of Sergeant Masson, remained in the area in order to provide support to the Light Dragoons Battle Group for a further 2 weeks.

SUMMARY

Although insurgents and local nationals were aware that ISAF troops were heading to the Loy Adera cemetery, the operation was marked, encouragingly, by a relative lack of kinetic action. The lack of insurgent activity was assessed to be the result of the casualties sustained by insurgents during the opening phases of Operation PANCHAI PALANG. Throughout

Extraction to BASTION at the end of Op PANCHAI PALANG. (MOD – Sgt C Halton)

Operation PANCHAI PALANG 3, the Battle Group dominated the region through deliberate patrols and active engagement with local nationals. Initial clearance of Route MARS was marked by the lack of IED finds. Despite the lack of an overt presence, local nationals indicated that insurgents remained in the area observing the Battle Group's movements.

With the withdrawal of the Battle Group from Babaji, Operation PANCHAI PALANG concluded. The opening phase of Operation PANCHAI PALANG began with the Battle Group's aviation assault and seizure of the Luy Mandeh wadi. It was only fitting that one of Task Force Helmand's most significant operations of Operation HERRICK 10 was thus drawn to a close by the Battle Group securing one final objective thereby enabling the containment and clearance of the entirety of Babaji.

Despite the success of the Battle Group during the critical periods of Operation PANCHAI PALANG, the Battle Group was not left unscathed. The death of Bombardier Hopson, 38 Battery, 40 Regiment Royal Artillery, deeply affected all members of the Battle Group. He was a warm, outgoing, and strong character who was irreplaceable. The pride in our successes was tempered and humbled by the grief of his death and the casualties suffered during Operation PANCHAI PALANG.

Op PANCHAI PALANG 3 – Personal Account – Private Willie Brown (23), from Fife, 2 Platoon, Alpha (Grenadier) Company

We returned from R&R and were ordered back to Babaji to gain more ground from the enemy. This time there was no sign of the enemy and there were lots of local nationals we went out to talk to. We did a lot of patrolling although we suffered badly from the heat because we had spent 2 weeks getting used to the weather back home! The op was generally a success but at a cost. We lost a good man, Bombardier Hopson (Hoppo), when his vehicle hit an IED.

Lance Corporal Aaron Graham (22), from Fife, 1 (Senior Highland) Platoon, Alpha Company

It's as hard as I thought it would be out here, but watching Ross Kemp he kind of glamorises a bit eh. It is busy and you do get a lot of contacts. And you hype yourself up and then you go out, and you're not disappointed.

The adrenalin is second to none, you canna beat it. First time I got shot at, I just giggled. Everybody did.

When we did take a casualty, I think that was when a lot of boys had a lot of fear then. Maybe this isn't an X box game, it's real. Maybe it's not a computer game, but to be fair, everybody kind of just switched on that bit more. More efficient with their drills. From the top down it's been enforced that our drills are done properly. We're training all the time and any amendments are enforced by the low level commanders.

Geraint Vincent from ITN interviewing WO2 (CSM) Paul Colville and Sgt Gus Millar (right).
Gus was tragically killed a few weeks later on a return visit to Babaji. (MOD – Sgt C Halton)

Corporal Craig Duncan (33), Minden Platoon, Alpha (Grenadier) Company

Afghan has been more exciting than what TELIC was. That's what you joined the army for, it's what you enjoy. The heat has been hard, and carrying all the kit.

There's good morale within the platoon, and the whole company, a good bunch of boys, a good laugh and that's why you enjoy the tour a wee bit more.

You crack on during contacts, your adrenalin takes over and you just crack on, it's just a day to day thing.

We're confident in our kit, as long as you do the IED drills alright, we're pretty much happy, you can't ask for anything else.

Private Robert Robertson (29), from Fife, Mortar Platoon, Charlie Company

I've been with the Battalion for 6 years but I've come out late to theatre. I had left the Army last year and re enlisted about 2 months ago. I just wanted a change but it's made me appreciate what I've come back to. There isn't much in civvy street nowadays. This is better than being on the dole.

I did Op TELIC in 2004, I've been under Mortar fire, I've been IED'd, had a sniper shoot at me. My expectations for out here are totally different. More IEDs and determined attacks.

Sergeant Eck Reilly (37), from Dundee, Mortar Section Commander, Charlie Company

We tend to use the 81mm mortar. It was proven how accurate it was on the last op we did there. We fired about 18 fire missions, about 248 rounds.

Private James New (22), from Dundee, Mortar Platoon, Charlie Company

I've been twice to Iraq before. I'm a No 1 in the Mortar Platoon. It's brilliant. I prefer it here on ops than at the Fort (being in barracks in Scotland). In FOB JAKER a 107 rocket landed about 15 m away from me the other side of the hesco bastion. I just heard the whistling coming over and so I dived out of the way and all I heard was a bang. I was in a sangar on stag at the time, the sangar was covered in smoke and dust. I just hoped there wasn't another one coming in.

Sgt Eck Reilly.

Privates Peter and James Muir (18 year old twins, Drummer and Piper) from Kilcardy. Both GPMG Gunners in Charlie Company.

Usually you have to wait 2 years until you go to a specialist company, but we went straight away. The pipe band needed numbers, so we went to the pipe band. And then we done our GPMG cadres, SF and that and then obviously went to the FSG for Afghanistan. I enjoy the ops. Being in camp is boring, I'd rather be on the ground.

We both get on well together, argue all the time but never seriously, just joking about banter. All our family are proud, we've had great granddads who were in The Black Watch and one of them fought in WW1.

Babaji were the closest near misses under contact and Kandahar we were pinned down for a wee bit, 12 hours. We thought it was brilliant. The best bit of being out here. I think we've been contacted every op we've been on, it's always the FSG that seems to get contacted cos we always get pushed out to the flanks. We seem to swap about from FSG1 to FSG 2 quite alot to make up the orbat. That last op we ended up being in the same FSG and we were both lead scouts. It's alright cos the mine detection kit is good eh. Bit nervous cos before we were doing it, an IED had gone off and killed 2 of the ANA boys, about 5 minutes before, so we were a bit nervous, but we got through it alright. The kit is good. Carrying the weight of the kit was a struggle at first, but after you keep going out on the ops you get used to it. It's not too bad, I think we were carrying about 130lbs. Everyone chips in with the weight, the kit gets spread out.

The new rations are good actually, I quite like them. The water flavourings are good, but they need to bring back the Yorkie though or Mars Bars.

What are you going to do on your R&R? 'Get pissed'. I've got my birthday on R&R, there's a big night out in Edinburgh planned for it.

Ptes James and Pete Muir of the Fire Support Group – one a piper, one a drummer.

INTERVIEWS CONDUCTED AFTER DEPLOYING ON OP PANCHAI PALANG ON THE VEHICLE PARK, CAMP ROBERTS

Lieutenant Harry Pearce (26), from Ledbury, Gloucester, 7 Platoon Commander, Bravo Company

I've had 4 very close shaves. The last op (PANCHAI PALANG) I took a fighting patrol out to the south west of the Platoon house, and Corporal Copeland and I were just resting up next to a mosque and we heard RPG incoming, and so we took a knee, and it landed about 3 – 4 m away from us, bent in half but it didn't go off and just came to rest next to us. Corporal Copeland and I just sought of looked at each other and notched another one on our cards and I've got 5 lives left so it's not too bad.

Sergeant Stephen Noble (32), from Edinburgh, Platoon Sergeant Minden Platoon, Alpha Company

What's your most important job as a Platoon Sergeant?
Extracting casualties. Rear protection, flank protection and controlling rates of fire when the Pl Comd's busy. The Pl Comd, Mr Gorie and I started working together in Kenya, he was straight out of the chocolate factory Sandhurst. We've spent a lot of time together, I've offered him a lot of advice and he's done well, a bit of a nudge now and then.

We got contacted whilst out for a swim. There was a small tributary next to the canal near our compound – compound ALAMO – 10 of us guarding a compound for 5 days. We were pretty much in contact for 5 days but we decided to go for a swim out the back during a lull in the battle and it lasted about half an hour. One of the Jocks McCue was butt naked, everyone else stayed in their combats to wash their combats, he decided to go for a swim naked. About 150 m down the river bed, a couple of insurgents decided to have a few pot shots and rattled off about half a mag each. Six Jocks ran back in semi naked, back into the half platoon compound. Rounds were still coming in but the Jocks were laughing because McCue was naked and he was trying to grab his boots and his kit and that, and run back on the 20m dash.

The Jocks go for nervous pisses before they deploy, and down water like its going out of fashion.

My job is made 10 times easier because I'm here with 30 volunteers.

Captain Harry Hood (40), from Dunfermline, Fife, RCMO, LO, Officer Commanding 6 Platoon, Bravo Company

"24 years in The Black Watch, a 'nice surprise' commissioning".

It was a good experience being a Platoon Commander. I was asked to step in because Lieutenant Andrew Halliday was injured as a result of an IED. I stood in for him on Op PANCHAI PALANG Phase 1 and Phase 2. We established the FOB and the Platoon house, and conducted patrols. It took about a week to get settled back into it again, it was good. Jocks are brilliant, they've been magnificent. Over worked and under paid. They're stars.

Jocks taking a dip in the Shamalan canal.

Have they changed much since you were a 'boy soldier'?

They're the same but they're having to mature a lot quicker. They're producing the goods on a daily basis and they never cease to amaze me how resilient they are and how they can get on with things, and how professional they are.

It's been very mentally and physically demanding, having to make the right decisions for 24 soldiers. It's been a challenge. Once I got settled back in, it was fine, I had a good Platoon Sergeant, Sergeant Danny Buist.

We had to extract for about a km under fire on Op PANCHAI PALANG, out of the killing zone, but their drills were fine, the Jocks were aggressive. We broke contact and a 500lb bomb was dropped.

Lance Corporal Lanna Monaghan (28), from Buckhaven, Fife, A Combat HR Specialist, Adjutant General's Corps (Staff and Personnel Support)

I was excited to come out here. I jumped at the chance and I've volunteered to go out on the ground. I've done female searching so far on Op PANCHAI PALANG. I did female search training with Alpha Company and the RMP JNCOs.

I was very apprehensive the day before going out on the ground. When we landed I was like 'where are they?' We were sat there in the middle of the field and I was just thinking 'where are they?'

I'm about to go and be attached to Delta Company in Musa Qal'ah. It's important that whatever cap badge in the Army you are, that you go out because you're a soldier first. You definitely have to experience the different elements of the Army.

Sergeant Paul Cooper (35), from Fife, Medical Sergeant, Headquarter Company

I've had a total of 9 casualties so far 3 months into the tour, and 2 of them have been very serious.

We were on Op PANCHAI PALANG, checking for mines, an ANA soldier went off the safe route to pick some grapes and he stood on a land mine and it blew his leg right off. So I dealt with that and kept him alive.

This is a lot harder compared to Iraq, I've not enjoyed being here. I think its a waste of human life. That's just my personal opinion. Young lads in the prime of their life, losing their lives. I don't think the British public understand what we do out here and what actually goes on behind the scenes. I agree that the Taliban need to be suppressed but at the same time it is a waste of young lives, I suppose that's the sacrifice that has to be made.

Platoon Sergeant – Snipers, Charlie Company

I've been in the Army for 10 years, I've been in the Sniper Platoon for 8 years. Out on ops it's good, back in camp not so good. 98% of the time it's training and 2% of the time you actually get to do your job on ops and I've just been lucky that I've had 2 TELICS and now I've got this HERRICK under my belt.

The enemy over here are a lot more diligent than what they were in Iraq. Iraq it was more like somebody will grab a rifle and fire at you. Over here they know what they're trying to achieve without themselves actually getting killed. Like that last op we were on, there we were getting engaged from a sniper from 2 buildings and our guys that were on the wall were looking for the guy, he was firing from a building behind so he had cover from us being able to fire back at him. He was firing 2 or 3 rounds from one building, then moving position, then firing onto another compound. So the guys would see the splash there, and then they would

Mark Austin (ITN) and Sgt Cooper –
The Battle Group's Medical Sergeant.

174

all fire onto that compound and then he'd be able to escape. Out here they've been doing it for so long, they know what they're doing.

I've had quite a few near misses. We were pinned down on one op in Sangin, OUBA 3 for the whole day, couldn't move and the only way that we broke that contact was calling up a Javelin. The last op PANCHAI PALANG, attached to 7 Platoon, we got contacted going down the canal and me and the platoon commander were sat talking and a round landed in between us.

My wife's quite used to it because of the other ops, but she doesn't put the telly on anymore.

Major Jeremy Sharpe (36), from Bristol, Battery Commander for the 38 Battery Tac Group, 40 Regiment Royal Artillery

Would you do anything differently in the next 3 months based on your experiences of the first 3?
Nothing fundamentally different. I think we as a whole BG have got things basically right. They're always refinements that you would make to the planning process, to the way that you execute, to the way you use and bid for assets. We're learnt an enormous amount from the Americans, from the Canadians and all the guys we've worked with and you take each of those aspects forward and build it into the next plan. So our plans now are at a far more advanced level than they were when we first started and that will continue throughout the whole tour I'm certain.

What's the most difficult thing about being here?
On a personal level, missing home. On a professional level, it's the constant need to challenge assumptions and ask what else we could be doing and avoid complacency. It's very easy, partly because the level of access we have to assets, to accept that this is the best way of doing it, and not challenge what we do. And I think we need to be better at questioning the way we've done things and taking it forward in the future.

The pleasure of working with a single BG as a BC for the entire time of my tour is enormous, the BG look after us exceptionally well and that's been carried through from Kenya all the way through to now and we genuinely feel part of the 3 SCOTS team.

I think we are making a difference in Afghanistan. We don't get to see as a BG the difference that we make because we're in and out over a relatively short period of time. But the reports that we've had from the various operations that we've conducted are that we are delivering regional effect. In terms of pure focus on the enemy, I believe we have delivered some significant blows at the tactical level to the insurgency and that's all you can really hope to do as a BG. We will make small contributions to the overall greater effort of either RC(S) or Task Force Helmand.

In terms of the kinetic effect that we've had, the guys have shown remarkable restraint. One of the key features of the training and one of the sort of adages that I've always used with them is that they should make positive decisions every time. It should never be a reaction to deliver a bomb from an aircraft or to fire the guns or to fire GMLRS. It should always be a positive decision based on the situation that they find themselves in. We operate under a series of rules of engagement, having reviewed every engagement that we've conducted I think all but one of them could very firmly be said to have been conducted under

Maj Jeremy Sharpe, Battery Commander. (MOD – Sgt C Halton)

the most basic rules of engagement, which is complete self defence. We had no choice, it was to save life. To save the lives of our soldiers, that we conducted those engagements. We've conducted at least one I believe under offensive rules of engagement, which we are well within our rights to do so, but every single one of them has involved the FST Comd on the ground or the JTAC who has been conducting the drop of the weapon, taking active steps to minimise the collateral damage, chosen a smaller weapons system or gone back to the company commander and said I think we can achieve this with snipers, or with Javelin or a smaller weapons system.

So it's never been a knee jerk reaction that we must get rounds away, that's actually something that's quite difficult for the guys to do. Professionally they want to drop as many bombs as possible, you are an artillery observer or an MFC or you're on the mortar line or you're one of my guys up in FOB EDINBURGH with the guns, and you want to make things go bang. That's what being a gunner or being a mortar man or being a JTAC is about. But the guys have an absolute understanding of the requirement to minimise our impact on Afghan civilians by the kinetic action that we take. We recently received more direction from ISAF on that which really reiterates what we've always known. It does create some conflict for the guys inside themselves, because they start to wonder whether they have been making the right decisions. I believe very firmly, and we've reviewed every action that we've done, that we have made the right decisions. In particular now we're very constrained in engaging compounds, people's houses. I don't think even with this new directive it would have changed anything we would have done in the past, I don't think any of the engagements we have conducted, we wouldn't now conduct. And of the engagements we've conducted, we have not conducted at least as many, if not more, for those very same reasons. There was another method of engaging the target or we didn't need to engage the target, or the collateral damage as a result of taking on that target would have outweighed the benefit of striking it. I firmly believe the guys absolutely understand that requirement, but it is very very difficult, you're asking guys to make decisions that put their comrades in, at times increased danger for the sake of not having a kinetic effect that might cause collateral damage and that is a very difficult decision to make. The guys have been very brave in making those decisions and have put themselves at risk in order to either deliver orders or get into a position where they can assist the company commander in making that decision.

The repatriation that we did, I was personally pleased that it was my guns that fired the salute at the repatriation ceremony in Camp BASTION. It means a lot to me. The guys feel enormously part of the Battle Group, we've been taken on under their wing and we genuinely feel part of it and integrated at every level, from me working with the CO down to Bombardier Ewans, one of the Scottish guys in my Battery, who is now pretty much part of 2 Platoon and fights every case to move him onto a different Platoon to provide fires for them.

It's a phenomenal tour - we've learnt a great deal, we've had some great experiences; it's been dangerous and challenging for the guys on the ground, but everyone whether they're in camp or whether they've been out on the ground, has contributed to some enormously successful operations.

Losing Bombardier Hopson was difficult for everyone in the Battery and across the Battle Group, he was not the first to fall and was not the last, the loss of Sergeant Gus Millar and Corporl Tam Mason was as keenly felt by the Battery as it was by the Battalion. Following each of these incidents the guys in the Battery took stock, paused to mourn and then got on with the job in hand. The strength to do this was in no small part drawn from the close bond we had established with the Battalion and this has continued after the tour, both the Battery and the family of Craig Hopson have received superb support since returning.

The Brigade Reconnaissance Force (BRF) – Captain Will Johnson (30), from Liss, Hampshire, Platoon Commander BRF

The BRF was drawn from across the Brigade and 12 members of 3 SCOTS were selected, mostly from the Recce Platoon. The BRF was immensely appealing, as it operated independently within Task Force Helmand and was free from the normal day to day trivialities that could make battalion life restrictive, especially on operations.

One of the biggest selling points, when trawling for volunteers, was that we would work directly to the Brigade Commander as his eyes and ears across Helmand Province, delivering the effects that he wanted, wherever he wanted them. Also, the extra training and resources made the deployment much more exciting. From the start of our training we were expecting

Capt Will Johnson with members of the BRF.

to be used to deliver influence effects among the population; trying to win over the locals to our side rather than simply fighting the insurgency. As it turned out this was easier said than done for the first few months of the tour.

As the Recce Platoon Commander in the Battalion I was looking forward to the tour, as the BRF was really the only unit where I was likely to be doing real reconnaissance work. We ended up doing far more than this. For the first 2 months we had a very 'kinetic' experience, coming under contact on nearly every mission. This was because we were shaping the ground and the enemy for Op PANCHAI PALANG. The enemy were reluctant to expose themselves unless placed under extreme pressure, which usually involved us driving towards their likely positions until they had no alternative but to engage us. Combined with airborne ISTAR platforms this was very effective in finding depth positions, reinforcement and extraction routes and identifying prestige weapons such as heavy machine guns.

It was a pretty exciting time for everyone, particularly as we knew that we were fighting in places were few people had been before, and that the information we were obtaining would make the big operations easier for the fighting units. We probed several of the positions that the RBG(S), our own Battalion, would later assault. It was frustrating however, not to be taking the battle into the enemy heartland, the green zone.

The tour changed quite dramatically for us after Op PANCHAI PALANG. There were simply not enough troops to hold the ground in Babaji that had been taken and so we were sent in as a dismounted company to disrupt the insurgency in depth and allow the ground holding infantry companies to consolidate their areas without enemy interference. This role lasted from the beginning of August until the end of the tour. I think that we all enjoyed this time, despite the heat, shortages of food and water and sleeping rough in compounds and ditches across Babaji. We were finally getting amongst the enemy and locals.

In terms of soldiering it was a fantastic experience as we carried out nearly every type of dismounted operation that we had trained for over our collective careers. We had plenty of scraps with the enemy, using our numbers and training to good effect; disrupting them far behind the 'front line'. More importantly however, we had a real chance to make an impression on the population. It was reassuring, in the face of the sacrifices that had been made during the tour, to see the locals come forward to talk about the future and engage with us about regenerating their communities. This happened many times in many places after we had convincingly beaten back the insurgency each time. It was classic power politics; if we could demonstrate that we were the ultimate force the locals were happy to support us and welcome our presence. This small sign of hope for the future was most welcome.

The final half of our tour was immensely positive. We saw signs of stability and regeneration across Babaji after the fighting of PANCHAI PALANG; the kind needed to win the campaign. However, the cynicism of the UK media and evident lack of public support for the mission (upon returning home) compounded a feeling of frustration that so much more could be achieved. Maybe next time.

Chapter Seven

Operation TYRUNA 2B

8–9 August 2009

INTRODUCTION

On Operation TYRUNA 2B, the Battle Group was once again paired with high calibre Afghan Forces. As Bravo Company was on R & R, Alpha Company was involved with the operation to disrupt and destroy insurgents in the village of Malmand Chinah, Ghowrak District, in Kandahar Province. Operation TYRUNA 2B was a short operation in which Alpha Company and Afghan Forces inserted into the area on the evening of 8 August and extracted in the morning of 9 August. Battle Group TAC was situated on a hilltop to the east of the village and Major Robin Lindsay, the Battle Group second in command, commanded the operation.

EXECUTION

08 August – 09 August 09 (D Day – D+1)

At 2224 hrs 7 American Chinook helicopters, 2 American Blackhawk helicopters, and an escort of 2 American Apache helicopters left Kandahar and landed on target at 2313 hrs; Alpha Company and Afghan Forces landed to the east of the village. Following a brief period of regrouping, Alpha Company and the Afghan Forces moved on to their respective target areas. 2 Platoon came under small arms fire as it was attempting to secure a compound. The platoon returned fire and killed one insurgent. Afghan Forces secured Objective AUGUSTUS and discovered compounds that had recently been used as narcotic facilities; all the equipment was destroyed. 2 Platoon captured one detainee, and

Major Robin Lindsay leading the Battle Group – with the CO on R & R, Robin took over command.

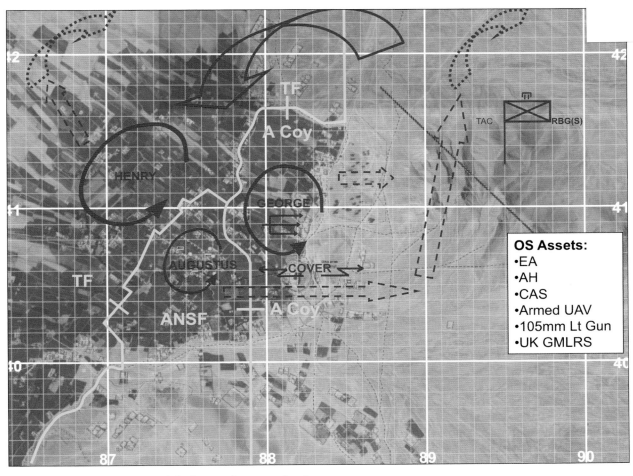

The green zone and dasht can be seen clearly.

US CH47s ready for take off from Kandahar.

Alpha Company extraction back to Kandahar Airfield.

Afghan Forces captured 3 detainees. Alpha Company and Afghan Forces extracted east of the village. All troops were back in Kandahar Airfield by 0700 hrs.

SUMMARY

The Battle Group successfully disrupted the insurgents in Malmand Chinah through a single wave of aviation assault. Intelligence following the operation suggested that the size and disposition of the ISAF forces and also the continued presence of the Apache helicopters dislocated and disorientated the insurgents and also discouraged insurgents from conducting any form of harassment. The lack of significant finds coupled with the information gleaned from local nationals on the ground indicated that the majority of narcotic and insurgent activity was taking place during the day and narcotic traffickers and insurgents moved away from the area at night. Further information derived from local nationals and our intelligence indicated that the Bazaar contained a number of IEDs and was also a focal point.

The rear gunner's view from the back of a CH47. As a Divisional asset, the BG worked with many different nationalities. Task Force Talon the US Combat Aviation Bde enabled most of the BG's ops during the second half of the tour.

Stephen Stewart, News Reporter, *The Daily Record* & *Sunday Mail*, Glasgow

He looked like a young Darth Vader – complete with black face mask – as he rattled off dozens of rounds into the darkness as we prepared to hit the landing zone. The teenage US Army gunner then turned and gave the thumbs up.

Everything inside our Chinook helicopter – the workhorse of Afghanistan – was bathed in a eerie, green light. The dull glow illuminated a fearsome sight that would have made the most bloodthirsty Taliban fanatic weep. Hundreds of Scots soldiers and a detachment of their US and Afghan allies were on their way to inflict an airborne surgical strike on the Taliban.

The Jocks – as the Scots are affectionately known – were armed to the teeth with machine guns, missiles, grenades, sniper rifles, high explosives and good old fashioned bayonets. Welcome to Kandahar as 3 SCOTS – The Black Watch – get ready for a massive operation under the cover of darkness against a Taliban Improvised

Journalist Stephen Stewart.

Stephen Stewart and photographer Lesley Martin before deployment.

Explosive Device (IED) and drugs factory in Sangin Valley – dubbed the "Valley of Death". Photographer Lesley Martin and I were the only journalists to join Alpha Company as they spearheaded a huge blitz on the Taliban's narco-terrorism network.

The swoop was a testament to the multi-national nature of the Afghan war – 18 UK, US and Australian helicopters took part in the raid. Nine Chinooks, 3 Black Hawks, 2 Sea Kings and 4 Apache attack helicopters swept across the desolate wastes of the open desert before targeting a remote and isolated compound area. Some 300 Scots soldiers, a US Army engineering detachment and scores of crack Afghan troops took part in the op.

When I was taken away for special training and shown how to apply a tourniquet if my arm was blown off, how to self administer morphine and apply field dressing to gaping wounds, I began to have second doubts about volunteering to witness the might of Operation TYRUNA first hand. But at exactly 22 minutes past 10pm on Saturday August 8 2009, we were there as the operation kicked off with the soldiers being led on to US Chinooks for the 40 minute rollercoaster ride from Kandahar to bleak Malmand Chinah in the infamous Sangin Valley.

I clung on to the canvas seat of the lurching twin rotor helicopter as the lights dimmed and eventually faded out completely and the troops donned their night vision goggles for a special night's sparring with the insurgents. Once the green night lights were turned off inside the chopper, we were left to brood over what lay ahead. With stomachs churning, thanks to a combination of nerves and the choppy ride, we were given the nudge and told to prepare to run off as the helicopter touched down at out target. I pulled down my ballistic goggles, adjusted my helmet and sweated furiously under pounds of body armour. As the Chinook blasted down on to the parched earth in the middle of a 80mph downblast from the twin rotors, we hurled ourselves into a field as the soldiers sprinted to their defensive positions.

We just had seconds to catch our breaths and take a swig from our water packs before it started: the deafening roar of an Apache helicopter's fearsome chain gun ripping into insurgent positions.

I heard another sound I wouldn't forget in a hurry – hundreds of crazed dogs barking as the massive column of troops begin to infiltrate the Taliban compounds. A crackle and pop sound – like bundles of hay being snapped in two – signalled small arms fire and showed that the Taliban knew we had arrived.

We made our way through a maze of sun-scorched compounds – all the time, making sure that we followed directly in the footsteps of the man in front.

I staggered through the solid ground punctuated by needle sharp bushes and jumped back in terror as a rabid dog which had its ears hacked off by its owner, leaped up to attack me.

My heart missed a beat as the chain – which I hadn't seen in the pitch darkness – took hold and dragged the devil dog back to earth. We then headed to a complex of houses moulded out of the rock hard earth as the soldiers began their drug and IED searches.

We slumped on the ground, greedily drank water and crunched boiled sweets to keep up our sugar levels as we waited for the houses to be cleared. Then, a white flash erupted, followed by a bang which shook me to the core and nearly knocked me over.

The crack Afghan units had just made their way into another suspicious home – this time, they had decided to go though the wall by blowing a gaping hole in it.

The sound of sporadic gunfire followed by suppressing shots resounded across the breathless valley for the entire mission that lasted almost 9 hours between Saturday night and Sunday morning.

Another massive explosion left me reeling and wondering about how we would cope with a rapid two-and-a-half mile march through terrain studded by jagged rocks, deep ravines – and most worryingly, deadly IEDS built to kill and maim.

We gathered our kit – which included rations and 7 litres of water – and moved out in single file. We marched out to the helicopter landing zone – always fearful that the next step could be our last. As we walked in moonlight on what felt like the surface of the moon, the sun gradually began to appear from behind the awe inspiring mountains of the Sangin Valley.

Shot through one of the soldier's night vision goggles, a soldier armed with a Javelin missile, a shoulder mounted anti-tank weapon, on watch at night on the roof of a compound in the middle of Malmand Chinah.

We had no time to worry about the possible dangers as we had to be at the landing site at just after 6am for our extraction.

With moments to spare, we knelt and down and awaited the churned up rocks and sand which would mark the Chinooks arrival.

Grabbing cameras and rucksacks we ran for the rear doors and into the chopper which sped off in a defensive move to deter any watching Taliban snipers.

It had been a rewarding night's work – sniffer dogs located a massive haul of 250 kg of wet opium worth more than $1.5m as well as a cache of weapons. It is thought 7 Taliban fighters were also killed during the operation. Major Robin Lindsay of The Black Watch, 3rd Battalion The Royal Regiment of Scotland, said the night-time blitz was an outstanding tactic.

He said: "This type of high intensity technique, where we airlift a large number of troops into a small area, effectively storming it, has been shown to work time after time. It proves to the Taliban beyond doubt that they have no safe havens even in the most remote, isolated places. We can hit them at will wherever and whoever they are. The money that would have come from the sale of the opium would undoubtedly have funded the insurgents' activities, further strengthening their hold in the area and their ability to launch deadly attacks on coalition forces. This kind of operation hits at the heart of the insurgency because it significantly reduces their capability to continue the fight. With fewer numbers and diminished resources, they are simply less effective."

One by one, the soldiers on the flight back began to slump on their weapons and drift into a deep and well deserved sleep.

After a small detour to drop off Taliban suspects captured during the raid, the Jocks swooped back into Kandahar.

Op Tyruna 2B Extraction.

Operation TYRUNA 2C

14 – 15 August 2009

INTRODUCTION

Operation TYRUNA 2C was initially intended to be 2 separate company level operations into Panjwayi District, Kandahar. However, aviation assets were unavailable to conduct 2 separate pulses into the area and as a result the operation became one single company level operation. Previous operations by Task Force Kandahar in the region had concentrated insurgents into the Panjway area and thus there was a strong assessment of a massing of insurgents in the vicinity of Talukan and Zangabad. In addition, prior reporting indicated that Zangabad was a key staging area where insurgents exercised shadow governance.

Bravo Company planned to conduct an aviation assault onto Objectives SHARK and BARRACUDA in the area of Zangabad, early in the morning of the 14 August. The company would strike targets in these objectives and conduct searches in the area with the deliberate intent to cause a response by insurgents. Insurgent response would allow the company to identify dispositions which in turn would enable further exploitation of the area. The company would then extract early in the morning of the 15 August.

EXECUTION

14 August – 15 August 09 (D Day – D+1)

At 0222 hrs, Bravo Company deployed in 6 Chinook helicopters arriving at 0255 hrs on Objective BARRACUDA. The Chinook helicopters returned to Kandahar Airfield to pick up the mortar line which was inserted into Canadian Patrol Base SPERWAN GHAR. 5 Platoon was positioned in the centre of the Company Group, the Fire Support Group in the west, 6 Platoon to the East and 7 Platoon in reserve with Company Main Headquarters. The company pressed south at first light and at 0530 hrs came under fire from small arms and RPG from multiple firing points. Throughout the day, the company remained in contact and made full use of all indirect weapons available: the Apache helicopter engaged insurgents with missiles, mortars were employed, and an Excalibur mission was prepared. Despite a furious day of fighting, the company also discovered a number of finds including anti-personnel mines, explosive materials, grenades, RPG warheads, and ammunition. The company extracted at 0345 hrs, however, UAV identified a number of insurgents on the extraction point which were prosecuted through air delivered munitions from an F 16.

SUMMARY

Insurgents became aware of the company's presence immediately on insertion but did not take any action until after first light. Insurgents proceeded to mount determined small scale harassing attacks. They used multiple fire points throughout the day, operating in groups of 2-3, and made use of small arms, RPG, PKM, and accurate single round sharp shooting possibly from a Draganov. The response indicated a prepared insurgent grouping, although the lack of IEDs encountered suggested that tactical surprise was achieved by Bravo Company. Further, the lack of any engagements prior to last light revealed that the insurgent force was not large and the day's fighting had caused a number of casualties and depleted insurgent's ammunition such that a period of consolidation was required.

The insurgent willingness to engage Bravo Company played to the company's strength and allowed the company to overmatch the insurgents in the area with a range of platoon level weapons, indirect fire, and air assets. Operation TYRUNA 2C was the last operation conducted by the Battle Group prior to the election period.

Op TYRUNA 2C – Post R&R Blues – Major Al Steele (33), Officer Commanding Bravo Company

At the start of the op we had 2 days of minor frustration as we arrived at the airhead only to be delayed. On the first night we were presented with the awful reality that because all of the hospital beds in Kandahar and Helmand were full we couldn't risk deploying. The Rifles were having an extremely hard time of it in Sangin. The second night the ANA failed to show. The third night everything went according to plan.

Having landed 2 hours before first light half, the company had broken into the village when at 0530 hrs we were contacted from 2 sides. 6 Platoon had got into a concealed position on the flank and found themselves almost on top of 2 fighters who loosed off an RPG. I managed to jump up onto a compound roof just in time to see it hit the low wall in front of one of the platoon's forward sections. Out of the dust of the explosion came the cry, 'get down' which in the confusion was interpreted as, 'man down'. It took several minutes to realise that we didn't have a casualty. By now 7 Platoon, who had been caught in the open, were in the safety of the compounds and the company had launched a ferocious counter attack with snipers and javelin missiles.

The contact continued with little respite throughout the day with all platoons playing their part. Of note, 7 Platoon pushed west to try and flank the enemy, finding some IED making parts and equipment taken from destroyed coalition vehicles and the snipers with 5 Platoon adopted some novel fire positions up a tree! By mid afternoon the fighting had tailed off and we began our preparations for extracting. With everything set, a message was received from Battle Group Headquarters in Kandahar that an insurgent grouping had been seen by UAV setting up an ambush at our chosen landing site. We were immediately given another pick up point and quickly changed the plan. Extractions are nerve racking at the best of times but with the heightened threat everyone was on edge. Despite a slightly confused pick up, that saw my second in command wading through a marijuana field, we made it out in one piece.

Op TYRUNA 2C – Personal Account – Lieutenant Martin Stanning (26), from Lossiemouth, 7 Platoon Commander, Bravo Company

Op TYRUNA 2C was my first operation with the Battalion having spent 5 months in the OMLT role. The last few days had been manic, moving into Camp ROBERTS, meeting the platoon, meeting the company, finding some kit, discovering the 'boardwalk', receiving orders, delivering orders, finding a rifle, zeroing the rifle, kit checks, more kit checks, ROC drills, rehearsals, another kit check, move to the flight line, move back to ROBERTS, Rolex 24hrs, another kit check, Timmy Hortons, back to the flight line, no ANA, return to ROBERTS, Rolex 24hrs, Green Beans, CSE show, back to the flight line, on the Chinook, take off, Oh God I'm leading a platoon on an aviation assault . . . this RBG stuff is awesome!

The move from a small patrol base north of Sangin, with its jerry can water and endless rations, to Camp ROBERTS could only be described as a culture shock, but not one to complain about though! Making the move from mentoring at company level to commanding at platoon level was an easier transition than I had expected, the age old saying of, 'have faith in your training' , would appear to hold true. It was good to be back with friendly faces and finally commanding Jocks.

Once on the ground getting used to the difficulties of manoeuvring the best part of 40 people into position was the first thing to tackle. Once postured and ready for first light I could start to settle. At 0530 hrs my peace was disturbed, the familiar crack, crack of incoming rounds. In the OMLT, my role in contact was almost that of a section commander;

Lt David Parsons (left) and Lt Martin Stanning (right) in between operations at Kandahar Airfield.

Lt Martin Stanning and 7 Platoon.

7 British troops to command but with a keen eye on the ANA giving guidance if and when needed whilst co-ordinating any indirect fire or air assets. It was a nice change to realise I had 3 section commanders who were more than capable and who have had to fight their own battles concurrently. On this occasion I rapidly discovered I had 2 sections in contact and a third working with the attached ANA section to clear compounds to our rear.

It quickly became apparent that it was not only my platoon in contact but in fact the entire company was in contact from a number of different locations. The morning continued in this vein with a wide range of weapon systems being used to great effect. I was hugely impressed with the platoon, having known them for under a week. Their appetite for work coupled with their tenacity and zeal in contact was reassuring to say the least. It was very apparent that I had inherited a fine fighting unit, a huge credit to those who had gone before me in command, Lieutenant Andy Halliday and Captain Harry Hood and of course to the Platoon Sergeants, Sergeants Ian Robertson and Danny Buist.

By mid day it had become clear that our intent to disrupt the enemy in an area they considered safe had been more than accomplished. It was decided that it was unnecessary to move on as initially planned. The extraction was due to take place during the night but the HLS options were narrowing, crops making the sites unsuitable. We would head south to an HLS, with 7 Platoon conducting a feint to the south west during the afternoon to deceive the enemy of our intentions.

At last light the company was ready to move and final confirmatory orders were about to take place. This is when the RBG(S) role came into its own. Due to our fortunate position within Regional Command South we have been able to receive ISTAR coverage for the majority of the time we are on the ground. In this case it proved its worth as the planned extraction HLS had been compromised and it appeared that in the region of 8 insurgents had set an ambush on what would have been an obvious route out. In this case we were able to readjust our plan and extract from an HLS to the north leaving air assets to strike the insurgents in the south. It became very clear to me at this point that not only had I been fortunate enough to inherit an awesome platoon but I was now part of an extremely well resourced Battle Group. I honestly believe I saw more ISTAR and air assets in those 24hrs than I had in the previous 5 months.

The final scene of this operation was the extraction, or my introduction to the unpredictable sport of a company lift by aviation at night. Multiple waves of aircraft lifting from multiple boxes at night lead to an extraordinary number of variables, the majority of which can be planned for. There are some factors which remain in the hands of the gods and hence make it quite sporting. This extraction was no exception. The company second in command had spent hours carefully planning the manifest and waves to ensure the correct people were in the right place at the right time. The MAOT had carefully cleared and marked 5 'ops boxes'. The first wave was positioned at the relevant boxes ready to board the aircraft and the second wave was postured to protect the HLS. Fifteen minutes prior to Y-Hour the attack helicopters started circling above providing yet another layer of protection.

The Chinooks then appeared through the darkness. No matter how much planning is involved or how good the HLS is from the ground, a pilot has to make a split second decision from his perspective in the air, including consideration of enemy, ground and a host of other factors and all in total darkness. Hence, on this occasion we had 3 aircraft trying to occupy 2 boxes and one landing between the other 3 boxes: it wasn't apparent where the fifth aircraft had gone at this point. There were Jocks being lead left, right and centre with commanders trying to locate the correct helicopter. The company 2IC was lost in a huge field of cannabis and all communications were unworkable due to the noise. Finally, order was restored, the MAOT calmed down and we managed to get all aircraft and all Jocks back to Kandahar.

First impressions of RBG(S)? Awesome. TYRUNA 2C epitomised the ability and conduct of aviation assault strike operations. RBG(S) uses its flexible, capable manoeuvre ability to fight a brave and tenacious enemy with all the assets at NATO's disposal. Our Battle Group has been fortunate to be at the pinnacle of light role infantry operations. It is for roles like this one that soldiers join the Army.

Lance Corporal Heather Johnson (19), from Innerleithen, A Combat HR Specialist, Adjutant General's Corps (Staff and Personnel Support)

Morale – We need to make sure our soldiers' pay and allowances are sorted out properly and running smoothly. The last thing you want is for them to be worrying whilst out on the ground.

Professionalism – stressing the importance of our professionalism in dealing with serious issues such as when a casualty comes in. We must be able to deal with people sensitively and in confidence.

Operation AABI TOORAH SE

16–23 August 2009

INTRODUCTION

The period of the elections was relatively quiet for the Battle Group as Regional Command (South) Headquarters gave clear direction to the Task Forces under its command. RC(S) outlined a plan of 4 tiers of security during the elections with a deliberate lead made by ANSF. Tier 1 was an Afghan National Police task to provide immediate security around the polling centres. Tier 2 was an Afghan National Army task and consisted of close framework security around polling centres or clusters of polling centres. Tier 3 defined the role of ISTAR

The Jackal Group in Lashkar Gah, the provincial capital of Helmand province, during the controversial Presidential elections.

either through UAV or screens established by Battle Groups. Tier 4 was the outer ring of security provided by ISAF. This support primarily involved posture, presence and profile patrols by battle groups distant from polling centres. Tier 4 also included District, Provincial, and Regional Response Forces to primarlily support the ANSF in response to incidents.

The Battle Group was tasked to provide the Regional Response Force which included 2 aviation assault companies based out of Kandahar Airfield and a mobile company based from Lashkar Gah. Over the period 17 – 19 August, the aviation companies and mobile company would be at a state of high readiness at 6 hours notice to move. On 20 August, Election Day, the aviation companies would be at a 60 minutes and 2 hours notice to move and the mobile company was at 30 minutes notice to move. From 21 – 23 August, the companies would return to the same readiness states as 17 – 19 August. The election period would conclude on 23 August.

EXECUTION

17 August – 23 August (D–3 – D+3)

The mobile company, Charlie Company, mounted in Jackals, arrived in Lashkar Gah in the evening of 16 August while the aviation companies remained in Kandahar Airfield prepared to deploy. In the days leading up to the election, the companies remained poised in their

respective locations. On Election Day, the aviation companies remained in Kandahar Airfield and did not deploy. However, across Southern Afghanistan, and in particular Helmand, the insurgents harassed and intimidated local nationals and ISAF troops. There were approximately 200 contacts, IED strikes, and IED finds during the day; historically there are 50 separate incidents on any given day and thus Southern Afghanistan witnessed 4 times more incidents on Election Day. During the morning of Election Day, Lashkar Gah came under attack from indirect fire. Charlie Company was despatched from Lashkar Gah to the west of the city to dominate the area and defeat the indirect fire threat to the Provincial capital. Charlie Company returned late in the afternoon. During the period 21 – 23 August, all 3 companies remained in their respective locations.

SUMMARY

Throughout the election period ANSF were in the lead and the ANSF provided intimate security to the polling centres. Although Charlie Company deployed, the fact that the aviation companies remained in Kandahar Airfield was noted as a success as it meant that the ANSF were able to contain the insurgent threat on Election Day.

A CH47 'buzzes' the Jackal Group. (Sgt N Collins)

Chapter Eight

Operation TOR SAHAKATCHA

29 August – 2 September 2009

INTRODUCTION

After the election period, the Battle Group was tasked to provide one company to support Battle Group (Centre South), the Welsh Guards, in the region of the Luy Mandeh wadi and Shamalan Canal. Alpha Company was to maintain the security along the Shamalan Canal as Royal Engineers collapsed a patrol base and denied a crossing point. Alpha Company would deploy to FOB WAHID on the 29 August and begin the operation on the 30 August and would extract from the area in the late evening of the 1 September or early morning the 2 September.

EXECUTION

29 August – 30 August 09 (D–2 – D–1)

Alpha Company arrived late in the evening of 29 August at FOB WAHID by aviation. The company coordinated with Number 2 Company, the Welsh Guards, and the operation was delayed until the 31 August. The delay provided the company with the opportunity to conduct its final preparations prior to conducting Operation TOR SAHAKATCHA.

31 August 09 (D Day)

Alpha Company deployed on foot at 0200 hrs from FOB WAHID to the west of the Shamalan Canal to initially establish a screen and subsequently move south along the canal. I Platoon was the lead platoon and established a screen in a compound west of the canal at 0500 hrs. The remainder of the company pressed south. Concurrently, elements of Number 2 Company were clearing the eastern side of the Shamalan Canal. Company TAC headquarters established itself in a compound and the remainder of the Company adopted screen positions and constructed sentry positions on the compound roofs.

At 0900 hrs, the company came under fire from insurgents. Prior to the contact, there had been no visible insurgent activity. The engagement was initiated by accurate small arms fire from unidentified firing points to the west. An RPG struck the roof of the compound occupied by 1 Platoon. The detonation filled the air with a huge amount of dust and debris which obscured vision. As the dust cleared, casualties became apparent: Private Kevin Elliott was dead, Sergeant Edward Nichol was lying face down and was injured but still vocal, Private Shaun Ross was injured but did not suffer life threatening injuries, and Sergeant Gus Millar was critically injured.

Insurgents continued to target the compound and the few still on the roof not injured attempted to provide immediate first aid and called for a medic. Lance Corporal Barry Green from the Javelin Platoon first checked Private Elliott and then moved on to Sergeant Nichol. The pair crawled over to treat Sergeant Millar and reported that he was bleeding excessively and they required more first field dressings. The medic, Lance Corporal Stacy Quinn, RAMC moved to the roof immediately after the explosion. After quickly assessing Sergeant Nichol's condition she moved on to Sergeant Millar who bravely gauged his own condition and waved her off to tend to the other casualties; shortly after Sergeant Millar succumbed to his injuries. Lance Corporal Quinn returned to Sergeant Nichol and on to Private Chisholm who was in pain and in shock. The Regimental Medical Officer, Captain Will Charlton (who had taken over from Captain Ryan Wood on his posting) and Alpha Company Sergeant Major, Warrant Officer Class Two Paul Colville moved in and took over the casualty treatment.

LCpl Stacy Quinn (26) from Edinburgh, Royal Army Medical Corps (RAMC)

All the Fijians in the Battle Group together, forming The Fijian choir, during the memorial service for Sgt Gus Millar and Pte Kev Elliot. (MOD – Sgt C Halton)

Capt Harry Gladstone reading his tribute to Pte Kev Elliot at the memorial service. (MOD – Sgt C Halton)

As care was being given to the casualties, the remainder of the company was in contact. 1 Platoon's compound was still coming under significant fire and Private Inia Nino and Private Brian King raced to the rooftop to join Lance Corporal Daniel Hatton who had remained in place and was attempting to identify insurgent firing points.

The Royal Engineers who were attached to Alpha Company were tasked to provide a safe exit from the compound that was out of sight of the insurgent firing point. Under a high volume of suppressive fire, Private Ross and Sergeant Nichol were extracted from the roof and evacuated back to an emergency helicopter landing site. Lance Corporal Hatton had identified some shrapnel wounds and he too was evacuated. Apache helicopters came on station before the American Blackhawk medical helicopter and the insurgent engagement ceased. The casualties were extracted at 1000 hrs.

Alpha Company was subsequently engaged by enemy fire a number of times throughout the day. Sergeant Nichol, who had suffered serious shrapnel injuries during the contact in the morning, had been evacuated back to the UK at 2040 hrs.

1 September 09 (D+1)

Alpha Company remained in place over night and began to extract from the area at 1000 hrs. As the extraction began the company came under contact and engaged insurgent firing points with mortars. The company had fully returned to FOB WAHID by 1300 hrs and awaited last light prior to extracting from the Luy Mandeh wadi. At 2230 hrs, Alpha Company began its return and all troops were back in Kandahar Airfield by 0155 hrs.

SUMMARY

The heavy rate of fire combined with the accuracy and manoeuvre suggested a well experienced insurgent grouping. Use of the ingress routes and the insurgent's ability to remain unseen for most of the day also suggested a tactical awareness of the geography in the area.

The loss of important figures within the Battle Group was difficult for all. Sergeant Millar, an experienced mortar fire controller, was an outgoing and endearing soldier; Private Elliott was a real character who was on the verge of leaving the British Army prior to the tour, but in the last month decided to renew his contract and deploy on Operation HERRICK 10; Sergeant Nichol's evacuation to the UK left 1 Platoon without a Platoon Sergeant which was quickly filled by Sergeant David Taylor from Charlie Company; Lance Corporal Green also sustained injury to his ear drum and returned to the UK; Lance Corporal Hatton and Private Chisholm were also injured but remained in theatre.

Op TOR SAHAKATCHA – Personal Account – Lieutenant David Parsons (23), from Eydon, Northamptonshire, 1 Platoon (Senior Highland) Commander, Alpha (Grenadier) Company

Our Company mission was to provide a block out towards the west and into the Chah-e-Anjir Triangle (CAT). The Welsh Guards had a patrol base by a crossing point along the

Lt David Parsons, 1 Pl, A Coy, arriving at his objective.

Shamalan canal, but due to its position and the intensity of insurgent activity the decision had been made to collapse it. We were essentially there to soak up the insurgent fighting and allow the engineers to collapse the patrol base. 2 and 3 platoon were going to clear a series of compounds and prior to that 1 Platoon would be securing a compound just to the north west and positioned to give them a bit of security out in the CAT. Once they had cleared the compounds and then set up positions out to the west, they hoped to sit back and destroy insurgent targets from a distance and we would collapse back through them in order to act as Battle Group reserve under the command of the Commanding Officer of the Welsh Guards.

The first task for my platoon was to lead the company through the forward line of enemy troops and into the CAT, which was an area entirely dominated by insurgents. We were warned by one of the Platoon Commanders that we would be moving close to a cluster of compounds where insurgents were believed to operate, and there was no doubt that the insertion would carry a high level of risk both in terms of the IED threat but also for an insurgent ambush. Corporal Natui, section commander of my 2 Section had the unenviable task of leading the platoon and picking a route through what we knew would be highly complex terrain. He carried this task out brilliantly and despite having to wade through waist high irrigation ditches in complete darkness, he led the company onto the objective without incident and without the insurgents having any idea that over 100 men had just pushed past them and into their safe-haven.

The compound that we entered was deserted and after a routine clearance of it, we moved in to establish our position whilst the other platoons moved towards us. As always the first thing done was to build up positions and then we had little to do but sit and wait for any insurgent response and most importantly ensure that we kept the pressure off the other platoons until they were settled in their locations. As they were clearing established firing positions, the IED threat was high and we needed to ensure that they weren't distracted.

Whilst the task that we were given was standard for what we have done out in Afghanistan, sadly the outcome of this job was a very heavy cost. A direct RPG strike could have happened multiple times during the tour and on many occasions we were lucky that bullets and grenades flew right by. The luck was with the insurgents on this day and it cost the lives of Sergeant Gus Millar and Private Kevin Elliott.

Despite the tragic loss of such brave men, the fact that shines out from that day and certainly what I try and look back on, is just how phenomenal all my Jocks were. These were guys, many just 18 years old, dealing with a situation that you would hope nobody would ever have to go through, let alone people so young. Not only was their focus and professionalism astounding but they did everything fully aware that the risk was far from over. As the team medics treated Sergeant Nichol my Platoon Sergeant and Private Ross my signaller, rounds were still flying overhead with remarkable accuracy. They had to expose themselves to the incoming fire in order to identify where the enemy were located and look to regain the initiative. One of the Jocks involved in this had joined us in theatre straight from training and was now in as serious a situation as a soldier might face, yet he did not flinch from his task and returned fire with devastating effect.

I look back on that day and it is still very vague. Certainly for myself, the shock of being close to where the RPG detonated followed by the realisation that such crucial members of my platoon were the casualties was something that all the training in the world could not have prepared me for. I think that it is partly for this reason that I am so proud of the guys. With their platoon sergeant as the main casualty, an integral source of leadership was out of the game. However, despite this being one of the greatest challenges that they will have to face, their efforts on that morning were awe inspiring. They stepped up in every facet despite their safety blanket of an experienced platoon sergeant removed; they worked tirelessly, without hesitation and gave no thought for their own safety. The fact that all the casualties were successfully extracted and no further casualties were sustained is testament to what a good job they did. With the gravity of the situation the potential was there for it to deteriorate and I have no doubt whatsoever that the actions of these young men prevented that from happening and ensured that the insurgents received a bloody nose.

It is the nature of the beast, that despite something like this happening, there is still a job to do and every soldier works on the mentality that the best way to serve their fallen comrades is to push grieving to the back of their mind for the present and do the best job possible in order that their efforts are not in vain. This is certainly a clichéd sentence but when the Jocks respond in this manner it is still so impressive. They had to work hard over the next 48 hours securing 2 locations and giving little rest to exhausted bodies and minds. One thing that was very apparent was the immediate bond and fellowship that is created when having gone through something like that. It was a close platoon before but after this incident the tight-knit feel was quite special.

I am sure that no one who was there in that compound will ever forget Op TOR SAHAKATCHA. With time the shock and sadness turns to pride to have served alongside those who fell and pride to have served with Jocks who truly surpassed themselves on that day.

Op TOR SAHAKATCHA – Interview – Lance Corporal Aaron Graham (22), from Wemyss, Fife, 1 Platoon, Alpha (Grenadier) Company

We took the objective and we went firm. We got the defences up and we were just observing. The other platoons had taken their objectives and my section was out on the track and set up an immediate VCP stopping movement up and down the track. We heard a loud bang and an explosion. We turned around, it was a bit confusing to start with, we turned around and there was a deathly silence to start off with. We could not get any comms. And then everything started to erupt and we learned that an RPG had hit the north eastern corner of the compound. To start with, I did not know what happened and I did not know if anyone was hit, but it turned out to be 2 KIA and 3 WIA. We went back on our normal SOPs after that and conducted the Casevac. I was rear protection for that. I did see the KIAs and so did my section which, for me as the commander I had to make sure they were alright and doing their job, but a lot of the confidence dropped, they took a big knock.

A lot of them were shocked. It was a big shock. The platoon sergeant is a father figure in a rifle platoon and he was always the one when times were hard to say, "Look boys, this is alright, we'll manage through it, soldier on." But he was not there anymore, so it was quite tough for the young boys, even myself, to crack on. You just have to get on with it.

I knew Sergeant Millar because he had worked with us before. He was a mortar fire controller, but I did not know him that well, I had a few brews with him. Kev Elliott, he

Sgt Gus Millar, Alpha (Grenadier) Company's Mortar Fire Controller.

used to be Alpha Company, he was good mates with my best mate Private Devine, so he was a big knock and Devine took it hard, and other people took it hard. Trying to motivate them was hard. Yourself and the commanders have taken a knock, you can't let show your weakness, which is quite difficult.

Different people respond differently. The stronger boys just get on with work, get a grip and crack on, and the younger boys who are not as tough you got to hold their hand a bit. Take them and say, "look, this has just happened, just pick yourself up, you'll have time to settle about this, but not until we get back or when it is safe."

Op TOR SAHAKATCHA – Personal Account – Private Willie Brown (23), from Fife, 2 Platoon, Alpha (Grenadier) Company

Dawn approached and the company was scattered to the 4 winds. I Platoon had taken a compound and was defending it. 2 Platoon was searching a cluster of compounds that had been damaged by constant fighting and strikes with guided missiles. 3 Platoon had taken a compound and got all the defences prepared and just when we thought everything was going to be quiet, "Contact wait out" came over the net. I Platoon had been hit by an RPG and the whole company was under attack.

My section (2 Section, 2 Platoon) was the only section not in contact that was close enough to I Platoon to help out. We moved forward under fire, hoping we were in time but when we got there we found that there were multiple wounded and 2 KIA: Sergeant Gus Millar and Private Kev Elliott. We had to extract the wounded and the dead while I Platoon had to give up the compound they had occupied. We could not extract through the entrance

Cpl Boila talking to his section at the end of the operation.

that we had entered as that meant exposing ourselves to the Taliban killing zone. The engineers had to blow a hole in the compound wall but they put so much explosives in, it wasn't a hole but the whole wall that opened up. As one of the wounded couldn't move to cover, I covered him while all the debris fell from the sky. Once the dust settled we all worked together to get the wounded and the dead out of there and to safety. Corporal Boila (my section commander) with the help of Lance Corporal Nicholson guided the section and the rest of 1 Platoon back to the safety of 2 Platoon's location. Here fresh hands took over from the men who had had to make their way through a maize field and were all exhausted and feeling the strain with all the kit and the heat of Afghanistan beating down on us.

After the mission was completed, we extracted back to FOB WAHID. The op was a success but it had come at a great cost to everyone. Soon after, Chinooks flew us back to Kandahar for rehab and re-supply. There was a chance to rest and then we got ready to go out again, taking the fight to the enemy just as we have always done being the fighting Jocks that we are.

Op TOR SAHAKATCHA – Personal Account – Private Kevin Dye (24), from Armadale, 1 Platoon, Alpha (Grenadier) Company

TELIC was very different compared to this. We had a few contacts on TELIC, here though they're willing to stand and fight you. It keeps you on your toes a bit. I'm a bit of an adrenalin junkie so I'm usually one of the first guys to jump on the roof. It's the role that I chose to be a GPMG gunner, so I'm always going to be one of the first to start firing. I've had a couple of confirmed kills. I felt a little bit of remorse but at the same time, at the end of the day, it's not one of our guys, its' one less of them.

Op TOR SAHAKATCHA – Highs and Lows in the Mortar Platoon, Private Martin Coulter (23), from Dundee, Mortar Platoon

As with all platoons we had our highs and lows. One of the most common highs that occurred regularly with the airborne ops was Private Shaun Ross's spectacular falls, usually in front of everyone while running for the chopper. With his bergan packed and weighing in excess of 50kg, Shaun would make it up the last 10m behind the chopper, then fall face first into the sand, some how always managing to finish on his back. By the time the last couple of guys were about to pass him, he had just about finished his impression of a tortoise stuck on his back and was making it to his feet to rejoin the group before we left him.

Further to this the Mortar Platoon was renowned for pranks, nicknamed "jihad", thanks to "mini me". One of the best 'jihad's' played on anyone was the one that the whole Mortar Platoon played on Lance Corporal Eck Little. Eck one day was heard after another incident stating that he would never be 'jihadded', which then set a challenge to the rest of the Mortar Platoon. So one day when he went away for his dinner, the whole Mortar Platoon took his bed space out of the tent that we were staying and placed it between the mortar ISO containers, which were near the other end of camp. The bed space was then reset up the exact way it was in the tent, complete with his shelves, mosquito net and foot locker at the end of the camp bed. However, upon heading back to the tent, mission complete, we bumped into the platoon sergeants in which they informed us that we had a brief.

While we were waiting at the front gate to move for the brief, word was leaked that the prank had been played on Eck and he was not amused. What made the situation worse was the fact that he was unable to go back to the tent to check on his bed space as we were leaving for the brief. However once we all got back to the tents, after the wind had picked up, and it was threatening to rain, Eck went into the tent and was confronted with a empty gap which used to contain his bed space. On realisation he erupted in rage and stormed out the room, to the amusement of everyone there. He then spent the next 30 minutes wandering around camp looking for his bed space until someone tipped him off to its location.

However the Mortar Platoon had also had its lows. The lowest point was when the Platoon Sergeant "Gus" Millar was killed by an explosion whilst out on patrol. I still remember clearly the day that it occurred. The majority of the Mortar Platoon had been left back at camp as other mortars were in the area. It was the lowest point of the Mortar Platoon, I think mainly due to the fact that we felt helpless that we had no been there to help a friend in need. However in true Mortar Platoon style we regained our composure and got on with the job in hand.

So it was safe to say with all its highs and lows, the Mortar Platoon was one of, if not the tightest knit platoon in the battalion.

Members of Mortar Platoon, Charlie Company.

Operation BURS SIMI

5 – 7 September 2009

INTRODUCTION

Operation BURS SIMI was an operation focused on defeating insurgent IED networks in Southern Afghanistan. The Battle Group was tasked to support the operation over the period 5 September – 7 September. The primary focus of the operation was to find and understand the insurgent IED network and thus enable target development for future strike operations; the operation in Objective FORCEFUL was the first of a series of deliberate operations in the Sangin area.

The Battle Group intended to launch Bravo Company and Charlie Company to the west of the Helmand River in the area of Karlz Kukah, south of Sangin District Centre. Bravo Company would secure Objective CAMERON in the south and the Charlie Company would secure Objectives GORDON and SEAFORTH. The Battle Group would deploy early in the morning on the 5 August. After last light, Bravo Company would move north and take control of the Charlie Company's locations. C Company would subsequently move to the dasht in the west with Battle Group TAC and extract early in the morning of the 6 August. The next day, Bravo Company would patrol east close to the Helmand River in order to provoke a reaction by insurgents.

However, on D Day the weather in Southern Afghanistan changed dramatically as sandstorms swept across the region. As a consequence, the intended resupply and extraction planned for the early morning of the 6 August was cancelled and the Battle Group returned to Kandahar Airfield as one group in the morning of the 7 August.

EXECUTION

5 August 09 (D Day)

The Battle Group deployed into Objective FORCEFUL at 0200 hrs on the 5 August. Following a brief period of regrouping on the helicopter landing sites, the companies moved to isolate their target areas and secure the objectives. Bravo Company identified the local elder early and conducted a shura with him. Charlie Company in the north discovered 2 small finds of wet opium which were destroyed. By mid morning, Bravo Company reported 4 RPGs fired ineffectively towards its location. In the afternoon, Bravo Company reported one further indirect fire attack by one mortar round which was equally as ineffective. Having exploited all opportunities in Objective GORDON, Charlie Company consolidated on Objective SEAFORTH to prepare for Bravo Company's move north in the evening. Late in the

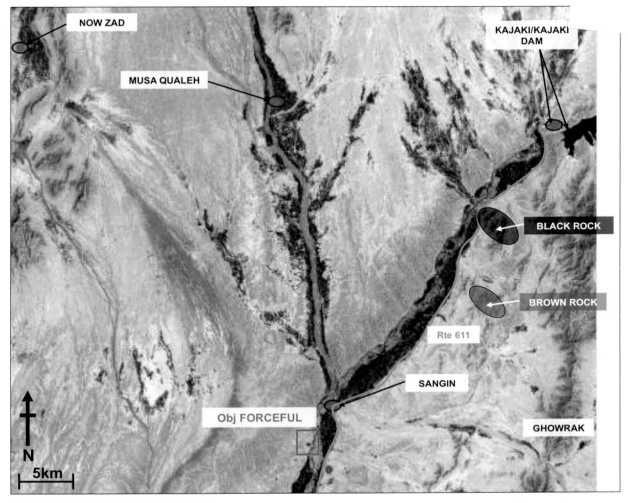

afternoon, the weather in parts of southern Afghanistan changed over the course of a couple of hours. Although Objective FORCEFUL was clear without any suggestion of sandstorms, the route to the area was affected and as a result neither resupply nor extraction took place. Bravo Company arrived in Objective SEAFORTH and both companies remained in place overnight.

6 August – 7 August 09 (D + 1 – D + 2)

In the morning, Charlie Company patrolled north. Without the planned resupply and extraction on the previous evening, rations became limited. In order to supplement the limited diet, a number of soldiers decided to improve their condition and purchased flour and chickens from a compound owner. Lance Corporal Viny Vunibobo and Lance Corporal David Cassidy prepared the flour to cook into roti, while Warrant Officer Class Two Gary Theyers butchered and cleaned the chicken. A resupply of rations eventually arrived in the afternoon and Bravo Company conducted its feint to the east with limited response by insurgents. Both companies remained in Objective SEAFORTH until after last light and extracted to 2 separate helicopter landing sites. Extraction by Chinook helicopter began at 2200 hrs and all troops had returned to Kandahar Airfield by 0200 hrs 7 August.

A patrol moving between compounds near Sangin.

LCpl 'Viny' Vunibobo and LCpl David Cassidy making bread – locally bought flour could be used to make the bread.

SUMMARY

Despite the limited engagement with insurgents, the operation provided situational awareness of the area which could then be used for target development. The operation, in conjunction with Operation GHARTSE BREESHNA conducted by 2 RIFLES, had a short-term effect of creating uncertainty in the mind of the insurgent. The operation also increased ISAF understanding of the IED networks in the Sangin area.

Op BURS SIMI – Personal Account – Captain David Mack (32), from Toronto, Canada, Officer Commanding the Mortar Platoon, Charlie Company

During Op BURS SIMI, I briefly took over the role of Operations Officer. I was the Mortar Officer, and as such, I would typically deploy with TAC on Battle Group level operations in order to coordinate mortar fire. I was quite fortunate as the majority of my fellow Mortar Officers on Op HERRICK 10 were tasked in completely different roles; one friend was an Operations Officer with 2 RIFLES, another had taken on a role as a mentor to the Afghan Army, another was mentoring the Afghan Police, while Captain Tom Anderson from the Welsh Guards had taken on a plethora of jobs including liaison officer in Lashkar Gah, a company second in command, and most recently as a Mastiff Commander. As the Mortar Officer in TAC, I had a strong understanding of the conduct of an operation through my mortar fire controllers that were attached to rifle companies and thus the switch to the role of Operations Officer was not significantly different to what I had already done, although the scope was much larger.

Op BURS SIMI was a relatively quiet operation, although Bravo Company was contacted by RPG rounds. On the evening of the first night, the Jackal Group and Battle Group TAC had intended to extract. However, weather across Helmand and Kandahar Province changed significantly and dust storms grounded all helicopters. As a result, all the troops remained on the ground for a further day. The only difficulty with this development was the lack of rations and water as the troops had brought out a day's supply with the intention of a resupply on the first night. As stomachs rumbled, resourceful Jocks began to look around for a means to supplement missed meals. TAC was housed in a compound where half a dozen chickens ran free and it did not take long for the intrepid Jocks to make deals with the compound owner. After an amusing 20 minutes in which the Jocks chased the hens around the compound, eventually a pair was caught. Warrant Officer 2 Theyers quickly got to work and demonstrated to the Jocks, butchering techniques. Concurrently, Lance Corporal Vunibobo and Lance Corporal Cassidy prepared flour into roti while Lance Corporal Ratukalou and Private Mudunovosa looked on gleefully, licking their chops.

On a personal note, I was still dealing with the death of Sergeant Gus Millar. He was my Platoon Sergeant and a very capable mortar fire controller. The operation provided me with a necessary distraction. It gave me a chance to refocus my energies and rebalance as other operations were not far off which would require my undivided attention.

Chapter Nine

Operation SPIN ARWA

14 – 19 September 2009

INTRODUCTION

Operation SPIN ARWA was part of Operation KHWANDHI LOYALAAR, aimed at defeating the insurgent IED threat. Operation KHWANDHI LOYALAAR intended to enhance freedom of movement through deliberate clearances, removal of emplaced IEDs and the disruption of insurgent networks. Intelligence reporting had established an increase in insurgent IED emplacement and ambushes along Highway 1, in Zhari District, Kandahar Province; from its vantage point atop Ghunday Ghar during Operation TORA ARWA, Battle Group TAC had witnessed many such incidents. In addition, 3 wadis in the area had been used by insurgents as defensive positions. Operation SPIN ARWA was set in Ops Box CONDOR, Sangsar, Zhari District, Kandahar Province.

The Battle Group planned to strike into Ops Box CONDOR through a 3 wave aviation assault starting in the early morning of the 14 September. Alpha Company would land first and strike deep into the green zone before clearing a southern wadi, called Wadi Spey. Bravo Company would insert at 0230 hrs north of the Afghan National Army Patrol Base Howz-E Madad and move south and subsequently clear insurgents from the second wadi, Wadi DEE. Task Force Thor, attached to the Battle Group for the operation, would link up with Bravo Company on Highway 1 and clear Route BANFF into the green zone. Finally, the Charlie Company, Battlegroup TAC, and the Mortar Platoon would deploy at 0330 hrs and north of Highway 1. TAC and the Mortar Platoon would move into Howz-E Madad (ANA Patrol Base) and Charlie Company would secure the northern flank of the green zone.

Once the 2 wadis were cleared, anticipated to be on the 16 September, Alpha Company would extract through Charlie Company and north into Howz-E Madad while Bravo Company would also move through Charlie Company and then press east to Patrol Base SPIN PIR. Charlie Company would later follow Alpha Company into Howz-E Madad and act as Battle Group reserve. The companies would remain in their respective patrol bases and conduct patrols in the area while also maintaining the capability to strike further east.

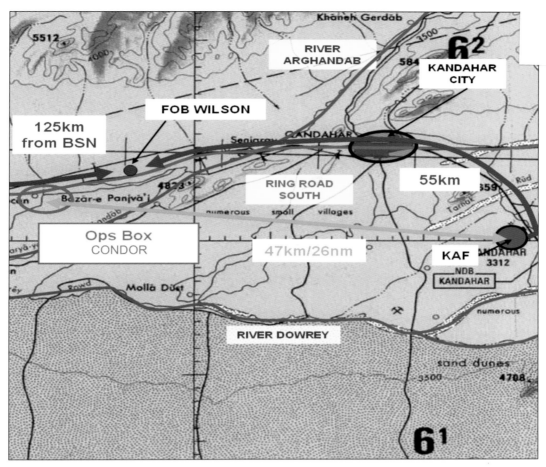

A large overview map showing the distance from Kandahar Airfield to the objective area. Slides like these were always used in the delivery of orders to the Battle Group.

EXECUTION

14 September 09 (D Day)

Alpha Company landed on task at 0058 hrs. Previous reports had confirmed an insurgent bed down location in a compound in Alpha Company's area. When the company landed on target, approximately 30 armed insurgents fled the compound to the north and west. The Apache helicopters that had escorted the Battle Group's insertion identified and engaged the insurgents with missiles and 30mm cannon. Alpha Company had entered its first compound by 0140 hrs as the Apache helicopters continued to pursue insurgents. Bravo Company landed to the north of Highway 1 at 0217 hrs and then began its move south in order to link up with Task Force Thor. By 0210 hrs, Alpha Company had seized initial objectives. At 0230 hrs Bravo Company had joined with Task Force Thor and began to make its way south down Route BANFF. Charlie Company, TAC, and the Mortar Platoon landed at 0330 hrs. Charlie Company moved south to secure the northern flank and TAC and the Mortar Platoon were established in Howz-E Madad at 0415 hrs.

Alpha Company had consolidated on its position and made significant finds including an AGS-17 (an automatic grenade launcher), an 82mm recoilless rifle, numerous AK-47 rifles, a trauma kit, explosive components, detonation cord, handsets and radios, an ammunition vest, body armour, ammunition and artillery ordnance, anti-personnel mines and grenades.

15 Sep 09 (D + 1)

Alpha Company exploited its success of the previous day and conducted rummages of the compounds in its area and discovered an IED factory. The insurgents in the area took some time to reorganise following their casualties during the morning of the insertion. Nonetheless, by mid afternoon Alpha and Bravo Company had received some harassing fire which was diffused through a series of mortar fire missions. Charlie Company also received fire from insurgents in the north. The Canadian Kiowa attack helicopters, which were in support of the Battle Group, engaged insurgents to break the contact.

After last light, the Battle Group began to regroup with the plan for Alpha Company to begin the clearance of Wadi SPEY the next day; the Reconnaissance Platoon would relocate to Bravo Company and the Company group would remain in the area to clear Wadi DEE and then move east to SPIN PIR; Charlie Company would secure and control the co-ordination point on the ground before releasing the Fire Support Group to come under the command of Alpha Company. At 2310 hrs, as the Reconnaissance Platoon began its regrouping with Bravo Company, Corporal Tam Mason, a Bravo MFC attached to the platoon, was severely injured by an IED. Immediately after the explosion Corporal James Couper and Private Barrie Durcan, a combat medical technician, rushed to Corporal Mason's aid. They applied tourniquets to both of his legs and administered morphine. Corporal Mason was stabilised and evacuated to Kandahar Airfield at 2348 hrs.

16 Sep 09 (D + 2)

As Bravo Company cleared Wadi DEE it received sporadic small arms fire and RPG contacts from the east, west, and south. The wadi was a well prepared defensive position in which trenches, IED equipment and dug outs were all eventually found in the wadi in the first 2 days of the operation. Bravo Company also discovered an IED in the wadi which was exploited by the Canadian Counter IED team attached to the company. The team arrived and meticulously continued the confirmation of the IED. After dismantling the device the team discovered a secondary IED. At 1210 hrs, shortly after detecting the second IED, Captain Lapointe, the team commander, triggered a third device which severely injured his right foot and injured Sergeant Hampton, his second in command. Lieutenant Al Philips, 5 Platoon Commander, led his team to Captain Lapointe and Sergeant Hampton. The 2 casualties were then extracted to an emergency helicopter landing site and evacuated back to Kandahar Airfield. During his extraction, Captain Lapointe's final words before being placed on the helicopter bravely warned the company of further IEDs in the area of the blast.

After the evacuation of Captain Lapointe and Sergeant Hampton, Bravo Company continued the clearance of Wadi DEE and recovered to SPIN PIR before last light. Alpha Company likewise completed its clearance of Wadi SPEY and on route to Howz-E Madad, the company identified a possible IED factory which was subsequently searched by a British

A large ammunition find – mostly RPG warheads but also hand grenades, anti personnel mines, mortar rounds and artillery shells.

An IED found by Bravo Company – the threat of IEDs was at the front of everyone's mind.

Cpl Dave "the boy" Roy, Bravo Company patrolling through a Marijuana field – plantations like these were good places for insurgents to hide from the all seeing Attack Helicopters.

Counter IED team. The company and Charlie Company Headquarters were secure in Howz-E Madad before last light.

17 September – 18 September 09 (D+3 – D+4)

Alpha and Bravo Companies conducted local patrols from their respective patrol bases to maintain the security of Highway 1 while also conducting preparations for company level operations planned for the 18 and 19 September.

Alpha Company conducted a company group patrol to the south west of Howz- E Madad in the area of Baluchan. The patrol was engaged by insurgents using small arms fire and RPG. Snipers returned accurate fire and suppressed the insurgent threat.

19 September 09 (D+5)

Bravo Company departed SPIN PIR at 0200 hrs to conduct a company group patrol to the south east of the patrol base and was supported by a troop of Canadian Leopard tanks. The insurgents were aware of Bravo Company's movements and attempted to place IEDs in the area. The insurgents were observed by armed UAV and were engaged by Apache helicopters in the act of burying the IEDs. Bravo Company remained in position prior to moving north before last light and were engaged by harassing fire from the insurgents.

Alpha Company conducted a platoon level patrol into the Howz-E Madad bazaar in the afternoon prior to preparing for its extraction later that night. The Battle Group's extraction by Chinook helicopters began at 2013 hrs and all troops had returned to Kandahar Airfield by 2200 hrs.

SUMMARY

Operation SPIN ARWA significantly disrupted insurgents in the Sangsar area in terms of attrition to manpower and materiel which relieved the pressure on the ANP seeking to establish themselves in the area. The seizure of numerous weapons, IED components and explosives reduced insurgent capability to place IEDs and conduct ambushes along Highway 1 in Zhari District. Also, the dislocation and defeat of insurgents in the area reduced insurgent targeted attacks on Kandahar City. The capture of 2 prestige weapons (AGS – 17 and 82mm recoilless rifle) was a boost to the morale of the Canadian OMLT troops in Howz-E Madad who were daily targeted by the weapons.

The Battle Group's success was due largely to the tactical surprise that was achieved through the aviation assault on the first day of the operation. The air support gained from Apache, Kiowa, and UAV proved to be devastating against the insurgents throughout the operation. Moreover, the Battle Group benefited from the armour supplied by Task Force Thor and Canadian Leopard tanks. Despite the multinational assets that were available during the operation, the men of the Battle Group were nonetheless vulnerable to the insurgent IED threat: Corporal Mason and Captain Lapointe were evacuated to the UK and Canada respectively; devastatingly, Corporal Mason died from his wounds 6 weeks later in the UK.

An insurgent AGS 17 (Grenade Machine Gun) captured by Alpha (Grenadier) Company.

Capt Will Charlton the Regimental Medical Officer for the second half of the tour and Lt Andy Wallace A Coy's Intelligence Officer – note the mark left by an AGS 17 strike above their heads.

Op SPIN ARWA: "Contact IED. Wait Out" – Lieutenant Colonel Stephen Cartwright, Commanding Officer

"Contact IED – wait out". This is the radio transmission I have most feared on the Battle Group (BG) communications network during our operations. Battle Group TAC HQ has deployed onto the ground with the aviation company on every operation, and therefore although we cannot always see where the companies are, we can always hear their engagements with the insurgents. When static, the HQ has been located in a compound or on a piece of high ground with good visibility. We have all learnt the sound of an IED this summer. The period of silence that follows has created one of the hardest emotional strains I have experienced. There is a loud explosion and everyone stops what they are doing. The majority of people in the HQ look at me. I always ask – "Did anyone report that they were initiating a controlled explosion". If the answer is no, the tension rises: there is no idle chat. After what seems many minutes, but is more likely just 30 seconds, a radio transmission is heard: "Hello 0, this is Emerald 10, contact IED. Wait out". It is a most dreadful, soul destroying time. There has been an explosion, initiated by someone under your command, during an operation that you have planned and given guidance on its execution. The responsibility is yours. If there has been an IED strike you are certain that someone, perhaps more than one person, will have been injured, most likely severely. There is a high probability that he might have been killed. You are helpless, there is nothing you can do until more information is passed. Within minutes the company is sending a request for medical evacuation (MEDEVAC) and with it comes details of the casualty. Names are not used on the radio 'net', but personal codes are. BG HQ has a list of every one of these code numbers and I personally know the name of who has been injured or killed within 10 minutes of the incident. My thoughts race; is it my fault, did we or he do anything wrong, how will those around him deal with the most dreadful situation that they find themselves in, will he have a chance of survival on his flight to the hospital.

As the Commanding Officer, my absolute priority was to take everyone home safely, and it is with huge personal regret that I have not achieved this due to the nature of operations this summer. The soldiers are all rather relaxed about direct fire weapons, their fire fights with the enemy, even though we have lost 2 of our own in an RPG attack. It is the IED attack they fear the most and I agree with their sentiment.

Op SPIN ARWA 1 – Reflections – Major Matt Munro (36), from Hampshire, Officer Commanding Alpha (Grenadier) Company

The initial assault devastated the insurgents. Six US Chinook (CH-47) laden with battle-hardened Jocks swooped out of the inky darkness and landed almost within touching distance of the Taliban stronghold. This caused mayhem amongst the Taliban ranks. In the initial exchanges upwards of a dozen Taliban were killed. Apache gunships targeted them with pinpoint accuracy, using their 30mm cannon and missiles. The weight of fire from the aircraft was staggering; it was like a fireworks show as heavy-calibre cannon and rockets ripped into the tree-lines around us as the Taliban tried to re-group. Some of it was very close to us but

Maj Matt Munro, OC A Coy (left) and Maj Al Steele, OC B Coy (right). (MOD – Sgt C Halton)

Sergeant McBride my Joint Tactical Air Controller had the situation well under control. 2 Platoon missed out on the action initially; their aircraft had dropped them some 650 metres off target.

As dawn broke on the first day ground call-signs began to exploit the compounds that they had assaulted into. They found an 'Aladdin's cave' of Taliban ammunition, explosives, medical supplies, communications equipment and weaponry. Significantly, a grenade-launcher and recoilless rifle, both of which had been used effectively against coalition forces in the area for some months were recovered. The signs of the hastily departed were everywhere. The Taliban dead lay in the adjacent field. Their eviscerated and broken bodies cooked in the sun and fed the flies. They were not dignified in death; bloated and foul-smelling, local national civilians carted them away in wheelbarrows.

On the first afternoon the insurgents tried to exact some revenge but their attack was not unexpected. With the company well disposed the rocket and small arms attack was met with a hearty rebuttal of well-coordinated machine-gun and mortar fire. One of my section commanders led his section in an attack on an enemy machine-gun nest. Like the rest of the company, his section had spent the latter part of the day in searing heat repelling a series of insurgent attacks. As dusk fell the position was engaged by a hail of accurate and sustained machine-gun fire from a grape hut only 120 m to the south. The enemy was positioned such that snipers were unable to prosecute the target and the enemy position was too close to consider using mortars to silence them. Two 66mm rockets were fired. Although this silenced one firing point, accurate bursts of automatic fire still emanated from another firing point within the same grape hut. Displaying exemplary courage, leadership and initiative, the young commander left the relative safety of the compound and led his section across open ground to clear the enemy from the position. Incoming rounds zipped around him and kicked up the dirt at his feet as he made his approach. He then saw a further grouping of 4 enemy moving along a tree line to reinforce the position. Reacting instinctively, he positioned a gunner to engage and neutralise this threat. Still under fire and given that the ground afforded him little cover, he dropped to his belly and continued to push forward towards the machine-gun position. By now he was totally committed and also exposed. He readied himself; he fixed his bayonet. He hurled 2 grenades through a doorway and then launched himself into the heart of the position and cleared it with bursts of automatic fire. This calculated and courageous act of controlled violence defeated the insurgents; the machine-gun was silenced and 2 insurgents lay dead.

As darkness fell the company moved north and extracted through Bravo Company into an area secured by Charlie Company. It was good to see some friendly faces, and the secure route and compound at its end were very welcome. A heart-stopping explosion signalled that Corporal Tam Mason, a Mortar Fire Controller working with Charlie Company had been seriously injured by an IED. His wounds were grievous (tragically he died in Selly Oak Hospital some six weeks later). We stole a few hours sleep before clearing a Wadi that the Taliban had mounted attacks from. This was slow work; short of sleep, wary of the very high threat and nervous because a savage sandstorm had blown in and reduced visibility to just a few metres, we were all relieved to get to Howz-e Madad, a Canadian Mentored ANA base. We spent a couple of days in Howz-e Madad, though we did venture south and fought the Taliban once again it was quite clear that our actions in the first 48 hours had had a crippling effect on their capabilities.

Op SPIN ARWA – Cavalry in the Infantry – Major Ben Cattermole (35), from Somerset, Officer Commanding Jackal Group (Charlie Company), Royal Scots Dragoon Guards

On the thin plyboard wall of the Company Commanders' office in Kandahar are pinned 4 black and white portaits. Ostensibly, these seem to constitute a sickly attempt by the British to show some form of multinational awareness, as the photographs of the Dutchman, the Australian and Englishman carry the same subtitle: "This man is your friend. He fights for freedom." The fourth picture, however, shows a Scottish soldier, complete with outsize Tam O Shanter, edited by some stalwart of anti-sentimality who had daubed in a red hackle, erased a tooth or two and stuck an alternative inscription over the text: "This man isn't your friend. He fights everybody." To infer too much from this montage would be academic, and a little boring – although I note with interest that it was an infantryman who had misplaced the apostrophe. As an outsider coming to the 3 SCOTS BG, however, it set the tone well. Scottish soldiers truly are a breed apart, but underneath any first impression, they are some of the most loyal, courageous and noble men with whom to serve.

So, as an Officer in Scotland's Cavalry, there was never any doubt when asked whether I would like to spend 3 to 4 months with Jackal Group of the Regional Battle Group (South) in Afghanistan. All too often, officers are 'trawled' from their units to join an operational headquarters, exchanging the challenges of command for the essential, but far less fun purgatory of hours glued to computer screens, where statistics, strap lines and staffwork are served, and process rather than outcome become all-consuming. To be offered the opportunity to command soldiers of the 3 SCOTS BG, with whom my own Regiment had served in Iraq in 2003, in Afghanistan, without having been through the mill of pre-deployment training, is rare in the extreme and not something to be passed up. Of course, even in Fallingbostel, Germany, we had heard of the extensive early summer exploits of the Battalion, but one is always healthily sceptical of media hyperbole. But little could have prepared me for the sheer breadth and success of the operations undertaken by the Battalion – and what they continued to achieve throughout their long 7 month tour.

I was rightly nervous of what I was letting myself in for. After all, I was not an infantryman, I had not been to Afghanistan and the media was, unsurprisingly, far from positive about our wider national and international efforts in Helmand. I was, however, reassured that the soldiers of D Squadron would be well led by the officers of the squadron, an excellent sergeant major and a team of high quality senior NCOs. Wading and crawling through the individual battle skills range in Hohne, regretting having not paid sufficient attention to my last real exposure to infantry training at Sandhurst some 13 years previously, however, it all seemed a little surreal. Leaving the family behind, not because I had to, but because I wanted to; replacing tank ranges and radio training for ranges where the targets shoot back and lost

Maj Ben Cattermole with the D Squadron Scots Dragoon Guards pennant.

communications can be fatal. One comfort was that my intended role was to be mounted in Jackal, a relatively new acquisition by the Army which offered superb off-road mobility and firepower. Visits to 3 Commando Brigade, who had put the Jackal to great effect over the winter, driver training on the dunes and beaches of north Devon and long hours spent reading back copies of the 'Infantryman' magazine reinvigorated my confidence a little. But there is little that one can do to prepare for taking command of soldiers half-way through a fraught and exhausting tour, soldiers who have been in the thick of combat, soldiers whom one does not know, soldiers with whom one hasn't trained and whose technical and tactical knowledge far exceeds one's own. Except to trust in them, since for all the gadgetry, newspaper headlines and bold political assertions that lay claim to the essence of modern soldiering, they are for nought without the people who make up our battalions and regiments.

Not so long ago, we concentrated our training on a recognisable enemy who fought us on relatively empty ground. But the enemy in Afghanistan is not so recognisable; he is, for the most part, one of the people among whom he lives and fights; and he fights us from beneath the ground with IEDs that are increasingly complex. And every time that the 3 SCOTS BG has deployed, it is to areas where the threat from this unseen but all-seeing enemy is particularly high, deep into insurgent safe-havens. Some soldiers have rightly been formally recognised for their gallantry and courage, but this may belie the bravery of every single man and woman who sets foot outside the confines of BASTION or Kandahar. One cannot fix bayonets against a pressure pad, only keep patrolling day after day, trusting in one's drills and those of one's comrades. The degrading effect of this constant pressure, which knows no relent, must never be underestimated – and yet this is what the Jocks, alongside their colleagues from all nations, have stoically endured, never knowing when the enemy might chose his moment to strike. And when he does strike, the next level of courage kicks in: rushing to the aid of a friend critically injured by an IED, private soldiers risking the threat of secondary devices to bring vital life saving first aid.

Even in the darkest moments, when casualties have tragically been taken, humour is never far away. The doctor, busy treating the wounded, passes his rifle to the Jocks giving covering fire. "Did you use it?" he asks, after the event. "Aye, sir, just ten to twelve rounds, eh." During the next lull, the doctor sets to cleaning his weapon, and is surprised at the amount of carbon and grime that was engrained into it. Needless to say, the opportunity to fire a weapon and not have to clean it had been to hard to resist, especially after actually firing ten to twelve magazines through it. But these same soldiers are not superhuman, they still share their personal grief, arms round shoulders, heads bowed as they listen to the Fijian choir sing words unknown, but which somehow mean so much.

Indeed, when I joined the Battalion in late July, towards the end of PANCHAI PALANG, I had time aplenty. The arrival in theatre of the 82nd Combined Aviation Brigade had given the Battle Group a massive uplift in the availability of helicopters – and understandably the focus was increasingly on aviation assault operations. The soldiers of Jackal Group were, therefore, required in their second role as dismounted fire support groups in the rifle companies. A week long foray down to Lashkar Gah, as a Jackal Group, seemed to put the concept of a mounted regional reserve capability back onto the planning table. So, when called down to

Coy HQ during Op SPIN ARWA with Capt Jon Kerr in the foreground.

Capts Dougie Bartholomew JTAC, Jon Kerr OC Javelin Platoon and David Mack OC Mortar Platoon.

Kandahar to plan for a battle group reconnaissance operation in the Sangin Valley, and having pored over the maps and consulted the various brigade troops who had travelled there before, I was confident that Jackal Group would be rolling again very soon, my squadron pennant fluttering in the dust-heavy wind.

Instead, there was no pennant – and the dust came not from the wind, but the down-draft of the Blackhawks and Chinooks that carried the Jackal-less Jackal Group far from Kandahar, and me even further from my comfort zone as a tank commander. Unlike staff college planning exercises, the faultlessness of one's logic and deductions would not win leather bound memoires of venerated Generals; this time the logic was academic; the conclusions all critical. And mistakes would send young soldiers to join the long-dead Generals. The planning tools taught over many hours in anodyne classrooms in Wiltshire do, however, pay real dividends, enforcing strict deliberation and consideration of most eventualities. But it was the trust that I could place in the highly experienced soldiers of the company that won through. When at the eleventh hour, intelligence indicated that a key enemy leader was in a compound just 100m from where we were due to land, there were no questions. When I needed someone to break cover and recover an ANA section who had chosen to advance line abreast against an insurgent firing position, there were no questions. When spotters were needed to direct helicopter fire, there were no questions. And when sections deployed on patrol, having been contacted twice in just a few hours on the same ground that they were to cover again, there were no questions.

The United Kingdom will no longer send a battalion to Kandahar to be the Regional Battle Group (South); instead, British forces will be concentrated in Helmand Province. The luxury of having 4 or 5 spare Chinooks for a battle group assault, the intelligence available from having 2 or 3 UAVs dedicated to the operation, the firepower of teams of Apache and Kiowa helicopters at one's fingertips – all will disappear. But the individual memories will remain for years to come, of personal challenges overcome, of friendships forged, of soldiers killed and broken. I only hope that whoever occupies this building sees the same 4 portraits and reflects on what makes the Scottish soldier such a fearsome and capable contender in battle, humorous and stoical, brave and dependable. It truly has been a privilege to serve with the soldiers of the 3 SCOTS Battle Group.

The 'Swimming Pool' in PB JOBOLAND, overlooking the Nahr-e-Bughra canal.

Chapter Ten

Operation MAR ZAY

30 September – 3 October 2009

INTRODUCTION

Operation MAR ZAY was set in the Lakari Bazaar within Task Force Leatherneck, the United States Marine Corps Expeditionary Brigade in Southern Afghanistan. The operation was conducted to continue the clearance of the Brigade's battlespace and disrupt insurgent operations. Concurrent to the operation, Task Force Leatherneck aimed to construct a patrol base 2.5 km north of the Lakari Bazaar.

The Lakari Bazaar had been identified as a significant insurgent facilitation node in terms of IED, arms and narcotics. Insurgents were known to operate in the bazaar during the day and insurgents imposed a tax on local national shop owners. Previous operations by Task Force Leatherneck had uncovered large quantities of narcotics, IED material and weapons.

The Battle Group planned to conduct a 3 wave aviation assault into the region of the Lakari Bazaar. Bravo Company would land first to the north of the bazaar and establish a screen along the eastern bank of canal Cobra. Alpha Company would land second to the south of the bazaar and also establish a screen to the west. Once the companies were on target, Bravo Company would secure Objective EASTGATE and Alpha Company would secure Objective KINGSGATE. Each company would meticulously search the compounds within their respective objectives and then Bravo Company would continue the process in Objective SILVERBURN and Alpha Company likewise in Objective WAVERLY. All insurgent material was to be destroyed in place with samples extracted as evidence.

The operation was to begin early on 30 September 09 and conclude on the evening of 1 October 09. However, following finds of ordnance and precursor narcotic chemicals Task Force Leatherneck Headquarters were concerned to the explosive effect on the bazaar despite the reassurances of the Explosive Ordnance Disposal Team on the ground. As a result the operation was extended for 24 hours to allow the Battle Group to separate the ordnance from the chemicals.

Members of 2 Platoon endure a sandstorm in the USMC's Camp Dwyer.

EXECUTION

28 September – 29 September 09 (D–2 – D–1)

The Battle Group was forward mounted to FOB DWYER on the 28 September by United States Marine Corps (USMC) air assets. On the 29 September, the Battle Group conducted integration training in FOB DWYER with Task Force Leatherneck prior to deployment. Final confirmatory orders were also given in FOB DWYER.

30 September 09 (D Day)

The insertion on Operation MAR ZAY was conducted as planned with all troops on the ground by 0435 hrs. Before first light, Alpha Company was in position with 2 platoons to the north of Objective KINGSGATE and a platoon and its headquarters were established in a screen to the west. In the north, Bravo Company had positioned 5 Platoon to secure the company's western flank and also provide overwatch of a canal crossing. 6 Platoon moved into Objective EASTGATE and secured the company's northern flank. 7 Platoon was colocated with Battle Group TAC on the fringes of the bazaar.

Lt Andy Wallace, as A Coy's Intelligence Officer, attends a shura.

After first light, both companies began the process of searching compounds in their objectives. Alpha Company engaged with local nationals who claimed that the bazaar was littered with IEDs to prevent ISAF forces from entering. Alpha Company intelligence suggested that there would be an attack against the Battle Group. At 0800 hrs, the snipers from Alpha Company identified 8 armed insurgents in the village of Tebbi which were engaged.

The Battle Group made good progress on the objectives. At 1035 hrs Bravo Company was engaged from Compound 328 in the village of Tebbi and continued to be harassed throughout the morning. At 1216 hrs, a 500lb GBU bomb was dropped in the vicinity of the compound, however, it failed to detonate. The insurgent quickly withdrew to a grape hut where he was met by 4 other insurgents. The armed UAV, which was observing the insurgent movement, fired a missile which destroyed the insurgents.

As this engagement was taking place, 7 Platoon made the first of a number of finds consisting of artillery ordnance, IED material, and drugs. The insurgents used limited engagements of single shots or bursts of fire in attempts to harass the Battle Group throughout the remainder of the day. Bravo Company continued to make numerous finds ranging from large quantities of drugs and precursor chemicals to weapons, ammunition, ordnance, and IED material such as detonation fuses, command wire, and battery packs.

By last light, the companies were established in secure locations. Resupply was being brought to the companies by Task Force Leatherneck. Unfortunately, the resupply points were incorrectly briefed to the pilots and as a result all the resupply for both companies landed at Bravo Company's location.

1 October 09 (D+1)

Early in the morning, Alpha Company repositioned to collect its resupply and begin the clearance of Objective SILVERBURN. Bravo Company established a screen along canal MAMBA and COBRA to disrupt any insurgent attempt to engage friendly forces. Alpha Company made further finds of IED material and drugs while Bravo Company were harassed by small arms.

The Battle Group was due to extract on the evening of the 1 October. However, Task Force Leatherneck Headquarters was not content for the Battle Group to destroy weapons, ammunition and chemicals in a compound in the bazaar as it was concerned the explosion might destroy the entire bazaar. The Explosive Ordinance Disposal Team had previously reassured that all the finds could be destroyed without collateral damage to the surrounding compounds, nonetheless, Task Force Leatherneck cancelled the extraction flights.

2 October – 4 October 09 (D+2 – D+4)

The Battle Group received an emergency resupply at 0300 hrs which was dropped at the correct locations. During the daylight hours the ammunition and weapons finds were separated from the chemicals in the bazaar. The chemicals and drugs were destroyed in the bazaar and the ordnance was brought into the dasht for destruction. 5 Platoon continued to receive fire from the village of Tebbi and 2 Excalibur artillery rounds were used to neutralise the insurgents. After last light, the Battle Group prepared for its extraction and moved to helicopter landing sites at 2200 hrs. The extraction began at midnight and all troops were in FOB DWYER by 0228 hrs. The Battle Group intended to return to Kandahar Airfield on 3 September, however, sandstorms grounded air transport. All troops returned to Kandahar Airfield by 4 September.

SUMMARY

Local national engagements confirmed that insurgent influence in the area was especially strong. Reporting of insurgent taxation of local nationals in the bazaar together with insurgents displaying an overt presence and conducting alternative governance was also corroborated by local national comments. Furthermore, the large finds of narcotics, weapons, ammunition, and IED material demonstrated a continued insurgent presence despite previous raids in the area. Undoubtedly, the clearance of the bazaar alongside the construction of patrol base north of the area will have severely disrupted insurgents in the area.

Operation MAR ZAY marked 2 important milestones. First, it was the first time that the Battle Group had operated with the United States Marine Corps. The operation restored a

A Coy destroying drug finds in the bazaar.

relationship with the United States Marine Corps that had begun during Operation TELIC 4 when its antecedent regiment, The Black Watch (Royal Highland Regiment), deployed to Camp DOGWOOD in support of operations around Fallujah, Iraq. Second, Operation MAR ZAY proved to be the last Battle Group level operation conducted by the 3 SCOTS Battle Group on Operation HERRICK 10. Although the companies would conduct 2 separate operations, the Battle Group as a whole did not deploy again.

Op MAR ZAY – Personal Account – Captain Euan Quin (30), from Bath, 38 Battery, 40 Regiment Royal Artillery

5 Platoon were tasked to protect the western flank and as this was the most vulnerable position I reinforced it by putting my Ack (Fire Support Team Assistant) Bombadier Richard McAuley and Lance Bombadier Craig Biggins with them to provide Offensive Fire Support. 5 Platoon were in frequent contact throughout the duration of the operation and on Day 1, I gained permission for Sergeant Ian Carlisle to engage with a 500lb bomb dropped from a UAV onto confirmed enemy who had been engaging 5 Platoon. Unfortunately the bomb failed to function but it forced the insurgents, still carrying their weapons, into a derelict grape drying hut. A missile was used to engage it and all 5 insurgents were killed with local nationals

coming into the area shortly after the strike and carrying away the deceased. On the third day, after several further attempts to engage with precision assets had been denied, I gained clearance to engage an insurgent firing point. Bombadier McAuley sent the Call For Fire and instructed the guns to "fire when ready' as 5 Platoon were once again in heavy contact. The round landed right on target and immediately put an end to the firefight. I was really pleased for Mac that his tour finished on a real high. He has been excellent all tour and battled severe pain in his legs to ensure that he deployed to support his mates in B Company. I could not have asked for a better Ack and I could not have asked for a better FST. They were all amazing in what we achieved and it was a special honour to have commanded them.

Capt Euan Quin on patrol with some of the members of the FST including Sgt Ian Carlisle and LBdr Craig Biggins.

Capt Euan Quin (right) and the FST on an earlier operation with the Bath Rugby Flag which went everywhere with them!

Op MAR ZAY – Late Start – Second Lieutenant Euan Eltringham (23), from Newcastle-upon-Tyne, Alpha (Grenadier) Company

3.30am and a combination of the rhythmic thud of the CH-53 helicopter, the awkward angle my body was perched on the seat and adrenaline made any form of sleep impossible. Looking around in the darkened atmosphere I could make out an array of expressions ranging from the intensely focused, to the jokingly calm, to those who at first seemed completely nonchalant before it dawned on me that they were indeed asleep. There had been a rapid turnaround since completing my Platoon Commanders Course after Sandhurst: - 3 weeks in total to complete the mandatory pre-deployment training, receive the kit and snatch a few moments to say the requisite goodbyes.

It was a far cry from the environment I had been operating in just a few weeks earlier – sitting in a classroom and trying to take in the information on the bright blue power-point slide which described in detail how to plan a live firing range. I had left Sandhurst for Brecon knowing full well that I was to join the Battalion in Afghanistan straight from training. At the start this simply manifested itself in an excitement I had rarely felt before. This was to be the culmination of a year and a half of work, and I was going to join the ranks of a battle hardened Battle Group that had a fighting spirit and ethos forged on battlefields in India, Korea, Western Europe and the North African desert.

As the course at Brecon progressed, there was a shift in the outlook that I was having. The culmination of the "Tactics" phase of the course encompassed a month long exercise in Belize, and being immersed in the military environment, my thoughts turned to the men that I would be commanding: How would they view me? Would they indeed be accepting? Do I have what it takes to lead them? All of these thoughts swirled around in the ether of my mind

Second Lieutenant Euan Eltringham conducting a shura.

Second Lieutenant Euan Eltringham talking to the local national population.

and I found myself, if ever unfortunate enough to make a mistake in the exercise, overly berating myself despite how insignificant it was. It would be fair to say that the upcoming deployment I was facing imposed a focus on all that I was doing.

The final stop on the merry-go-round of views that I was thinking came when we were finally up at Fort George, having received a phone call from the Adjutant informing us that our flights were going to be brought forward to the 10th September. It was only then it really hit me, the magnitude of where my fellow new subaltern and I were going. It just didn't seem real, how could it have come around so fast? There was still so many questions floating around that I didn't quite have the answer to, and it was a case of harvesting information from others who we met both on the pre-deployment package and up at the Fort itself. This final phase wasn't a lengthy one however – there wasn't really time for that and it soon made way for (again) excitement, but the difference this time however, was that this has remained since and has yet to be diminished.

Those opening scenes that I described at the start of this piece, were those that greeted me on my first deployment on the ground. Arriving so late in the tour I knew I wasn't going to have many opportunities on the ground, and indeed I had already missed Op SPIN ARWA by 2 days. Although I was only going to be shadowing, I was still relieved to be going out on the ground with the Battalion. Op MAR ZAY wasn't a very kinetic operation – I was not subjected to enemy fire except for a lone indirect fire incident which even then was nowhere near. I am immensely grateful to have been of part of this experience, it is something I will cherish and use to build on my future career, wherever that may take me.

It would be misleading to think that my experience was unique and not shared by anybody else in the Battalion. There were a number of young Jocks who made an even greater leap into the unknown and came from their infantry training at Catterick, to the sweltering heat of an Afghan summer and the intense cooking pot of campaigning that the Battle Group was going through. One of these was Private Darren Bernard, a native of Kenneway, just 18 years old and serving with 2 Platoon, Alpha (Grenadier) Company. I first met Private Bernard on a quiet Tuesday afternoon in Camp ROBERTS, and his experiences

Pte Stevens (left) and Pte Darren Bernard (second from left) from Kenneway, 2 Platoon, Alpha (Grenadier) Coy.

highlight the enormous burden placed on those young men joining the Battalion just a number of months after leaving the confines of 'Civvy Street'.

Talking about his experiences on tour generates a certain nervousness at first, Bernard is a naturally quiet young chap, but gradually he talks more freely with an openness that is both refreshing and poignant. "I really enjoyed training at Catterick." he enthused, when probed on his experience at the training depot where all young recruits hoping to join the Infantry go: "Any chance to get out in the field was great but the live firing was probably the best". Bernard had completed a stint at Harrogate in preparation for joining the Army and always knew that 3 SCOTS was the Battalion he wanted to join. Once that had been confirmed to him, the instructors were keen to point out that although the training he was going through was physically demanding, it was going to be even harder out in theatre: "but I guess that was to be expected, so I had already prepared myself for that", Looking at him, and indeed at many of the young Jocks of the Battalion, it is hard to imagine their sinewy, calf-like frames carrying the 50kg average weight that the modern infantry soldier has to patrol with but they do so with unwavering resolve and despite the incredible heat that accompanies the day in Afghanistan.

After talking a while, I could see that the changes in feelings were not uncommon, with Bernard admitting that it was at the pre-deployment package when it hit him that he was bound for a warzone where the Army has been experiencing intense fighting and now entering a deadly counter-insurgency phase. On arrival in theatre at his new home, there was a real 'shock of capture' sense to those first few days. "It was a struggle getting to know all those new names and faces but I was lucky to go out on an op fairly soon after so I could mix in with the guys". However, that introductory phase wasn't without its perks, "I was surprised with Kandahar. It was the size of the place that struck me – it even had a Burger King and that!"

That first experience out on the ground for Bernard brought about that common sense of excitement that soldiers feel when about to do the job that they been training all their careers for (no matter how long or short). "There was going to be less tabbing, so I was really pleased" he says with a wry smile across his face "that was a bonus about being in the vehicles". Bernard was to be one of the platoon's 'IED clearance men'. This would involve him clearing routes by detecting IEDs with the metal detector. "I hadn't really thought about how dangerous it was at first, I didn't think I was invincible, I was just, maybe, unaware of how real it all was now". The feeling of invulnerability wasn't to last long however, "The Mastiff that hit an IED was in pretty bad shape, I realised pretty quickly from then on what was in store for me over the next few months". Quick to show that this was not something that phased him, he pointed out that the first time he was shot at "I just looked around at what all the other lads were doing… and then we had a bit of a giggle".

I was lucky that I never had anything traumatic to deal with so soon in my Army career, but young Bernard did not share the shame fortune. At the same time as him, in a different part of Catterick, there was Private Robert McLaren, a strong, charismatic young man who was also destined for the Black Watch Battalion. It was one of those fairly innocent, chance encounters that brought the 2 new recruits together explained Bernard "We were stood next to each other in the NAAFI queue, buying juice" he recalls with touching accuracy. Talking further about what his friend was like he describes a young man who possessed a natural maturity and a natural flair, sense of humour and skill at his job that won him the respect of his peers as well as popularity in the platoon. "The next week we were up in the Fort and found out that we were going to the same platoon, we even hoped to be in the same section but that didn't happen".

Looking down at the floor, and shuffling his feet, it is clear that the events on the day that Private McLaren died are difficult for him to recall, but nevertheless summons up what seems to me like yet more strength from the unshakable bank that these young Jocks seem to possess. "We were on a bund line with a grape hut 200m to our right when we all heard the bang", that bang was the detonation of that most indiscriminate weapon – the IED – by Private McLaren as he entered a compound to get a better view of the firing point. "There was a lot of talking on the radio until the OC cleared the net, at which point his personal code number was read out". It is something that this young man shares with too many other young men in the British Army, and compared to men of 5, 10 and 20 years experience seems tragically unfair a weight to place on shoulders so raw. That wasn't the end of the saga, during the contact that followed they were subjected to attacks by Chinese rockets: "That was the most scared I have been out here. I was nervous after hearing what had happened to Rab, but knew that there was nothing I could do. I was just so shocked, I never expected something like that to happen to him." Maybe the fighting provided a distraction to take the mind off those horrible thoughts, Bernard later recalls how the resupply gave him plenty of time for him to keep going over what had happened, and as he puts "I don't know how it is going to affect me, I'll just have to wait and see, I still think about it now".

I look at those Jocks who have been thrust into such a hostile environment and I can see already the maturity that they have developed. It has been earned in the least desirable of circumstances, and indeed in some cases the worst possible. However, for them to keep going out and doing their job with such understanding and spirit is still one of the greatest things I have seen in my short time but will take something quite spectacular to surpass.

Op MAR ZAY – Thoughts whilst flying – Captain Samuel Newson (28), from Prestwood, Buckinghamshire, Second in Command Alpha (Grenadier) Company

A prelude to battle, a voyage into danger.
A bridge, a stepping stone to safety.
A Watershed.

Flying marks a transition; a geographical dislocation often of vast distance, in time often brief but sometimes lengthy. A change in circumstance and consequence, both extreme and serious. A leap from a place of security to a barren hill, into a dark night holding unknown and unseen danger.

The flight, be it 10 minutes or an hour, to the infantryman is dead time. He can't go back, can't change anything. What is happening on the ground is irrelevant; he can do nothing until the ramp goes down only wait, wait and think.

I find myself thinking about the future. About loved ones, plans made and adventures to come. There is often a shadow, a hint of sadness, a vague imagining that these things may not come to be. Not fatalistic but a vivid awareness of how important that future is to me.

To entertain such thoughts en route to battle, might to some seem indulgent and unwise. I believe it is inevitable, part of what makes us human. It keeps us tethered to reality and reminds us that there is something to go back to, something that gives what is to come meaning.

I don't know what others have thought about amidst the noise and isolation of the insertion flight, what I do know is that those thoughts are tucked away as one steps off the ramp and on to the ground. Held in stasis, whilst focus and action are required, to be re-explored in a quiet moment or in lighter mood on the journey back.

I have no doubt there have been speeches formed in the mind which reticence would shackle. Their simple, honest eloquence would so delight and beguile the intended that once home I hope I am candid enough to give them voice.

Op MAR ZAY – Personal Account – Private Martin Coulter (23), from Dundee, Fife, Mortar Platoon, Charlie Company

In this op I was going to be heading out as a rifleman in 5 Platoon, to help make up numbers for injuries and to cover for the gaps created when some of the TA lads had left. My over all feeling before the op was that of excitement, however there was a little apprehension.

I was excited for a number of reasons. The main one being that I was heading out as a rifleman. This was slightly different compared to what I had been used to on the mortar line and a job that I had not done for some time.

The job of 5 Platoon was to move into the border of the green zone, overlook a Taliban strong hold and set up a platoon house. The platoon was acting as a cut off to stop the Taliban advancing to positions to launch attacks on to the rest of the battalion that was clearing a bazaar to the east. We knew just from this that we would be expecting some contacts, and the pre op brief later confirmed this.

I was looking forward to working as a rifleman and seeing how I would cope in this situation. Coming under contact excited me the most: the chance of firing my rifle. To be honest looking back I had been in that situation many times before. However I think it was the excitement that I might get to fire my rifle instead of my mortar made it feel slightly different. I think this was fuelled slightly by wanting to feel satisfied that I had revenged the death of my Platoon Sergeant Gus Millar and the injuries sustained from a IED to MFC Corporal Tam Mason, that I felt at the time that was missing from impersonal firing of the mortar.

Apart from the plume of dust and the sight and sound of the explosion, you rarely get to see the direct consequences of the effect of mortar rounds and as result there is an unconnected feeling after being told that you had inflicted damage upon the enemy. I wanted to experience a more personal level by firing my rifle, and see the direct consequences of the fire fight upon the enemy. However I was not going to let this cloud my judgment and actions, as I knew that it would be unprofessional and could lead to me making mistakes on the battlefield.

I was looking forward to heading out and seeing a bit of the green zone and farming areas. The green zone was a lot easier to cope with, compared to areas that I had been in with the mortar line. In past operations the mortar line had been dropped off in the middle of the desert, which was usually a couple of miles away from the green zone. The only shade was provided by a poncho which acted like a green house in the hottest parts of the days, with temperatures easily exceeding 50 degrees. In addition I wanted to see some of the locals. I had experience of them in the past, and to be honest they are good people. They did not want this war, they wanted peace, and to be honest 99 percent of them wanted us there. They feared the Taliban, their beatings and punishments, which sometimes resulted in death. They knew that if we were not there they would succumb to the rule of the Taliban, so they where usually warm and welcoming towards us.

Another major cause for my excitement was the weight of the kit I was carrying. The mortar kit that I would usually carry as a number one was in excess of 25kg, with the base plate, C2 sight, a greenie (2 mortar rounds in a green container) as well as any other additional kit that was needed for the mortar line. Further to this, during the hotter parts of the summer I would carry up to 8 litres of water, a day's rations, body armour and personal kit that I needed for the op. So from that it can be calculated that I was easily carrying over 50kg of kit. In fact on one op I was weighed and I was carrying just short of 70kgs of kit. However this op I was only carrying my personal kit plus a stretcher, the bare minimum.

There is always a little apprehension before every op. Each op is different and no matter how good the intelligence is, my experience from previous ops suggests that something unexpected would always pop up. It tended to be more so with the types of operations that the Battle Group was conducting. We were conducting strike ops with a specific task, usually clearing an area of Taliban, doing a drugs raid, or deliberately disrupting the enemy. Although we might have had more assets than usual to conduct the op, we were going into areas that had hardly been visited by coalition forces, so usually all there was to go on was maps and aerial photos. This usually meant that there was always a chance that the op would start off with a bang and stir up a hornet's nest.

My main apprehension was that I was heading out with a new platoon and that I was going to be an outsider. I knew that some of my rifleman skills and drills might not be as sharp mainly due to the fact that I had not been under contact as a rifleman. In addition I didn't know any of the lads, how they work together as a team etc. However on arrival at the platoon I found them very friendly and open, a lot like the Mortar Platoon.

I had the usual apprehensions that every soldier faces upon going out on any op. Not knowing if this op was going to be the last op. Would I be coming back intact? The injuries sustained by my friend Corporal Tam Mason in the last op that I was on and hearing the explosion that caused his injuries will haunt me for some time, in addition the death of Sergeant Gus Millar meant that these apprehensions were very real to me. However like every soldier you just knuckle down and get on with it.

Lieutenant Alex Phillips (26), from Ingham, Norfolk, 5 Platoon Commander, Bravo Company

Some of the Platoon I've had since the beginning of my time with the Battalion, and some joined as recently as a few weeks ago. Kenya was awesome in terms of training, for rifle platoon commanding. In terms of preparation for here, yes and no, it's very different.

I feel confident, there's nothing really that phases me out here which is obviously easy to say sat here in a chair but when you're on the ground, you just sort of deal with each situation as it happens. It's just a shame at the end of the tour I hand over, and that's just about when I'll have mastered being a Platoon Commander.

Not many people get to come here on Op HERRICK as a rifle platoon commander, but you really are doing your job here. The Jocks are awesome, it's amazing seeing how different people deal with it, from an 18 year old having just turned up from Catterick on their first op, really nervous and now they're more than confident and capable with getting on with it. It was a really weird atmosphere when we first arrived as everyone was really nervous, obviously hearing the stories and reading about it, but once you've experienced it, you kind of get used to it, and then it breaks you in.

I was more nervous when I first got here about doing the right thing than anything else, because of the responsibility of having the guys under your command. All you care about really is making sure you do everything right so that they're alright.

I'd do anything for them, just because they're my guys. Jocks have been stepping up to the plate for hundreds of years, and just if you think they're not ready, they are, and they're always capable of stepping up.

I think everyone has had quite a few near misses. You don't even realise it at the time, anything from Chinese rockets going off 2m away from you, or contacts where rounds are pinging. I sort of brush it off because it's just so surreal. Gregor Mill always says I never change when I'm in contact, or just in camp, I'm always the same. I just find it amusing, but that's easy to say if no one gets hurt. It's all fine until then of course.

Pte Connor Nichols (20), from Preston, 5 Platoon, Bravo Company

My mum's proud, proper proud of me being in The Black Watch, 3rd Battalion, she's really supportive. She's got all my R&R planned out already.

The first op and the last op I came under contact. The first one going down the road, then I got contacted from the right so I hit the deck, faster than I've ever done before, I was absolutely shitting it. I was shaking. I was still returning fire like but it was scary. It was close, they were hitting the trees around us and that. Bob McTurk was right next to me,

Lt Alex Phillips, Lt Rob Colqhoun and Lt Harry Pearce, Alpha (Grenadier) Company.

he was celebrating and cheering. I was confused like mad I didn't know how anyone could cheer through it. It relaxes you a bit when you realise everyone else can be relaxed round it.

On the last op, we got rocket attacked and that was scary. We were sat in a compound, starting to relax a little, everyone's chilling out, getting their head down and then rockets starting to come in. Everyone thinks when they're back in training it'll be mint coming under contact and that, and that you'll be able to do alright. But you do shite yourself. I think everyone did that came with me. Everyone around me had been in contact before and knew what to do. They were all on the ball. I trust everyone here, they would all look out for you.

Lt Harry Pearce and Lt Alex Phillips in Camp BASTION just after an incoming rocket alert clearance alarm.

Chapter Eleven

Operation HALQAY FULAARDEEN
(RING OF STEEL)

27 September – 11 October 2009

INTRODUCTION

Operation HALQAY FULAARDEEN was a Task Force Helmand operation to isolate Babaji area and support the Light Dragoons Battle Group's clearance of the area. Battle Group Centre, the Danish Battle Group in Helmand, was tasked to disrupt insurgents north of the Nahr-e-Burgha (NEB) canal. The Jackal Group was placed under the command of Battle Group Centre to support the disrupt mission north of Nahr-e-Burgha canal. The Jackal Group was tasked to find and deter insurgent movement in northern Babaji and the tunnels underneath the Nahr-e-Burgha canal. In addition, the Jackal Group was to conduct movement control along the canal.

The central patrol base established by Battle Group Centre was known as Patrol Base JOBOLAND. The Jackal Group planned to move to BASTION prior to deploying to Patrol Base JOBOLAND with liaison officers established in FOB PRICE. The Fire Support Group and the Jackal Group Headquarters would initially deploy to Patrol Base JOBOLAND at 1100 hrs on 27 September. The following morning the remainder of the Jackal Group and the logistic support vehicles would then deploy to Patrol Base JOBOLAND.

Once established in Patrol Base JOBOLAND, the Jackal Group would manoeuvre its 2 platoons into routine conducting 2 different roles. One platoon would conduct framework patrols from the patrol base and also monitor and control crossing points along the Nahr-e-Burgha canal. The second platoon would find and disrupt insurgents further afield from Patrol Base JOBOLAND. The platoon would maximise opportunities for local national engagements and understand the region. The platoon would also find and be prepared to control alternative crossings along the Nahr-e-Burgha canal. Each platoon would alternate in roles.

The Jackal Group zero their many weapons on the Camp BASTION range.

EXECUTION

27 September – 11 October 09

Once the Recce Platoon was in Patrol Base JOBOLAND and the logistic support vehicles were back in BASTION, the Jackal Group started its operations routine on a 72 hour rotation. One platoon remained in Patrol Base JOBOLAND and manned sangars and conducted framework patrols in the vicinity of the patrol base and Tunnel 4 on Narh E Burgha canal. The other platoon conducted patrols and was given the freedom to exploit mission command into a large area of operation. The patrols tended to concentrate in the area of Tunnel 3 on Narh E Burgha canal. The Jackal Group sought to counter the insurgent threat through a combination of mounted and dismounted patrols and by conducting spot checks and searches day and night.

Local national engagement was a critical focus during the 2 week period. Atmospherics were generally positive towards ISAF patrols. Local nationals were comfortable speaking with the Jackal Group. However, some local nationals demonstrated a reluctance to engage with the Jackal Group closer to the canal as there was concern of being observed by insurgents.

SUMMARY

Unlike the majority of the Battle Group's operations, Operation HALQAY FULAARDEEN was a defined ground-holding mission consisting of normal framework operations. The reinforcement of Battle Group Centre with the Jackal Group enabled a Battle Group level operation in the Upper Gereshk Valley while simultaneously assisting in the security of the Babaji area.

The Jackal Group returned to BASTION on the 11th of October. Once back in BASTION the Jackal Group was warned of a possible final operation over 19th – 20th October. However, this operation was cancelled and the Jackal Group began the tedious but important process of preparing its kit and equipment for a final handover later in October.

With the conclusion of Operation HALQAY FULAARDEEN, the role of the Jackal Group came to an end. The Jackal Group gave the Battle Group a third manoeuvre element that was mounted in Jackals and also dismounted for aviation assaults. The Jackal Group provided the Battle Group flexibility as a mobile group which could cover difficult terrain at great reach from central battle group logistic nodes.

Op HALQUAY FULAARDEEN (RING OF STEEL) - Diary Entry, 27 September – 09 October 09 – Captain Harry Gladstone (26), from Dumfries, Officer Commanding Machine Gun Platoon Commander, Charlie Company

We deployed as a Jackal group in support of the Danish Battle Group Centre South. They had a company based in a PB called JOBOLAND. Joboland is on the north side of Babiji and covers 2 sets of tunnels which can be used to cross the NEB canal. It is named after a famous theme park in Denmark. The Danes first arrived while fighting the Taliban to the south. They said that it was like a theme park because you could swim in the pool and then shoot at the

Capt Harry Gladstone talking to the local national population.

enemy later on! The NEB canal is an enormous canal built by the Americans in the '50s which brings water from the Helmand River out into the desert. It has created a huge area of agriculture now called the Afghan Development Zone.

The FOB is only 2 kilometers away from FOB WAHID which we used for Op PANCHAI PALANG. It was suspected that the tunnels were being used by the Taliban to move themselves and supplies in and out of Babaji. The locals in the area were still indifferent about ISAF forces and scared of Taliban. It was our job to disrupt the enemy and win the support of the locals so that they provide us with information.

The Company moved as 2 platoons, with the FSG deploying first on the 27 September. We went to JOBOLAND via Highway 1. We were met by the Danes who had a mixture of armoured vehicles including Humvees, armoured fighting vehicles, and Panthers. They offered to take us straight on a familiarisation patrol. I split my platoon in half so that half were on guard and half were on patrols. I took the patrols half with the Danes, on the familiarisation patrol. We visited a set of tunnels called NEB 3 which ran under the NEB canal.

On the route back insurgents from the south of the canal fired one RPG at my vehicle. The RPG malfunctioned and went shooting off into the sky over our heads. I was expecting a volley of small arms fire any minute and had the machine gun in my shoulder in anticipation, but it never came. Corporal McLaughlin, who was my gunner at the time, fired a couple of rounds at the contact point. We continued on our patrol and returned to FOB JOBOLAND. The Recce Platoon arrived and assumed the job of mobile platoon and started patrolling the wider area.

Whilst on guard we carried out a number of small patrols lasting about an hour each. One of our tasks was to carry out spot checks on NEB 4 which is one of the tunnels under the NEB canal. I took Jackals down to the canal for these checks. We searched everyone who approached us and questioned them on the Taliban and asked them questions like "where do you live?", "why are you crossing the canal?", "what do you think of ISAF?" and "do you have enough water?" We asked one man what the Taliban were doing on the other side of the canal. He said, "The same thing as you, trying to get the people to support them."

We moved to mobile patrolling after 3 days of guard. I stopped all my vehicles to the north of NEB 3 and patrolled on foot from there. I also sent a vehicle patrol down to NEB 3. Colour Sergeant Latta led this patrol and unfortunately got stuck in full view of the canal and also the enemy. I sent another 2 vehicles down to help get them unstuck. As the vehicles were leaving, the enemy fired a couple of bursts with AK47s. Nobody was hurt and the fire stopped before anyone could return fire.

During the night we mounted an 8 man OP. I placed the OP in a tree line beside a drainage ditch. Unfortunately this meant that the mosquitoes were unbearable. We were also extremely cold having not brought any warm kit. During the night we had the Command Launch Unit (CLU) trained on the tunnels to pick up any heat sources, but did not see anything.

In the morning we moved to FOB PRICE. In FOB PRICE we were able to use the internet, eat good food again and use the showers. We returned after 24 hrs to NEB 3. We remained at NEB 3 for 2 hours and then visited some locals nearby. One of these locals told us that his neighbour had had the Taliban to tea one day. It turned out that he hated the Taliban because they had used his last compound as a firing point and then it had been flattened by a British rocket.

We also met a local leader who said he was trying to encourage his people to help fight the Taliban by reporting IEDs. He said his message to his people was "People do not be afraid, go outside and find the IEDs so you can tell others." He complained of having too small a congregation.

I also a met an old man. He told us that he had been told to stay inside at night by the Taliban after 2200hrs. He said that the Taliban often move around with their faces covered. I asked him about elders in the area because there are none. It is very clear that the area needs elders. We tried to get him to take on the responsibility but he complained that he does not have time to be an elder. He also complained about the rise in tax which would go along with an increase in local government. We returned to FOB JOBOLAND to take over guard.

During the guard phase Sergeant O'Brien took a patrol to NEB 4 which was shot at on the way back to JOBOLAND. I took a patrol to the north to investigate some markers on the road. I was concerned that they might be markers to warn locals of IEDs. We could not get an answer about the IEDs from the locals but as we left they kicked all the stones away. We put the area out of bounds. It was very clear that people were still not happy to hand over information.

I carried out one more phase of patrols. I returned to visit the old man I had met earlier. He took us round the back of his compound so that the Taliban could not see him talking to us. He was very afraid of Taliban but we could not find out why. We asked when he had last heard of a local being punished for speaking to ISAF troops. He said it happened a long time ago. He got very angry and said it is not worth the risk; they could come and kill "this son here", while pointing to his son. "If there was not Taliban intimidation then I would form a council in order to run the area."

We visited a compound and ended up having a shura. About 5 old men came out of nowhere wanting to discuss issues. The first issue on the menu was their ailments. One was going blind. We gave him aspirin and he was happy. Another had cold fever and we gave him Diorylyte. When they did get down to business they said that it was great having us in the area because it meant that the Taliban could not be there. They thanked us for providing security. They complained about us driving on their fields.

I also met a young teenager waiting for a shop to open. He was very open about many issues including the Taliban sometimes wearing uniform. I can only assume that teenagers do not have any memory of Taliban persecution before the invasion. The next day I saw an almighty explosion in the area of NEB 3. After quizzing locals it turned out that a dog had set off the IED.

We returned to BASTION without further incident after 2 weeks. The operation was extremely interesting because we spent so long engaging with locals and trying to win their support. This is the kind of thing which a ground holding battle group would do all the time. For us, a strike battle group, it was a great change. In 2 weeks we only scratched the surface of understanding local pattern of life. It is clear that the NEB area needs elders. I had begun to realise how little I knew about Afghan communities. I did not know how elders are appointed, if at all, and how they are paid. It is clear that to do this job well would require more fluent Pashtu and a very good knowledge of community structure. Talking to people is very important in winning a counter insurgency campaign. The majority of people in

Afghanistan do not care who wins the war; ISAF or the Taliban. They are more concerned with living and raising their families in a safe environment. They will favour the side which they think will win.

Op HALQAY FULAARDEEN – An Observation of the Contrast Between Operations in Iraq and Operations in Afghanistan – Captain Jon Kerr, Officer Commanding the Javelin Platoon, Charlie Company

To a non military person, the British Forces' campaigns in Iraq (Operation TELIC) and Afghanistan (Operation HERRICK) may seem similar or even the same. And to an unobservant or ignorant soldier there may not appear to be any difference – both in a hot, far away country where one sleeps in a crowded, stuffy, 20 man tent not knowing what is going to happen next week, tomorrow or even in the next few hours. So his kit is packed ready for anything to happen, ready for the unexpected. Living in these cramped conditions and being on such a high state of readiness, over a 6 month period is stressful, emotional, tiring, at times mind numbing and yes, there is no difference between life on operations in Iraq or Afghanistan, or anywhere for that matter. The life of a soldier on operations has probably not changed over decades, maybe even centuries.

So what is the difference between Op TELIC and Op HERRICK? What are the differences between any operational tours?

The obvious difference is the weather, which in the case of TELIC and HERRICK is not very much.

Capt Jon Kerr, OC Javelin Pl, C Coy.

The main difference therefore is the terrain and of course the enemy.

When I was in Iraq on TELIC 10 I was a Warrior Platoon Commander with the 2nd Battalion The Royal Welsh. 2 R Welsh were 1 Mech Brigade's Manoeuvre Battle Group operating mainly in Basra city. The weather was unbearably hot and dry. When preparing for TELIC 10 I asked a friend who had done a summer tour of Iraq what the weather was like. His response was hot, very hot. He said that driving in the day was like someone holding a hair dryer to your face. He wasn't wrong. That summer in 2007, like all summers in that part of the world, the temperature reached the low 50s. The midday temperature in the turret of a Warrior or Challenger reached 70 degrees centigrade.

Our area of operations – Basra city – included metalled roads up to 6 lanes wide with a central reservation all the way down to dust tracks barely wide enough for a Landrover. Off road in that part of Iraq consisted of salt marshes, and therefore a no go to any vehicle. Basra was a busy place with a population of over 3 million, crammed with buildings rarely higher than 2 or 3 stories and intersected by roads and alleyways. Perfect ground for an insurgency to grow and thrive. The enemy were insurgents, maybe from Iran, maybe from somewhere else in Iraq or maybe home-grown in Basra. Either way he was cunning, ever evolving his tactics and brave – *Insha'Allah* was his motto meaning 'If God wills it.' He blended into the population that he was trying to influence, he lived among them, he dressed the same and he spoke the same language.

At the time, fighting in Basra had reached an all time high since the invasion in 2003. This meant that only armour could go into Basra. So we were trying to win a counterinsurgency with tanks and armoured personnel carriers. Operations had changed from foot patrols consisting of soldiers wearing soft hats mingling with the people to armoured companies and battle groups punching into the heart of the city to strike a known insurgent commander's dwelling. Operations like these meant tens of Warriors and Challenger Tanks setting up inner and outer cordons that would protect the platoon carrying out the strike from the countless hoards of fighters trying to stop them. The outer cordon bore the brunt of the backlash. But the bullets from their AK 47s and PKMs did very little to the exterior of the armoured vehicles firing back at them with 7.62 mm chain guns and even 30mm high explosive shells. And thanks to new armour technology their rocket propelled grenades were no longer much of a threat either. Their IEDs were however.

One of the best weapons in any insurgent's arsenal is the IED. It can be made from every day products quickly and easily and it can be laid hidden for days or even months. In Basra the insurgents had developed their IEDs from large devices that contained a large amount of home made explosives (HME) to small devices that were designed using anti armour technology to concentrate the force of the explosion onto the side of an armoured vehicle. These explosively formed projectiles (EFPs) were the main threat to us, and the thing on everyone's mind. The molten slug produced from an EFP could, if directed at the right spot, cut through a Warrior like a hot knife through butter. And because they were small they could be made quickly and transported around the city easily and rapidly by IED teams on motorbikes. Operating in pairs, the IED teams could be informed, by the all-seeing dicking screen, that there was a Warrior company coming their way. They could then lay the IEDs in our path and sit and wait on the end of a command wire or leave the passive infra red sensor to do it's work. We became good at spotting the IEDS - this meant we could stop and call for the engineers to come and blow the devise up or de-activate it,. If they weren't spotted however, due to being hidden too well or simply missed, then they frequently detonated and occasionally, if placed well, hit their intended target – the crew of the vehicle. Sadly this tactic used by the enemy was sometimes successful and soldiers were killed. But because of the immediate threat, and because of the fatalities, our tactics, techniques and procedures evolved to counter the IED threat and lives were undoubtedly saved.

As well as the IEDs there was also a sniper threat. The 2 and 3 story buildings that lined our routes into and out of Basra provided perfectly concealed firing points for snipers. And the countless alleyways, doorways, nooks and crannies in the city provided excellent cover for insurgents to hide and spring ambushes from. Thankfully though my time on TELIC saw the beginning of the end for British forces in Iraq. In mid August that year there was a ceasefire of sorts and operations into the city stopped. In mid September the 4 Rifles Battle Group handed over Basra Palace to the Iraqi Army and left for good. So we ended the tour by conducting ops to the south of the city all the way down to the Kuwaiti border. And thankfully, like the operational tempo the temperature came down too.

Sixteen months later I deployed to Afghanistan on Operation HERRICK 10. This time I was with my own Battalion, 3 SCOTS. During the first week in Afghanistan I saw so many similarities. It was hot, dusty, the tents were exactly the same, we drank water out of half-litre plastic bottles, we queued up 3 times a day to wash our hands in the same yellow soap then get the same vacuum-packed plastic cutlery and oval paper plates only to layer it up with the same greasy bacon and sausages and rubber eggs boiled in oil. And in the evening you could have G1098 cheesecake - no matter where you go in the world the Army will provide the same cheesecake.

So, like many other soldiers who had been to Iraq at some stage, as I assembled my Osprey body armour (which had got no lighter) I wondered how this tour would differ from my last. I knew the terrain would be slightly different, although places like Gereshk and Lashkar Gah were similar to Basra, they were just towns and we only ever passed through them. The natural landscape was very different however. When we inserted into target areas by Chinook helicopter I noticed vast mountains silhouetted against the night sky, and once in the target area, again the terrain was different. Most of our ops were conducted in the 'green zone.' The green zone is a belt of vegetation that straddles the river Helmand all the way from the Kijaki dam, through the Sangin valley, through Gereshk and Lashkar Gah, through Garmsir to the fish hook and beyond. The majority of southern Afghanistan is arid dessert but the irrigated ground either side of the River Helmand is fertile ground, ideal for growing crops such as wheat, maize and poppy. Because the ground is irrigated crops can be grown there, because crops can be grown there people live there and because people live there the insurgents live there. And so we have to operate in the green zone either because we're trying to influence the people or because we're trying to strike the enemy. Either way soldiers have to operate in and amongst irrigation ditches, boggy fields, and on the plethora of hard tracks and paths that criss cross the green zone. And it is on these tracks and paths that the insurgents place their IEDs.

The insurgents in Afghanistan though are not trying to punch holes in Warriors or Challengers, these heavy vehicles would not get very far in the green zone, all the insurgent in Afghanistan has to do is make an IED capable of blowing off a couple of legs, maybe an arm or two or even kill someone. And because we are patrolling in the green zone on foot an IED strike can be followed up effectively by an ambush using AK47s, RPKs, PKMs, DShKs and RPGs.

So because of the difference in ground the enemy use different tactics and likewise so do we. When caught up in fire fights our tactics are much more conventional than in Iraq. Soldiers are having to revert to the field craft they were taught in training or on the hills in Brecon. Commanders are having to deal with far more complicated ambushes over far more complicated ground and against a much more formidable, determined enemy, sometimes at the point of the bayonet.

So when one compares a long list of things like food, water, accommodation, weather, equipment, welfare etc not much is different and rightly so. Today's soldier has some of the best equipment available to him and today's Army is used to being on operations so the little things that make so much difference to soldiers' moral are set up and in place. But our operations are shaped by the ground we cover and the enemy we are up against, and because the ground is different and the enemy more cunning and tenacious our operations are different - longer, more complex, physically more demanding and, at times more violent. During my time in Iraq and Afghanistan, like all soldiers, I've experienced a wide range of feelings and emotions. I've missed home, family and loved ones. I've been under pressure and experienced fear. But on both instances I've witnessed and been a part of bonds forged under extreme circumstances and been part of a team from the Commanding Officer right the way down to the Jocks.

Sergeant Kevin Stobbs (28), from Newcastle, 38 Battery 40 Regiment Royal Artillery

Even before March this year when we came out here, we did a lot of pre deployment training with the BG out in Kenya and a couple of exercises up in Otterburn as well.

I left Kenya 2 weeks early to go on my JTAC course which is training to bring fast air in. That's the job I'm doing out here. My main role is therefore the coordination of fast air and bringing fast air and attack helicopters in to support the ground troops. This includes UAVs. We look into general areas, compounds of interest and to follow troops on the ground and just overwatch. We can also go kinetic by giving the jets the 9 Liner and the talk on to drop bombs on to specific targets. You get trained to a very high standard and most of last year I spent on exercise and also in America. It took me about 8 -9 months to train to be out here for this specific role. In reality I think that's too short, you really need over 12 months just to get your head around things.

Because of my guns (Royal Artillery) background I've spent a lot of time out on the ground with Charlie Company. I've been attached to the snipers, FSG, Charlie Coy TAC and I've been out on the Jackals as well. It's been good.

We put Joint Tactical Air Requests in before we go out on the ground – for any fast air assets or any UAV assets we need and then failing that, if there isn't anything up in the air and we do come under contact, I get on the radio and declare an Air TIC. Once an Air TIC is declared they will push any fast air that's in the area straight to my call sign and help the troops in contact.

What has been your most memorable moment?
I'd say dropping the first bomb, because that's what you get trained to do. It was also quite worrying at times as well, because you want everything to go alright, you want the bomb to go in the right place. The control was very by the book and it went where I wanted it. When

I dropped the bomb I was quite happy that there were no civilians in the area because we'd been in the area for 3 days, there was very minimal civilian movement, once we moved into the area you could see the women and children move out of the area.

Acting Sergeant Chris Halton (26), from Pontefract, Army Photographer, Royal Logistics Corps

I have have been a professional Army Photographer since 2006. I was sent to Afghanistan in 2009 as a SNCO to work in the Public Affairs Office (PAO) in Regional Command (South). Although this was not my first operational tour, it was the first time I had been deployed as a photographer.

During my tour in Afghanistan I was attached to the 3 SCOTS BG on numerous occasions to document the work that they did on operations as well as more local events such as handover ceremonies and repatriations. Although this was not a direct role for me, the BG often requested that I join them for such operations as PANCHAI PALANG and TORA ARWA.

The most challenging aspect for me was working on the ground with an infantry battalion as I had never had the opportunity to do so before. Being a trained soldier is one thing but working with the infantry as a photographer meant I had to be self sufficient and not a burden to them whilst trying to do my job. I was there to photograph and capture the events as they unfolded and to tell the story of the men and women trying to help make a change in the lives of the Afghanistan population, and this meant I had to be aware of what was going on around me at all times. I had to know the inner workings of each and every section and platoon of the BG. Sometimes this was under very dangerous circumstances such as being under contact. I saw the emotions on the faces of those that have lost friends and I saw how it made them stronger and brought them all closer together as a family.

I learnt a lot from my time with the 3 SCOTS BG. I got to see first hand the hard work that everybody goes through from the rifleman that is on sentry to the medics that are tested daily with new injuries and illnesses. I saw how a young 19 year old rifleman grows into a more mature solider within just a few weeks because of everything he has experienced and I was able to go through the same experiences with them. The BG looked after me every step of the way while I invaded their life and their space, to be able to do my job. After just a couple of days, I trusted these soldiers with my life and I would have followed them anywhere, knowing I was amongst some of the very best trained soldiers in the British Army.

Chapter Twelve

Operation BURS SIMI Pulse 1 & 2

9 – 10 & 14 October 2009

INTRODUCTION

Operation BURS SIMI Pulse 1 was the first of 2 company level pulses conducted in October and in line with the over arching Operation BURS SIMI series, of which the Battle Group took part in September 09. Alpha Company was tasked to the village of Do'Ab, Sangin, approximately 2km north of Sangin District Centre and at the south end of the Musa Qal'eh Wadi.

Do'Ab was assessed to be situated on the insurgent transit route between Musa Qa'leh and Sangin. Reporting from previous operations also indicated that insurgents staged through the area in order to conduct operations in Sangin.

Alpha Company intended to conduct a pre-dawn aviation assault into Ops Box ATLEE. The company would initially seize its objective and then secure the target area; 1 Platoon was tasked to secure Objective CYCLOPS, 2 Platoon to secure Objective MEDUSA, and 3 Platoon to establish a screen in Objective SIREN. The goal of the operation was to stimulate insurgent activity and increase an understanding of the insurgent IED networks which would develop targets for future exploitation. The operation was scheduled over the period 9–10 October.

EXECUTION

9 October – 10 October 09 (D Day – D + 1)

The company lifted from Kandahar Airfield at 0230 hrs and arrived on target at 0330 hrs. At 0337 hrs, the Blackhawk helicopter that escorted the Chinooks observed insurgents departing 500m north of 3 Platoon's landing site. The insurgents, armed with small arms and RPG, were manoeuvring tactically through a tree line and attempting to flank 3 Platoon. The Apache helicopter continued to monitor the insurgents and at 0415 hrs engaged with its 30mm cannon and one missile.

The platoons took up positions in their objectives and waited for first light prior to conducting compound searches. At 1154 hrs, 1 Platoon in Objective CYCLOPS was engaged by heavy machine gun fire. The fire was highly accurate and pinned down rooftop sentries but no immediate firing point was identified. The sentries were forced to crawl off the roof due to the accuracy, weight and impact of the fire, with rounds penetrating the compound walls and sandbags. Close air support was brought on station and the heavy machine gun threat was mitigated. The remainder of the day the company continued with compound searches. At midnight, the company moved to its extraction point in the dash and had arrived in Kandahar Airfield at 0300 hrs.

SUMMARY

Operation BURS SIMI Pulse 1 met with limited direct insurgent action and restricted to one engagement by a heavy machine gun. Nonetheless, the operation had the desired effect of sparking an insurgent reaction which was targeted by ISTAR. The operation also flushed out insurgents from their bed down locations to the immediate north of Do'Ab which were successfully prosecuted.

Operation BURS SIMI was the last deliberate operation conducted by Alpha Company. However, the company was deployed one last time on 14 October. During an operation conducted by Afghan Forces in the area of Malmand Chinah, a Chinook helicopter made a hard landing damaging rotor blades and rupturing the fuel tank. The company was tasked to provide protection until the Chinook could be extracted. The company deployed on the ground at 1005 hrs and established a defensive perimeter around the helicopter. Initially, another Chinook helicopter attempted to lift the damaged helicopter but was unsuccessful. Also, during the attempted lift the company was engaged by insurgents. At 1630 hrs a MI26 helicopter successfully lifted the helicopter and the company extracted from the area at 1752 hrs.

Two snipers and members of the Fire Support Group observing the ground around them from the roof of a compound. (MOD – Sgt C Halton)

The CH47 having made an emergency landing is unable to fly and therefore is guarded by A Coy while it is prepared for lifting.

Another CH47 attempts to lift the stricken Chinook.

Finally the CH47 is rescued by a Mi-26.

Op BURS SIMI – One last Op – Personal Account – Captain Samuel Newson (28), from Prestwood, Buckinghamshire, Second in Command Alpha (Grenadier) Company

The company had done its last operation; we had waited patiently in the dasht for our last helicopter pick up, boarded the Chinooks with no small amount of relief and headed back to Kandahar for the last time. There was undoubtedly a little disappointment that we had been on our last outing though we could all now relax and look to returning home.

Of course things never pan out as expected. A Chinook had landed hard in a wadi not far from Sangin, the troops aboard had the area secured but were not configured to hold the ground for any length of time.

We were still the divisional reserve so one more operation beckoned. I will admit for a moment I was angry, I didn't want to go out again. We had all made it and I just wanted to go home. But that passed quickly and we all set to preparing for the off.

Having prepared the company and snatched a few hours sleep we were ferried into the area to take over. We landed and had a quick chat with the in situ commander before dispersing the troops to the high ground to overwatch the Chinook and mitigate the threat from the nearby village. A downed helicopter attracts a fair amount of enemy attention and the radio scanners suggested that during the night upward of 40 fighters had gathered in the nearby village.

The snipers as ever proved useful fixing the enemy and preventing movement. The attack helicopters and A10 ground attack planes circling also prosecuted a number of targets who could have threatened the helicopter. The aircraft recovery team worked hard to extract the Chinook, with a huge Russian helicopter being called in to lift the weighty fuselage. The Jocks swept up some of the larger pieces including the rotors and we lifted off to get back to Kandahar. The whole job lasted around 9 hours and turned out to be a rather fun last job.

It is testament to the company as a whole that we could switch from preparing to return home to flying into unknown territory within hours, the Jocks unfazed by the change in direction and eager to get out for one last chance to battle the enemy.

Op BURS SIMI – Stepping Up – Lance Corporal Scott McFadden (22), from Kirkaldy, Alpha (Grenadier) Company

Prior to training for Afghanistan I was told I would be stepping up to be a Section 2IC for HERRICK 10. At first I was not sure what it was going to be like but I was looking forward to the task in hand.

We went to Kenya and that was the first time I really got to do the job I had been asked to do. Every day you do the job, the easier it gets. At first I was a little unsure if the guys in my section were going to do anything I had asked them to do because I was the same rank as them but they just got on with it and done the things that needed doing. Now deployed on Op HERRICK 10, I find the job has its ups and downs like everything else in life. For example on the tour I was given acting rank which meant I got paid more money but now I'm always on the re-supply as that is the 2IC's job to go and get the kit.

The op I remember most was in Babaji as part of PANCHAI PALANG. We were on a patrol heading back to meet the rest of the Company and get set up for the night. It was a really hot day reaching around 50 degrees and the guys in my section were feeling the heat especially with the weight of the kit they were carrying. The further on we went the hotter it seemed to get and then one of the guys collapsed. He was in a bad way and needed to be extracted, so as the Section 2IC I had to make sure his kit was handed over and everything we needed was there. Once the kit was distributed we were ready to set off again. We came across a small river and most guys managed to get over it without getting wet. I misjudged the width of the river and the weight of my kit and ended up falling in. Looking back it was quite funny but at the time I 'snapped', wishing I was not the Section 2IC and had not took that extra kit.

LCpl Scott McFadden from Kirkcaldy, Alpha Coy.

Now at the end of our tour, packing up our things to go, I will soon hand back my acting rank and have the JNCO Cadre to look forward to at the start of next year to train me to become a Section 2IC. With my experience I will hopefully pass that and I can come and do this job all over again!

Op BURS SIMI - Living in the Field in Afghanistan – Private Vincent Byrne (32), from Banff, 2 Platoon, Alpha (Grenadier) Company

There are many things that separate humans from animals, one of the main differences being our ability to survive in any climate on any continent in the world. It is this adaptability that ensures soldiers can function and carry out their duties to their full extent, for example whilst living in the field in Southern Afghanistan.

From the moment your chopper drops you off you are self supportive in sometimes extreme conditions. Whether the temperature is above 50 degrees Celsius or the rain is driving down in sheets, whatever you carry in your day-sack is all that you have till you get picked up again. The kit is heavy, and there is normally only minimum room for comfort kit to last for the duration, that's if you are lucky.

During the day the heat can become unbearable to work in, so finding shade in a compound through the hottest hours is a must. This gives the guys a chance to rest and re-hydrate and can also reduce the amount of heat illnesses sustained.

Compounds are also a good place to set up for an overnight stay and a well chosen one can give good protection from the elements, a chance to remove helmets and most importantly, good sentry positions for all round defence at night.

In cooler months 6 litres of water is adequate per day but during summer months at least 8 litres need to be carried. The addition of a Life Saving Bottle or Survival Straw per section is needed in case the next replen is delayed. There is normally plenty of water available though from local sources but usually the colour of it is enough to turn all but a thirsty soldier away.

Warm climate ration packs are a blessing: no more melted chocolate before you get the chance to eat it and the difference in choice can lift morale for soldiers new to the field. Eventually though, the paper menus at the top of the box are grabbed and the favourite boxes are gone leaving some poor soul with bean salad for lunch AGAIN!!! If you deploy by air assault, re-supplies normally occur daily to replenish food, water and broken kit where possible but if you are vehicle mounted you will need to carry it all with you.

To carry this burden, along with ammo, HE, radios, night sights, ECM, batteries, socks, wash/shave kit, marking kits, stretchers, team medic packs, cleaning kits, torches and the rest, a good quality day-sack with a chest strap is advised. The strap helps stop the weight constantly pulling your shoulders back and considering most soldiers carry upwards of 40 kilograms in their day-sack alone, this item is a must. Add to this body armour, helmet, weapon and the intense dryness and heat, fitness tests at home seem a walk in the park albeit a long way away.

The body armour itself, although weighty soon becomes un-noticeable, that is until you need to try and climb a wall or get in a decent fire position to start fighting the enemy. Unfortunately it isn't too compatible with the Mk6a helmet as it stops squaddies getting their heads right back when in prone position. Sunglasses with different coloured lenses are required too, not just to darken the surroundings during the day but also protection from fragmentation and from all the dust and debris kicked up when the helicopter flies low over your head to extract you after a long few days or weeks out on the ground.

The main thing though that keeps you going, and which is seen both in the green zone in Helmand and on the plains of Salisbury, is the camaraderie between the troops that exists even in the toughest of environments. With all the kit we carry, it's this simple thing that probably makes it all bearable.

Op BURS SIMI – My time with The Black Watch, 3rd Battalion Royal Regiment of Scotland – Private Graham Johnson (22) a Territorial Army soldier from Inverness, Mortar Platoon, Charlie Company

Writing this as I am at the close of the tour – after having returned body armour, ammunition and morphine – I am wholly grateful for the opportunity of serving with undoubtedly one of the finest Infantry Regiments in the world. Much is said of the closeness of Scottish Soldiers and their renowned spirit, not that other regiments do not have spirit in equal measure but the sum of the parts seem to add up to more. The historical reasons of fighting for pride and upholding the honour of family, village and clan are infused in the Scottish Soldier today; though in a subconscious manner, seemingly the spirit lives with the Regiment, simply through the very being of the Regiment and its history. I am not a military historian, therefore, other than make this observation on reflection of my experiences, I shall not dwell. It is not something I would have been able to comment on first hand had I not served and experienced the events during training for and then an operational tour such as we have had on Op HERRICK 10 with 19 Brigade.

There have been many aspects of this tour that have given insights into myself and others, the workings of the Army as it currently is, the uniqueness of the Army's regimental system and The Royal Regiment of Scotland. Sometimes we have cried, more often than not laughed. We have lost friends both fatally and with very serious injury. A lot has been in the press about the "war", and about "heroes" but in our absence it has perhaps gone unnoticed by ourselves. Likewise the general public is guided by what is written or shown in the media. Too much may have been made of too little, misguiding rather than guiding opinion. It is impossible to truly describe to the public quite what the circumstances we work in are – as is evident by the line of questioning by reporters whom declare themselves "experts" in their field. It is good that the Armed Forces and its tasks have become a subject for public discussion moreover than the discussion of the political will behind the Army's deployments, but some of the discussions need to remain in the private domain. I for one do not think of anyone as a hero. People in the Army are not any different to people leading civilian lives with regards heroic deeds. We are no more heroic than anyone who has served in the Army in any of the previous decades it has been in existence. When an Army is deployed it will suffer casualties - this should not be a surprise to the press or public. Armies have always had to adapt to what kit they need, and what tactics they need and when they do the enemy adapts himself likewise to counter this new materiel or threat - and so the cycle continues.

I have thoroughly enjoyed my time serving in this Regiment, should I ever deploy with another I do not think it will quite live up to my expectations, there not being a finer Regiment in existence. I have enjoyed serving in Afghanistan, and hope that a political will of strong support continues from the international community, and the Afghan people to continue with the development and growth of its democratic society. The locals I have met certainly deserve more than they are getting, and will I am sure help themselves where they can to improve basic living standards for all. It is a land of opportunity.

Corporal Bob Meredith (30), from Newburgh, Fife, A Combat HR Specialist, Adjutant General's Corps (Staff and Personnel Support)

Although I was based primarily in Camp ROBERTS, Kandahar within the Regimental Administrative Office, I was given the opportunity by my Company Commander, Major Munro, to deploy out on the ground. I deployed on one of the operations alongside the

Cpl Bob Meredith (far right), A Combat HR Specialist attached to A Coy, with members of his Coy on return from the operation.

infantrymen in my company. It was an exhilarating experience and gave me first hand experience of what the Jocks and attached arms experience outside of the wire. My role as a Combat HR Specialist is essential in providing the administrative support needed by the soldiers in my unit, for example ensuring they receive their pay on time, their allowances are correct and any welfare related matters are dealt with quickly and sensitively. It was an honour to serve with the 3 SCOTS BG, especially on operations in such a busy and challenging environment.

The Battle Captain – Regimental Signals Officer, Captain Alastair Colville, from Perthshire

The majority of the time spent in the operations room is simply monitoring the ongoing operation and providing support to the watchkeeper who is silently logging everything that goes on. The room has been likened to a large chicken hut due to the American habit of constructing everything from wooden frames covered in plywood. Despite the agricultural look it is wired up with up to 6 Satellite radios, a secure satellite phone and many computer systems allowing us to talk to all the different nations in theatre.

Everyone faces one wall as if to confirm the concentration on the current situation. There are 3 50 inch TV screens beaming the latest situation. Each Battle Captain brings his own style and manner to the room for his period on duty. Some are compulsively tidy and some less so, but all retain a firm grip on the current situation.

The normal routine is occasionally interrupted by the imposition of Op MINIMISE. This is the controlled suspension of communications home when a casualty is taken somewhere in theatre. As the single point of truth for the Battle Group the watchkeeper has the task of confirming the imposition with Camp ROBERTS. In the Ops room it will raise interest and as the details flow like a chatroom window on a big screen people drift in and out asking the news. Pained faces normally appear as the details of the injuries are read from the screen. No names are given and everyone quietly checks to see which unit has suffered.

Having sat beside the screen for the duration of the tour, lines like '…triple amputee, no radial pulse…' have become sadly commonplace. It never lessens the horrendous feeling in the pit of your stomach when you pause for a second and think

what that means. If he survives, and there have been amazing stories of recovery, the poor man will spend the rest of his life with horrendous injuries. Either way a family will be getting some very bad news soon. The reminders of sacrifices made are ever-present.

The sound of 'Contact, casualties, wait out' has been heard from the radio speakers a few times. There follows what seems like an eternity as everyone in the Ops room yearns for the information so that they can help speed up the process of evacuation. A calm silence descends and the key officers are informed. The Battle Captain checks the accuracy of grids and sends the information to RC(S) who task the helicopters. It is difficult but very important to present a calm voice on the net and reassure that you are, of course, doing everything possible to get the helicopter there as soon as possible. The relief when the casualty is lifted is tempered by the need to start the paperwork for any serious incident and these are always best filled in straight away.

Casualties are not the only incidents and the successes have been numerous; be they destroying insurgents who have been firing at the Jocks, finding IED parts or denying large amounts of drugs. It is the human aspect to the casualties which makes them so sadly memorable. Soon the calm hum of the air conditioning reclaims the position as the soundtrack of the ops room.

Chapter Thirteen

Life in Kandahar

KANDAHAR AIRFIELD

Kandahar Airfield is a chaotic multinational base. Almost every NATO nation has representation including British, American, Canadian, French, Dutch, Danish, Slovakian, Bulgarian, Hungarian, and Czech troops, and there is even a Malaysian officer who works in Regional Command (South) Headquarters. In addition, many of the workers are recruited from Nepal, Sri Lanka, Philippines, and India.

Regional Command (South) controls and commands Southern Afghanistan from its headquarters in Kandahar Airfield. Also located in the airfield is Task Force Kandahar headquarters, the Canadian brigade that controls Kandahar Province. However, the heart of Kandahar Airfield is known as "The Boardwalk" which consists of a number of stores and fast food restaurants such as Burger King, Pizza Hut, Subway, and Tim Horton's. At the centre of the boardwalk are volleyball courts, a basketball court, and a dry hockey rink, as well as a stage that is used for numerous concerts and performances.

Kandahar Airfield is constantly expanding and growing and underwent major changes in the summer as the US Army Stryker Brigade deployed from the camp and the US Army Combat Aviation Brigade (CAB), which provided a significant helicopter capacity, took up residence on the airfield. The sandy ground in the west of the airfield had been replaced by rows upon rows of American Humvees and armoured engineering equipment. In addition, when the Battle Group first arrived in Kandahar Airfield the foundations for the Role 3 Hospital were being poured, however, by the time the unit left the building structure was complete, bricks were being placed on the external walls and the lighting and electrical cables were being installed. Also, the gravel roads of the airfield that covered the soldiers in dust as they marched to the central cookhouses had been covered by tarmac by the end of the tour.

Also, a number of the original buildings of Kandahar International Airport that were built in the 1960s and predate the Taliban and Soviet control can still be found on the airfield. Kandahar Airfield Headquarters is housed in a building named the Taliban Last Stand (TLS), as the building proved to be the last position held by the Taliban in the area.

Finally, one cannot fail to mention the stench of rot that dominates the airfield. The sewage facilities were unable to fully support the large number of people living on the airfield.

CAMP ROBERTS

Camp ROBERTS was the centre of the Battle Group's life. Named after Major Alexis Roberts, who was killed in 2007 while serving with 1st Battalion The Royal Gurkha Rifles, it provided the Battle Group with an essential centre for activity in which all members of the Battle Group were accommodated. Various departments, such as the Quartermaster's Department, the Mechanised Transport Platoon and staff from the Adjutant General's Corps were all based in Camp ROBERTS. The camp provided a location for the Battle Group to conduct rehearsals, while the companies maintained offices where orders were delivered. The camp also acted as a staging area where troops would assemble prior to a deployment and in which resupply loads was prepared.

Physical fitness was a priority while the troops were not on operations and Camp ROBERTS provided room to conduct physical fitness and also housed a gym consisting of free weights, a weight machine as well as treadmills, cross trainers, and spin bikes. Also, welfare

A typical bed space in Camp ROBERTS. Very comfortable compared to those conditions when deployed forward.

The BG was augmented by 46 members of the Territorial Army.
They performed numerous tasks across all parts of the BG.
(Maj G Shaw)

The 3 SCOTS Padre, Capt David Anderson with the Jocks as he hands out the welfare parcels in Camp Roberts. *(Maj G Shaw)*

Physical training was conducted in Camp Roberts and Camp BASTION in between operations. There was also excellent gym facilities in both locations for all troops, available 24 hours a day. *(Maj G Shaw)*

facilities such as telephones, computers with internet access, and televisions were all available in Camp ROBERTS.

In addition, a tent was dedicated as a chapel and was consecrated by the Padre as St Andrews in the Field. It was from the chapel that the welfare parcels were distributed. The chapel also took on the role of a classroom that was used by Lieutenant Mike Goodall to provide the Jocks with important educational qualifications.

Camp ROBERTS also hosted many guests of the Battle Group including the Secretary of State for Defence, Mr Bob Ainsworth.

BATTLE GROUP MAIN HEADQUARTERS

Battle Group Main Headquarters was located in the Regional Command (South) Compound and consisted of the operations room, the planning room, and the intelligence cell. The Battle Group Chief of Staff, Major Robin Lindsay, managed the operation of the headquarters and coordinated support for the troops while deployed. Major Rupert Whitelegge was double hatted as OC Charlie Company and the BG Operational Plans Officer. He played a key liaison role with all the staff in the Regional Command (SW) HQ, setting the conditions for the BG's next operations in terms of programming the resources required. He was replaced mid way through the tour on posting, by Major Ali Hempenstall. Main headquarters stayed in touch with the troops on the ground through a vast array of telecommunication equipment that was maintained by the members of the Communication Information Systems Platoon. Daily briefs took place in the planning room and this was also the location in which battle group orders were delivered.

A1 Echelon staff in Camp BASTION. Although based initially in Kandahar, the BG's A1 Echelon staff frequently deployed outside the wire on operations, including from Camp BASTION.

Capt Brian Cooper QM(T) and Capt Michael "Titch" Robb MTO with a day's supply for the Battle Group in the field.
(Maj G Shaw)

LCpl Vunibobo, the 3 SCOTS BG postman.
(Maj G Shaw)

A Combat Critical Load being hooked up to a CH 47 Chinook helicopter.

QUARTERMASTER'S DEPARTMENT

Although the role of the Quartermaster's Department is traditionally centred on logistical nodes such as Kandahar Airfield and Camp BASTION, the difficulties faced by the Quartermaster and his troops in providing essential life support to the deployed Battle Group cannot be underestimated.

Resupply was necessary every 24 hours as the Jocks were unable to carry more than a day's worth of rations and water as a result of the heavy loads of radios, ECM, ammunition, and body armour. In order to be resupplied, troops on the ground established effective communication with the headquarters in Kandahar Airfield. The companies requested water, rations, batteries, ammunition, and replacement equipment for what had been damaged or destroyed during the day; Battle Group planners estimated the water consumption rate to between 8 - 10 litres a day per man. The Company Quartermaster Sergeants and their crew would then assemble the resupply demand in Camp ROBERTS into combat configured loads. These palletized loads were subsequently brought down to the airfield and rigged to be carried as under-slung loads beneath Chinook helicopters. Although this process was developed in Northern Ireland in order to resupply patrol bases, the process has been complicated by greater distances, extreme weather conditions, and different contributing nations that often have different methods of delivery as well as weight and size restrictions.

On operations such as PANCHAI PALANG, a logistical convoy of 55 vehicles deployed to transport the Battle Group's supplies. This convoy, called A1 echelon, was capable of sustaining the Battle Group for 5 days with all nature of supplies from foot powder to ammunition to water and rations. Ground resupply provided some challenges as the vehicles were limited to what sort of terrain that could be crossed and the necessity for protection for Jackals and Vikings.

WO2 (CSM) Paul Colville, WO1 (RSM) Lawrie McDougall, Cpl Lennard Maillet, MCpl Devin Batchelor, Sgt Bjorn Dittman, WO2 (CSM) Paul Dargavel, Lt Alex Phillips. *The 3 soldiers in the middle are all serving in The Black Watch (Royal Highland Regiment) of Canada.* (WO2 Dargavel)

Operational Mentoring and Liaison Team

MAJOR NIGEL JORDAN-BARBER
Officer Commanding, Delta Company

CONTEXT

D (Light) Company deployed to Afghanistan as an Operational Mentoring and Liaison Team (OMLT) to the Afghan National Army (ANA) on Op HERRICK 10. Initially commanded by Major Angus Philp, the Company was handed over, mid tour on his posting to Major Nigel Jordan-Barber. The OMLTs from across 19 (Light) Brigade were battle grouped under the Commanding Officer of 2nd Battalion Mercian (2 MERCIAN). The OMLT Battle Group was based at Camp TOMBSTONE, next to SHORABAK, the home of 3rd

Musa Qal'eh District Centre. (Sgt G Hogskins)

Brigade of 205 (Hero) Corps of the ANA, 3/205 Bde. The 3/205 area of responsibility was roughly equivalent to Task Force Helmand's (TFH). D (Light) Company was assigned OMLT 3 with the permanent callsign AMBER 30. The other OMLTs were provided by a variety of 19 (Light) Brigade infantry units augmented by Regular and Territorial officers and soldiers. OMLT 3 was assigned to mentor 3rd Kandak (Kdk) of 3rd Brigade (3/3/205 Kdk) in MUSA QA'LEH (MSQ) district of Helmand Province. 3/3/205 Kdk's area of operations was co-terminus with Battle Group (North West), initially 2 Royal Gurkha Rifles (RGR) and subsequently 2 Royal Regiment of Fusiliers(RRF).

OMLTs are employed as a means of developing the ANA as part of the Security Sector Reform programme, which aims to reform Afghanistan's security institutions in enabling them to play an effective, legitimate and accountable role in the internal and external security of their country. The functions of the OMLT include training, mentoring, liaising and enabling the ANA in the planning, resourcing and execution of routine and deliberate military operations. It should be noted that although OMLT does not include C for Command, from time to time our young officers were required to command and lead ANA Warriors either by necessity or circumstance. By its very nature the OMLTs are embedded within ANA units, and sub-units. D (Light) Company initially deployed as 5 teams to mentor the Kdk headquarters element (AMBER 30), 3 rifle companies (AMBER 31, 32 and 33) and the Heavy Weapons Company (AMBER 34). Very quickly it was clear that sustaining five teams would be very difficult and the opportunity to reduce down to 4 was seized when 3rd Kdk's Second Company was withdrawn back to SHOROBAK as a Brigade reserve company. The remaining four 10-man teams retained the majority of the D (Light) Company members although Captains Kennedy, Stanning and Harrison also from 3 SCOTS were employed as team commanders elsewhere in the OMLT BG, later accompanied by Captain McVey from The Royal

Building a roof sangar at Satellite Station North. (Sgt G Hogskins)

Lt Russell Doughty in his mentoring role with the Afghan National Army. (Sgt G Hogskins)

Highland Fusiliers, 2 SCOTS with Sergeant Watling (7 SCOTS) and Lance Corporal Watt (3 SCOTS) in support.

AMBER 30's role was to mentor the Kandak headquarters element, with the OC responsible for the Commander and senior officers, the CSM (as an acting RSM) responsible for the RSM and Senior NCOs, the Company 2IC for the operations and intelligence staffs. The remainder of the team played an essential part in the smooth running of the Kandak, for example liaising with medical and supply staffs to prepare the Kandak for operations. The key figure in the Kandak was clearly the Commander, Colonel Mohammed Rasoul Kandahari. A gruff, likeable bear of a man, he was a Mujahedin fighter during the Soviet occupation, and was at one time a prisoner of the Taliban. Colonel Rasoul's fierce reputation was well-respected by the mentors and the British Battle Group, and from time to time it appeared his men feared him more than they feared the Taliban. Joining him on operations was an experience in itself: always keen to be leading his men from the front he was sometimes between his own men and the insurgents at the height of the fighting. He enjoyed a joke and smile at the most bizarre moments, and was always keen to tease the British for their lack of tactical speed because we carried too much kit. The Kandak was very well led and trained by him, but was let down by a horrifically inefficient supply system which struggled to provide sufficient stocks of anything.

AMBER 32, commanded by Captain Olly Lever, mentored 1st Company to the north of the District at Satellite Station North (SSN), a purpose-built base, with good facilities and plenty of space. SSN dominated the interface between the green zone and the desert to the north east of MSQ. Routinely attacked with small-arms and indirect weapons, the team in SSN were truly on the front-line from the beginning of the tour. In spite of being short of a formal company commander, 1st Company was ably commanded by 2 junior officers who shared the responsibility and established fantastic working relationships with the OMLT.

LCpl 'Chuck' Brady of Amber 32. (Sgt G Hogskins)

LCpl Brady's 'Hell's Kitchen' – LCpl 'Kenny' Everett and LCpl 'Chuck' Brady cooking in satellite station North – LCpl Brady cooked every night as it helped pass the time. (Sgt G Hogskins)

Accommodation in satellite station North. (Sgt G Hogskins)

AMBER 33, under command of Acting Captain Tom O'Sullivan with Sergeant McLeod as 2IC were allocated to 3rd Company in the west and south west of the District. They were initially based at Patrol Base South West (PBSW), in the small village of GHUND KALAY. PBSW was a small base centred on a civilian compound with some purpose-built force protection sangars and barriers. Although 'embedded', the team had their own living space within the PB. Conditions were fairly cramped, with one small room serving as operations room, cookhouse, medical centre and welfare area. In the manner of all Jocks on any operations their means of improving their lot was provided by a self-funded satellite television receiver, pumping out Iranian and Pakistani channels, as well as the odd English language gem. Following Operation MAR LEWE 2, AMBER 33 moved further south to Patrol Base TALIBJAN named after the RSM of 3rd Kdk who was killed in action fighting insurgents during our tour. PB TALIBJAN was another small compound, but doubled in size by a large Hesco Bastion wall with sangars, and purpose-built "habs" for all the accommodation and living areas. An al fresco dining room was set up, designed and built by Captain O'Sullivan and Sergeant Frodsham. During the period of the build at PB TALIBJAN the team had to live amongst the ANA; this proved to be very challenging. However culturally aware we would care to claim to be, living in the personal space of another soldier is probably stressful enough, but doing so with the inevitable collision of two vastly different cultures proved to be very difficult indeed. Far from improving relationships, the enforced closeness provided lots of friction which eroded the goodwill on both sides.

AMBER 34, under command of Acting Captain Doughty, and later Mr Hieghton-Jackson, started their tour in Patrol Base YUBRAJ with Heavy Weapons Company in the south and south east of the District. They moved to Patrol Base ATAL to the southern end of the village of YATIMCHAY following Op MAR LEWE 1. ATAL was by far the least developed PB, with very little in the means of purpose-built force protection, although Afghan mud-walled compounds are extremely resilient.

Amber 34 playing volleyball in US patrol base. (Sgt G Hogskins)

The Death of Acting Sergeant Sean Binnie

On 7 May 2009, AMBER 32, commanded by Captain Lever deployed from SSN to conduct a domination patrol in the area of TOWGHI KELI known as the Desert Compounds to the north east of the PB. The patrol was in support of a deliberate operation on the West side of the MUSA QA'LEH wadi, in order to deter the enemy from interdicting the operation which was assessed to be at risk from an enemy ambush from the area of TOWGHI KELI. During the advance North by AMBER 32, AMBER 30 took up an overwatch position on MOSQUE HILL. At around 1000 hrs, it was reported that an enemy activity in the area was increasing, and that IEDs had been put out to delay ISAF troops.

At 1058 hrs, AMBER 32 was approached by 6 local nationals on motorbikes. When they failed to stop warning shots were fired. Shortly afterwards the ISAF observation post at ROSHAN TOWER positively identified enemy fighters on a feature known as BUNKER HILL and at 1116 hrs engaged a group of enemy fighters with JAVELIN and 105mm Light Gun in the direct fire role. At 1120 hrs as AMBER 32 moved through a series of alleyways the ANA surprised a group of enemy who fled north, at which point the ANA and ANP gave chase. In doing do, they became isolated and were soon pinned down by enemy fire in one of the

Amber 32 preparing a model, in satellite station North, for a Company level operation. (Sgt G Hogskins)

Amber 32 on patrol. *(Sgt G Hogskins)*

compounds, taking 2 casualties in the process. It was also reported that 4 of the ANA had been captured. AMBER 32 pushed forward, with Sergeant Binnie in the lead. Captain Lever was told that the ANA advance and clearance had stalled because they were short of grenades. Captain Lever drew a grenade and was about to go forward when Sergeant Binnie, calmly but firmly, said "give it here, Boss", then went to deal with the enemy himself. The situation was made more complex by the presence of women and children in the compounds and the building where Sergeant Binnie had identified the enemy. Sergeant Binnie had the presence of mind and discipline to clearly assess the situation and confirm the exact location of the enemy fighters. Despite also carrying ECM, Sergeant Binnie scaled a compound wall and placed Lance Corporal Everett to cover his final approach. With enemy fire still coming from the building, he moved along the wall and posted a grenade through the compound doorway, sustaining a fatal gunshot wound as he did so. The grenade killed the 2 enemy inside and proved the turning point of the battle. Lance Corporal Everett followed up and cleared the remnants of the enemy from the position before the enemy broke contact, allowing the ANA and ANP to extract in good order and without sustaining further casualties.

The Memorial Service of Sgt Binnie led by Padre David Anderson. Colonel Greville Bibby, Deputy Commander Task Force Helmand, Maj Angus Philp, OC Delta Coy and the RSM WO1 Dougall are to the Padre's right.

Op MAR LEWE Phase 1

Op MAR LEWE Phase 1 was launched on 29 May 2009, following a joint Afghan National Security Forces (ANSF) and ISAF planning process. The plan was to clear and then hold the village of YATIMCHAY to the south of MUSA QA'LEH District Centre, accomplished by fixing the insurgents in YATIMCHAY itself whilst putting a screen into the east and a feint to the west and then clearing the village in detail. The 'hold' was to be achieved by placing Heavy Weapons Company and AMBER 34 into the village, in a new PB, to be known as ATAL. The 'hold' would allow the influence of the Government of the Islamic Republic of Afghanistan (GIROA) to be extended further away from the MUSA QA'LEH District Centre.

The operation for the OMLT started with a night move by vehicle and on foot into an assembly prior to moving to assault the village. The ANA exploited any opportunity to kill insurgents and it proved very difficult for the OMLT to be able to identify the Forward Line of Own Troops (FLOT) as small fire-fights broke out in all areas: the major problem was deconflicting own forces' fires to support the assault. Furthermore the inherent difficulty of being such a small team was demonstrated when only 12 mentors were required to keep an eye on and 'control' over 160 ANA warriors and ANP soldiers. The biggest problem, however proved to be OMLT tactical mobility on foot, burdened down by our personal protective equipment, electronic counter-measures, radios, ammunition and water. One of the major successes beyond the pure tasks of clearing and holding YATIMCHAY was the discovery of 2 major improvised explosive device (IED) factories in the village, including numerous designs not yet seen in the province

Op MAR LEWE Phase 2

Op MAR LEWE Phase 2 began on 10 August 2009 to re-balance the FLOT in the south of MUSA QA'LEH District. The success of the establishment of PB ATAL and subsequently PB MINDEN had been determined, but the laydown of troops in the District was out of kilter. In the south east, GIROA influence extended some 6 km from MUSA QA'LEH whilst in the south west only 3km. The intent for Op MAR LEWE Phase 2 was to establish 2 new patrol bases to the south of the FARADH MANDHA Wadi approximately 6km from MUSA QA'LEH. The joint ANSF and ISAF operation followed an extensive period of planning, and the tasks were allocated to C Company 2 RRF to launch an assault to clear the village of SHAH MUSH SHILA (SMS) from the north across the wadi, and to secure the high ground to the south of the wadi and the 3rd Kandak to clear the village of DEH ZOHR SOFLA (DZS) and then link up with C Company on the high ground. The hold would be achieved by establishing 2 PBs to be manned by 3rd Company.

LBdr Greening (left) and Bdr 'Robbo' Robson of 40 Regt RA – Members of the OMLT Fire Support Team – LBdr Greening was later shot in the back during Op MAR LEWE 2 but was saved by his body armour plate. (Sgt G Hogskins)

CSgt Beaton dishing out the Werther's Originals
to a local national boy. (Sgt G Hogskins)

Unmentored ANP, Heavy Weapons Company (AMBER 34) and 3rd Company (AMBER 33) moved on foot from Patrol Base South West (PBSW) and moved into a Forming Up Point (FUP) to the north of DZS, closely followed by the Kandak HQ and AMBER 30. During the move into the FUP lights were spotted in SMS and it was assessed that the insurgents were aware of the upcoming assaults. When the companies broke into DZS they found many compounds which had been prepared as fighting positions, but for some reason the Taliban chose not to fight. The ANA and ANP moved very quickly through the village and concentrated on a couple of compounds which had been used to fire mortars and rockets at MUSA QA'LEH District Centre in the previous couple of days. After a very successful and quick clearance of the village the Kandak joined up with C Company. Two compounds at the southern tip of DZS were chosen to become a joint ANP and ANA checkpoint, to be named MOHIB after an ANA soldier killed in action, and a further compound to the south of SMS was chosen to be Patrol Base TALIBJAN, named after the 3rd Kandak's RSM killed alongside MOHIB.

Whilst PB TALIBJAN was being established that afternoon it came under a period of sustained indirect fire, which coupled with small-arms fire and rocket attacks over the next week, set the tone for the occupation and hold of the high ground without significant resistance from the insurgents.

Op MAR ZINA – ANA Clearance of Ahmad Khwazi

PB TALIBJAN was established on the high ground to the south of the FARADH MANDHA Wadi following the success of OP MAR LEWE Phase 2 to rebalance the FLOT to the south of the BG(NW) AO. For the next week PB TALIBJAN came under effective small arms and indirect fire attacks by day and night from compounds in the east and south east. ANA intelligence assessed that the village of AHMAD KHWAZI, to the east of PB TALIBJAN, was the focal point of insurgent activity against PB TALIBJAN, and the ANSF checkpoint to the south of DEH ZOHR SOFLA, CP MOHIB. During the fighting on the night of 17 August 09 an ANP soldier was killed during an attack on CP MOHIB.

On 18 August 09 3rd Kandak led a deliberate joint operation to clear AHMAD KHWAZI. 3rd Coy would advance to contact from the north, deliberately diverting insurgent attention in order to allow Heavy Weapons Company and a platoon from 2 R WELSH at PB MINDEN to cross the MUSA QA'LEH Wadi and occupy a blocking position to the south of the village. 3rd Coy would then clear the village from north to south, concentrating on 2 objectives, SILVER and GOLD, clusters of compounds at the southern edge of the village. At 0800 hrs, 3rd Coy accompanied by AMBER 33 entered the village from the north, and immediately came under effective small arms fire. In the initial confusion the ANA company commander lost control of his troops, but the situation was recovered by Captain O'Sullivan who gathered the remnants of the company and led an assault against the first enemy position. Immediately, Heavy Weapons Company accompanied by AMBER 34 crossed the wadi in order to occupy the blocking position. They were followed by the R WELSH armoured infantry platoon whose dismounted element provided a block facing south to prevent insurgent reinforcement, whilst the armoured vehicles remained in the wadi to secure the route back to PB MINDEN.

Following the first contact, 3rd Coy positively identified 2 enemy fighters moving south through the village and engaged in an aggressive pursuit which led to them bouncing a further 2 enemy prepared positions. On reaching the Objective SILVER, 3rd Coy conducted a succession of hard knock entries, during which a grenade started a fire which in turn detonated a large cache of ammunition and explosives in a compound that was assessed to be a shop. Attention quickly turned to Objective GOLD, which required the company to cross 450 m of clear ground flanked by high maize and other crops. The assault to Objective GOLD was supported by ANA small arms fire support, and OMLT shoulder-mounted weapons. The clearance of Objective GOLD yielded approximately 500kg of ingredients for home-made explosives and other components, which was sufficient to make 25 IEDs. Shortly after Objective GOLD had been cleared, 3rd Company was suppressed by a huge weight of fire from the south. The firing points were in dead ground to the block and Heavy Weapons Company moved north in order to engage the insurgents. In the ensuing fight one enemy fighter and one Afghan National Police (ANP) officer were killed.

The Headquarters element of 3rd Kandak, accompanied by AMBER 30, now came into the fight clearing the ground between Objective GOLD and the block. Enemy resistance was strong and intensive fire-fights broke out all along the wadi edge and the area of the beach. The insurgents found themselves strong defensive positions in and about a kariz line (a series of ancient wells and irrigation boreholes) and slowed the clearance significantly. The Kandak commander personally led the assault on each identified enemy position, and the insurgents were quickly cut off between the advancing troops, the block and the Warriors in the wadi. The final enemy position proved to be the most difficult and the ANA requested OMLT assistance, at which point Colour Sergeant Smith, acting CSM for the OMLT, immediately volunteered and moved forward to clear the final enemy position using grenades.

In the immediate aftermath, it was clear that the clearance had accounted for at least 10 enemy forces killed in action, and 3 military aged males taken as prisoners. Only partially elated, the Kandak withdrew taking with them the heavy burden of their fallen ANP comrade. Heavy Weapons Company and the R WELSH platoon withdrew first taking the prisoners with them. The HQ element and 3rd Company then withdrew back to PB TALIBJAN. Approximately 45 minutes after clearing the area to the south of the village, AMBER 30 and AMBER 33 came under effective enemy fire to the rear from 3 firing points at ranges of between 50 and 200 m, approximately 1800 m short of PB TALIBJAN. During the course of this latest engagement, Lance Bombardier Greening, the signaller in AMBER 33's Fire Support Team was struck in the back by a rifle round, which penetrated his daysack and camelback but was stopped by the rear plate of his Osprey Body Armour. After attempting to break contact over 500 m of open ground, the Warriors assigned to protecting the Engineer build at PB TALIBJAN were called forward and they, with the liberal use of 105mm smoke, covered the remaining withdrawal.

Over the course of the next week PB TALIBJAN and CP MOHIB were not subjected to any insurgent attacks, indicating the successful nature of the clearance of AHMAD KHWAZI. What must be acknowledged that even after enduring the death of at least 10 of their fighters, the insurgents were willing and able to mount an effective harassing counter attack on the withdrawing troops. The following day the Afghan intelligence confirmed that 13 enemy fighters had been killed during the operation, but the 3 detainees were released due to lack of evidence.

D (Light) Coy was on the front-line of the insurgency for the entire tour, with very little respite, other than that won by heavy fighting and risky, but essential deliberate operations. All 4 teams in MSQ and the others across Helmand have been at the cutting edge of developing the ANA. Its continued success will be our legacy. By living, eating and fighting alongside the ANA warriors, we have made a significant contribution to the eventual success of Afghanistan as an independent state. What we must never forget are the personal sacrifices made by brave men like Sergeant Sean Binnie, those who have been wounded and our Afghan comrades, including the interpreters who were wounded and killed alongside. We know that the friendships and comradeship that have developed between the mentors and the warriors will last for a long time to come.

Rear Operations

The role of Rear Operations cannot be underestimated. While the remainder of the Battle Group was deployed to Kandahar Airfield and focussed on operations in Afghanistan, Rear Operations, under the command of Major David Bruce, remained in Fort George with a multitude of responsibilities.

One very important aspect of Rear Operations was to prepare individual soldiers to join the Battle Group in Afghanistan. Over 90 soldiers arrived in theatre after the initial deployment; some of these soldiers may have been under 18 and therefore not permitted to deploy until their birthdays, while others may have completed their basic training in the spring and therefore required appropriate pre-deployment training. External preparation included deployment training in the south east of England, mandatory annual tests in Aldershot, and range training in Northern Ireland.

An equally essential facet of Rear Operations was the responsibility to receive the members of the Battalion who were injured and killed during the tour. Under the guidance of the Unit Welfare Officer, Captain Lorne Campbell, hospital and home visits were organised for casualties and the families of soldiers killed in Afghanistan. Warrant Officer Class Two Kevin Stacey took the lead in conducting the funerals and he and his team were at RAF Brize Norton to receive each of the fallen soldiers.

One cannot forget the importance of "The Home Front" and the moral support that soldiers receive from their families. Moreover, the separation that exists during a tour is equally as difficult for those who remained at home as those deployed. The Unit Welfare Office took on a crucial pastoral role in nurturing the families of the Battle Group and organised numerous outings, activities and social events in Inverness. During the deployment, 8 family members were introduced to The Queen and The Duke of Edinburgh at the Culloden Visitor's Centre. Also, The Duke and Duchess of Rothesay visited Fort George and all in attendance were given the opportunity to visit the Royal Couple later in the summer.

Although the role of Rear Operations lacked the glamour and danger of operations in Afghanistan, it nonetheless provided a critical life support system for the soldiers in Kandahar Airfield and the families at home. The soldiers of the Rear Operation are recognised for their service by the remainder of the Battalion.

HRH The Duke of Rothesay chatting with the Commanding Officer's wife Susan Cartwright.
(Mr Mark Owens 2 Div MOD)

HRH The Duke of Rothesay chats to the rear party and families.
(Mr Mark Owens 2 Div MOD)

Rear row – Capts Mark McClelland-Jones, Pauline Murray-Knight and Lorne Campbell and 2Lt Andrew Heighton-Jackson
Front row – Lt Col (Ret) Roddy Riddell, Maj David Bruce, HRH The Duke of Rothesay, HRH The Duchess of Rothesay, Lt Gen (Ret) Sir Alistair Irwin KCB CBE.
(Mr Mark Owens 2 Div MOD)

Afterword

Lieutenant Colonel Stephen Cartwright, Commanding Officer

It was announced at the end of the October 2009 that the UK would no longer fill the RBG(S) role, as the manpower was to be reinvested into Helmand Province as part of a troop increase for Op HERRICK 11. The Battle Group remained on its reserve tasking until it returned to the UK in the first week of November.

After a 3 week period of leave, the Battalion reunited in Fort George in early December and entered a period of 'rehabilitation'. This period concentrates on the recovery and reconstitution of the individual as well as the Battalion's equipment. The first key event was a homecoming parade through Inverness, followed by a Service of Thanksgiving in Inverness Cathedral and a reception from the Lord Provost in the Town Hall. Despite the rain, the people of Inverness turned up in their thousands to show their support. This support was repeated the following week when the Battalion marched through Aberfeldy, Forfar, Kirkcaldy, Dunfermline, Dundee and finally in Perth, the traditional recruiting ground of the Battalion's antecedent Regiment, The Black Watch. Despite the seasonal fog and low temperatures, it was an amazing uplifting experience; the fierce burning pride of the Jocks was clear for all to see as their chests swelled as they heard, and then saw, the crowds that had turned up to cheer their return. The support that the people of Scotland have for its armed forces is genuine, strong and heartfelt.

After a second period of leave over Christmas, the Battalion's Royal Colonel, The Duke of Rothesay, his Royal Highness the Prince of Wales, along with Lieutenant General Graham, the Colonel of the Royal Regiment of Scotland and the Representative Colonel, Brigadier Riddell-Webster, presented the Battalion with their Afghanistan Medals on a freezing cold day in Fort George. The Duke of Rothesay also presented the new Elizabeth Crosses to the families of those killed on operations with us, and joined the soldiers and families for lunch and a

The Duke and Duchess of Rothesay pose for a photo with the rear party and families.
(Mr Mark Owens 2 Div MOD)

People of Inverness showing their appreciation for the Battalion on the first of the 7 home coming parades. (Mr Mark Owens 2 Div MOD)

Cpl "Biscuit" McLeod, Alpha (Grenadier) Company's Signals Detachment Commander.
(Mr Mark Owens 2 Div MOD)

Charlie (Fire Support) Company at the Aberfeldy Highlander after the Aberfeldy march. The Aberfeldy Highlander marks the spot where The 42nd Regiment of Foot (The Black Watch) first formed up in 1739 to form a regiment from the, already operational, independent Companies. (Mr Mark Owens 2 Div MOD)

The Battalion formed up in Fort George ready to receive their Afghanistan medals from HRH The Duke of Rothesay. (Maj G Shaw)

performance of the new 'Kandahar Reel' by the Officers' Mess. The dance was devised by Captain Andy Colquhoun and his cousin Lt Rob Colquhoun. The idea came during an initial period on standby operations where they developed ideas on the back of notebooks during pauses in the fighting. The double rotor blades of the Chinook helicopter and the single blades of the Black Hawk reminded them of the 'hands across' figure in dances and it was written with their fallen comrades very much in mind.

For those in the Battalion that were injured during the tour, the rehabilitation continues in earnest. The medical and welfare support to our injured is truly first class and that support will be in place for as long as the Battalion's soldiers require it.

The last Op HERRICK 10 event was the announcement of the Operational Honours and Awards. The Battalion's role in Afghanistan last summer was formally recognised with the Battalion picking up 19 awards. These included 4 Military Crosses (Lieutenant Phillips, Corporal Reynolds, Corporal Clarke and Corporal Sharpe) and 7 Mentioned in Despatches. Poignantly this included a posthumous Mention in Despatches for Acting Sergeant Sean Binnie, in recognition of his bravery in the face of the enemy which resulted in his death. A brief summary of some of the citations is included in the book.

The Pipes and Drums of The Black Watch, 3rd Battalion and the Band of The Royal Regiment of Scotland. (Maj G Shaw)

Members of the Royal Artillery, Royal Engineers and Royal Signals, who served with the Battalion in Afghanistan, march in the ranks. (Mr Mark Owens 2 Div MOD)

The Pipes and Drums of The Black Watch, 3rd Battalion lead the Battalion on 7 homecoming marches. (Mr Mark Owens 2 Div MOD)

The Colours are marched into the Cathedral to start the Homecoming Service, 3rd December 2009. (Mr Mark Owens 2 Div MOD)

HRH The Duke of Rothesay presenting Pte Staci Hynd AGC(SPS) with the Operational Service Medal. *(Mr Mark Owens 2 Div MOD)*

Mrs Jackie Smith, the Battalion's Civilian Office Manager, is presented the Commander In Chief's Commendation by HRH The Duke of Rothesay. *(Mr Mark Owens 2 Div MOD)*

The Battalion presents arms during the Royal salute to HRH The Duke of Rothesay. *(Mr Mark Owens 2 Div MOD)*

The WOs' and Sgts' Mess pose for a photo with HRH The Duke of Rothesay (Royal Colonel), Lt Gen Graham CBE (Regimental Colonel) and Brig Riddell-Webster DSO (Representative Colonel). (Mr Mark Owens 2 Div MOD)

Operations of course continue in Afghanistan, and the progress from the summer of 2009 is self evident. The gains from Operation PANTHER'S CLAW have been further developed by the UK's 11 Brigade during Operation MOSHTARAK, and more widely the US operations in Helmand have secured more of the Afghan population in Central Helmand. The increase of US forces will also put more ISAF forces into the North of Helmand in the Musa Qal'ah area and the Sangin valley. General McCrystal has announced that Kandahar Province will increasingly become the focus of ISAF attention, working in tandem as always with improvements to the economic development and governance. Each Battle Group operation in 2009 achieved tangible results at the time and these results are being built on as the campaign continues. Progress is being made.

There is little time to dwell on the events of the tour, although the military lessons have been recorded and personal experiences will be held in memory banks for many years. The Battalion's training programme for 2010 includes a period of training in Kenya in the summer before becoming the UK's Spearhead Lead Element Battalion for 6 months from September 2010. Every regular Battalion in the Royal Regiment of Scotland, supported by its 2 territorial Battalions, will be deploying to Afghanistan in the next 2 years. Some members of 3 SCOTS will deploy with the other Battalions less than 18 months after they left Afghanistan but the majority will deploy again with 3 SCOTS in late 2011. The training has started already and almost everyone will be in a new post as a result of career progression; there is much to be done. The experience remains in general terms but a new team will be built over the months before the next deployment. Operational success for a Battle Group is built on many aspects - training, equipment, intellectual study and the people that work together to a common goal. Arguably team work is the most important factor and it was the collective performance by the Battle Group that will be remembered the most by those who served together.

The 3 SCOTS BG was most fortunate in many ways to experience the uniquely challenging and exciting role as the 'flying squad' of Southern Afghanistan. The Battle Group was at the forefront of operations throughout Southern Afghanistan and Helmand in particular during a key year of the Afghanistan campaign that will only be able to be set into real context as the years pass. It has been the operational experience of a life-time and at the personal level, I have been humbled by the resilience, commitment and professionalism of the men and women I have been most privileged to command. My last and most important word is to the memory of those we did not bring home; they made the ultimate sacrifice for their friends. We will remember them.

Eulogies

EULOGY of 24914269 Sergeant Gus Millar

Sergeant Stuart 'Gus' Millar, 40, of The Black Watch, 3rd Battalion The Royal Regiment of Scotland, was killed on Monday 31 August 2009 whilst patrolling in Babaji District, Helmand Province, during an insurgent rocket propelled grenade attack.

Sergeant Millar joined the British Army in November 2000, after service in the Territorial Army. Following training he joined the Mortar Platoon of 1st Battalion The Royal Highland Fusiliers. He served in Northern Ireland, Falkland Islands, Cyprus and Iraq. He moved to 3 SCOTS Battalion as a mortar fire controller in Belfast in July 2007 and deployed to Afghanistan in April 2009.

Sergeant Gus Millar was a dedicated and professional senior non-commissioned officer. A career mortarman, he loved his job and during this tour had been able to put all his experience and years of training to the ultimate test in the most demanding of environments. Keen to prove the effectiveness of the men he had trained, Gus was the first mortar fire controller of the Battalion to engage a target. Ever enthusiastic to launch his beloved mortars, his booming voice monopolised the net as he took any and every opportunity to

Sgt Gus Millar, A Company's Mortar Fire Controller Killed in Action while on operations in Babaji.

call in fire. He had a remarkable sense of duty and has been the continuity in the development of the Mortar Platoon over the years. Sergeant Millar was a natural leader whose welcoming nature drew others into his company. He set the standard for the Jocks, but had the ability to empathise with those under his command – often taking the role of a big brother. But he had a bite when required, and the Jocks knew not to cross the line.

In his role as a mortar fire controller, he was at the very front of the action throughout the summer, famously being caught on the ITN news on the first day of Operation PANTHER'S CLAW, complaining that a long fire fight with the insurgents had delayed his 'morning brew'. It was typical of the man: in the thick of the action, professional expertise to the fore, combined with his wonderfully positive and humorous style. Sergeant Millar was great company, whose endearing Glaswegian patter was guaranteed to raise a smile in even the most trying of circumstances. He was a wonderfully kind and dependable man: the solid rock amongst the shingle.

Sergeant Millar was killed by a rocket propelled grenade during Operation TOR SAHAKATCHA in Babaji. Positioned on a roof to gain situational awareness, Sergeant Millar was the lead mortar fire controller and was attached to the senior Highland Platoon. A loyal and trusted comrade but above all a true friend, he leaves behind a hole that can never be filled.

Sergeant Millar married his wife Jillian last year. They have a very young and beautiful daughter, Grace. He showed a recent picture of them to the Padre, beamed with pride and tucked it into his notebook, minutes before he deployed on this operation. Our deepest thoughts and prayers are with Jillian and Grace as well as Gus' family and friends. Whilst the pain of this loss to them is unimaginable I hope they will draw considerable strength from the fact that we all will cherish some wonderful memories of the humorous rock that Gus was. We will all miss him terribly.

Sergeant Millar gave his life in the service of his comrades, for The Royal Regiment of Scotland, his country and the people of Afghanistan. We all consider ourselves truly privileged to have known him, to have served with him.

EULOGY of 25171259 Sergeant Sean Binnie

Sergeant Sean Binnie, 22, of The Black Watch, 3rd Battalion The Royal Regiment of Scotland was killed on Thursday 7 May 2009 in a firefight with insurgents near Musa Qaleh, Helmand Province, where he was serving as part of a team mentoring the Afghan National Army.

Sergeant Binnie joined the Army in 2003. Following basic training he joined the Battalion in Warminster and moved with them to Belfast at the end of 2005, taking part in the operation to close down British Army bases in the Province. He has served with his Battalion in Iraq and the Falkland Islands. Sergeant Binnie passed the arduous Section Commanders' Battle Course last year and took command of his section in time to deploy on Operation HERRICK in Afghanistan in March, living and working amongst the Afghan Warriors.

Sergeant Binnie was an enthusiast by nature, with a strong determined streak not always seen in one so young. He loved his job and was always the first to volunteer for extra courses – often doing them during leave as he claimed that otherwise he simply got bored. He was very much his own man but also a team player, which made him an excellent Junior Non Commissioned Officer. He was very robust, both mentally and physically, and carried others along with his force of personality. He also had a great sense of humour and could laugh at himself as well as with others. Sean was a sociable man with a deprecating sense of humour and a wide circle of friends. His soldiers liked him, but they also respected him as did all who served alongside him.

Acting Sgt Sean Binnie – Killed In Action whilst storming a compound in Northern Musa Qal'eh.

Sergeant Binnie was part of a small team bound together by trust and self-respect, built up over their arduous training in the last year and in their first months here in Afghanistan. The manner of his tragic death was typical of the man. The Afghan National Army he was mentoring was in trouble and with no thought for his own safety, he went forward to engage the enemy and get his comrades out of danger. It was an act of great courage and selflessness, in the finest traditions of The Black Watch Battalion, but no less remarkable for that and for which he made the ultimate sacrifice.

Sergeant Binnie gave his life in service of others in the career that he loved. He died in the defence of his friends and his comrades in the Afghan National Army. His death is a great blow for everyone in The Black Watch, 3rd Battalion of The Royal Regiment of Scotland.

The Battalion's deepest condolences and prayers go to Amanda, his wife, and his extended family.

EULOGY of 25202313 Corporal Tam Mason

Corporal Tam Mason, 27, of The Black Watch, 3rd Battalion The Royal Regiment of Scotland was very seriously injured by an improvised explosion device during an operation in Kandahar province on 15 September 2009. Tragically, he died of his wounds in Selly Oak hospital, Birmingham on 25 October 2009. He leaves a wife, Kylie and mother Linda.

Corporal Mason, originally from Rosyth in Fife, joined the Army in February 2005. After completing basic training he joined the Battalion in Warminster, Wiltshire. He deployed to Afghanistan on Operation HERRICK in 2006 before returning for a promotion course. He qualified as a Mortar Fire Controller in 2007 and was promoted to corporal. He deployed again to Afghanistan in March 2009.

Corporal Mason was a highly motivated and exceptional JNCO. On Operation HERRICK 10, Corporal Mason was at the top of his game; he was at his physical peak and thoroughly embraced the Scottish warrior ethos. Corporal Mason was a rugged, experienced, and hardened soldier who had been involved with the fiercest fighting that the Battle Group had witnessed. Often in the midst of a fight, Corporal Mason would heroically expose himself to enemy fire in order to get a vantage point to call in fire missions and strike the enemy with mortar fire. Technically, a superb mortar fire controller, Corporal Mason's confidence in his own abilities was founded on natural talent. Corporal Mason could always be relied on to remain cool and collected on the radio when calling in fire missions despite being in very difficult situations and under intense pressure. In addition, Corporal Mason was able to apply wisdom in challenging circumstances and was able to make the difficult decision of using appropriate and justified force.

He had set his heart on Special Forces selection next year and no-one would have betted him against reaching his ultimate goal.

He was an immensely popular and modest man and he will be sorely, sorely missed. Our deepest thoughts and prayers are with his wife Kylie and his family who have been with him by his side as he fought for his life. It has been a desperate time for them all and we pray that they can take some comfort from the fact that their Tam was a hero and that he is now resting in peace. We will all miss him terribly but he will not be forgotten.

Corporal Mason gave his life in the service of his friends in the Battalion, for The Royal Regiment of Scotland, his country and the people of Afghanistan.

Cpl Tam Mason, Cpl Ramsay and Pte McIntosh of the Mortar Platoon.

Pte Kev Elliot – A member of the Fire Support Group. Kev was killed along with Sgt Gus Millar by an RPG strike.

EULOGY of 25136352 Private Kevin Elliott

Private Kevin Elliott, 24, of The Black Watch, 3rd Battalion The Royal Regiment of Scotland, was killed on Monday 31 August 2009 whilst patrolling in Babaji District, Helmand Province, during an insurgent rocket propelled grenade attack.

Private Elliott attended Braeview Academy, Dundee where he was a keen boxer and footballer. He joined the Army in 2002. After basic training he was posted to Bravo Company, later moving to Charlie (Fire Support) Company. He had previously served in Iraq and Northern Ireland.

Private Elliott was an awesome fighting Jock, who was very much in his comfort zone on demanding operations in Afghanistan. He was excellent in the field and had a brilliant sense of humour. He was naturally fit and most importantly he was very loyal to his friends. He lived his life one day at a time and it is fair to say that he did not especially enjoy 'peacetime soldiering': like many a Jock that has gone before, he was a lovable rogue.

He was on the verge of leaving the Army earlier this year, but his inclination to be in the thick of the action was too tempting and he caught the last transport to Afghanistan with his mates. When asked why he decided to sign back on he simply said "I didn't want to miss the boys." Private Elliott loved operations and he was a big team player. It was no surprise to hear that in this tragic incident, he was the first man on the roof in the defensive position, the first to volunteer to protect his colleagues in a dangerous area. That sums up the man; he took life seriously when it was important to do so, and he was a first class field soldier as a result. He would never let his friends down.

Private Elliott leaves his mother Maggie and his father Sandy, his siblings Craig, Thomas, Luke, Natasha, Kirsty, Layren, Alex and Robyn and his grandmothers Margaret and Joan. We offer our deepest thoughts and condolences to all his family and friends and that they might gain some strength that he has died in the service of others, doing a professional job that he loved.

Private Elliott's loss will be hard to accept by all who knew him well. We will not forget his sacrifice, giving his life protecting his friends, representing his Regiment and his country, and so that the people of Afghanistan might have a better future.

EULOGY of 30029105 Private Robert McLaren

Private Robert McLaren, 20, died during an assault against Taliban forces near Kandahar on 11th June 2009. The Black Watch, 3rd Battalion The Royal Regiment of Scotland was conducting an offensive operation against the insurgents in one of the most dangerous parts of southern Afghanistan. Alpha (Grenadier) Company had been engaged in close combat with the insurgents for several hours. With his section pinned down by accurate rifle fire from two sides and the target of indirect rocket attacks, Private McLaren thrust forward to improve his position and relieve pressure on his comrades. He was killed by an improvised explosive device.

Private McLaren from Kintra, by Fionnphort on the Isle of Mull was schooled at Bunnessan Primary and then Oban High School. Pte McLaren joined the Army in November 2007 and trained first at the Army Training Regiment in Winchester and then as a Royal Engineer in Surrey. Pte McLaren ultimately decided to pursue a career as a Scottish infantryman and

Pte Robert McLaren. Killed in Action during Operation TORA ARWA 1.

attended and passed (with distinction) the Combat Infantryman's Course at the Infantry Training Centre, Catterick. He passed out of 7 Platoon on 3 April 2009 and was posted to 2 Platoon, Alpha (Grenadier) Company on operations in southern Afghanistan.

Private McLaren made a tremendous impact in the short time that he served with Alpha (Grenadier) Company. On his first operation, just a month out of recruit training, he left an indelible impression on his brother Jocks when in his first contact he fearlessly and decisively engaged insurgents at close range. He was killed taking the fight to the enemy just two weeks later. Had his life not been cruelly cut short Robert was destined for a successful military career. He had an obvious aptitude and enthusiasm for soldiering which set him apart from his peers. He will always be remembered as a capable, courageous and decent young man.

Private McLaren was buried at the small Creich Church in Bunessan on Mull. Hundreds of mourners paid their last respects. The service was broadcast to two village halls to allow residents to pay their last respects at what is understood to have been Mull's first military funeral since the Second World War.

EULOGY of 25145037 Bombardier Craig Hopson
38 (Seringapatam) Battery Royal Artillery
40th Regiment Royal Artillery (The Lowland Gunners)

Bombardier Craig Hopson was born in Castleford West Yorkshire on 11 March 1985 and joined the Army in January 2002, following training at ATR Pirbright and Larkhill he joined 129 (Dragon) Battery, 40th Regiment Royal Artillery in Topcliffe.

A motivated and intelligent soldier he quickly gravitated to the Tac Group and quickly progressed in both rank and trade. In 2008 he moved to 38 (Seringapatam) Battery on promotion to Bombardier and completed his Level 4 Targeting Course. He was an extremely talented young man and there is no doubt that he had the potential to reach the very top of his chosen career.

During his time with the Regiment, Bombardier Hopson completed two operational tours of Iraq, one of Cyprus and he was enormously proud of deploying in role as a Fire Support Team Assistant to Afghanistan with the Regiment for the first time.

Craig was a vibrant individual with a sense of humour and heart to match his stature. He made an immediate impact on everyone who was fortunate enough to come into contact with him. He had a ready smile and was the first to start with friendly banter in any situation; his irreverent sense of humour was legendary.

He attacked everything in life with verve and determination whether at work, on the rugby field or in the bar. On the sports pitch he had a deceptive turn of pace would turn his hand to any sport with great success but his true love was for Rugby League in which he represented the Army on a tour of Australia.

"Hoppo" enjoyed hiding his light under a bushel, his brash exterior thinly covered a man of intelligence, courage and compassion; he was the consummate professional. Immensely strong, calm under fire and technically excellent, his team remember him as a man they looked up to and aspired to emulate. On operations he was a man in his element doing the job he loved; effortlessly coordinating multiple missions in a most complex environment. The

Bdr Craig Hopson. Killed in Action during Operation PANCHAI PALANG.

support he provided to Alpha (Grenadier) Company earned him the deep respect and friendship of everyone in the Battle Group. His booming voice across the battlefield will be missed by one and all.

Craig had just returned from R&R seeing his baby daughter Amelia for only the second time, his enormous pride in becoming a father shone through whenever he spoke of his family.

He died at the very front line of Operation PANCHAI PALANG in Babaji, as the most forward artillery observer of the entire Brigade. He has given his life for his friends, for the Battle Group and his Regiment, and for the people of Afghanistan so that they may have a better life.

Bombardier Hopson died as he lived: leading from the front, determined and committed. He was one of the best of us and we will carry on strengthened by his memory. He will not be forgotten.

Honours and Awards Citations

EXTRACT FROM OPERATIONAL HONOURS AND AWARDS LIST NO 34

Lieutenant Colonel	Stephen John	CARTWRIGHT	Order of the British Empire
Corporal	Craig Richard	SHARP	Military Cross
Corporal	Christopher Sean	REYNOLDS	Military Cross
Lieutenant	Alexander John	PHILLIPS	Military Cross
Corporal	Richard	CLARK	Military Cross
Acting Sergeant	Sean Conor	BINNIE	Mention in Dispatches
Corporal	Samisoni Naisabo	BOILA	Mention in Dispatches
Warrant Officer Class Two	Paul David	COLVILLE	Mention in Dispatches
Lieutenant	Andrew John	HALLIDAY	Mention in Dispatches
Corporal	Paul	INNES	Mention in Dispatches
Corporal	David Joseph	ROY	Mention in Dispatches
Major	Alasdair Fortune Lyon	STEELE	Mention in Dispatches
Captain	Nicholas Peter	COLQUHOUN	Jt Commander's Commendation
Lieutenant	Robert John	COLQUHOUN	Jt Commander's Commendation
Captain	William Edward	JOHNSON	Jt Commander's Commendation
Lieutenant	Thomas James Peirse	KENNEDY	Jt Commander's Commendation
Captain	Olivier Lory	LEVER	Jt Commander's Commendation
Lieutenant	Thomas William John	O'SULLIVAN	Jt Commander's Commendation
Corporal	Alexander Thomas	WELLS	Jt Commander's Commendation
Bombardier	Richard	MCAULAY	Jt Commander's Commendation
Captain	Rik	GROVES	Jt Commander's Commendation
Major	Mathew	MUNRO	Commander British Forces' Commendation
Warrant Officer	Edward	DUFF	Commander British Forces' Commendation
Sergeant	Ian Lawrence	CARLISLE	Commander British Forces' Commendation
Acting Sergeant	Daniel	BUIST	Commander British Forces' Commendation
Corporal	Shelley	PARDOE R SIGS	Commander British Forces' Commendation
Corporal	Steven	PATTERSON	Commander British Forces Commendation
Acting Corporal	Alexander Peter	KANE	Commander British Forces' Commendation
Acting Corporal	Gareth	EVERETT	Commander British Forces Commendation
Lance Corporal	Daniel Wishart	HATTON	Commander British Forces' Commendation
Lance Corporal	Stuart Ian	NICOLSON	Commander British Forces Commendation
Lance Corporal	Stacy Dionne	QUINN RAMC	Commander British Forces' Commendation
Lance Corporal	Bryan	SCALLY RAMC	Commander British Forces' Commendation
Land Corporal	Dean	FORSYTH	Commander British Forces' Commendation
Acting Lance Corporal	Scott William	MCFADDEN	Commander British Forces' Commendation
Private	Daniel	DURIE	Commander British Forces' Commendation
Private	Rudi James	BRECHIN	Commander British Forces' Commendation
Private	Tony Mark	BROWNLESS	Commander British Forces' Commendation
Private	Stuart	TURNER	Commander British Forces' Commendation
Warrant Officer Two	Kevin	STACEY	Commander in Chief's Commendation
Mrs	Jackie	SMITH	Commander in Chief's Commendation

OFFICER OF THE ORDER OF THE BRITISH EMPIRE
LIEUTENANT COLONEL STEPHEN JOHN CARTWRIGHT
THE ROYAL REGIMENT OF SCOTLAND
Commanding Officer Regional Battle Group (South)
Southern Afghanistan Apr- Oct 09

Over a busy and demanding 6 month period on Operation HERRICK 10, Lieutenant Colonel Cartwright, as Commanding Officer of The Black Watch, 3rd Battalion The Royal Regiment of Scotland, has led his soldiers in 13 dangerous Battle Group operations. Throughout, he has planned and conducted his operations with great measure thereby, crucially, limiting the extent of collateral damage. His positive approach and tactical success have been widely praised with his Battle Group's performance recognised as comparable with a Special Operations Force. This reputation owes much to the outstanding leadership shown by Cartwright during some complex and dynamic expeditionary operations.

MILITARY CROSS
CORPORAL RICHARD CLARK
THE ROYAL REGIMENT OF SCOTLAND
Aviation Assault Company Section Commander
Southern Afghanistan Jul – Oct 09

Corporal Clark led his section in an attack on an enemy machine-gun nest. Clark sized up the situation and, one after the other, fired two 66 mm rockets. Clark's speed of thought alerted him to the need to act quickly and decisively before the enemy infiltrated any closer. Displaying exemplary courage, leadership and initiative, he left the relative safety of the compound and led his section across open ground to clear the enemy from the position. In this incident and others Clark's courage in the face of the enemy and leadership have ensured the success of the mission. His initiative, speed of thought and above all his utter disregard for his own safety in the face of the enemy has been extraordinary.

MILITARY CROSS
CORPORAL CHRISTOPHER SEAN REYNOLDS
THE ROYAL REGIMENT OF SCOTLAND
Section Commander
Babaji District, Helmand Province Apr – Sep 09

Corporal Reynolds has repeatedly demonstrated extreme bravery and outstanding technical ability as a Section Commander during offensive operations in Southern Afghanistan. On one occasion, Reynolds deliberately exposed himself to enemy fire in order to personally observe the insurgent firing point. Realising the imminent danger that the enemy posed, Reynolds engaged with his rifle in the face of considerable enemy fire, until his ammunition was fully expended. He then picked up a Light Machine Gun and again, fully exposed to the enemy fire, engaged from the rooftop. Throughout the tour, Reynolds has shown extraordinary bravery, whilst understanding the risks to which he was exposed.

MILITARY CROSS
CORPORAL CRAIG RICHARD SHARP
THE ROYAL REGIMENT OF SCOTLAND
Section Commander
Helmand Province Aug 09

Corporal Sharp was the lead section commander, responsible for providing flank protection for the IED disposal team who were clearing a route for the Jackal reconnaissance vehicles. As Sharp's team began climbing over compound walls into the main street of the village, the enemy opened fire with machine guns and Rocket Propelled Grenades (RPGs). The nature of the terrain was such that the rest of the BRF were unable to provide much fire support, which resulted in Sharp having to lead his section through what became a desperate 12 hour struggle for the village. Sharp, cajoling and encouraging his section, personally moving back and forth to carry out ammunition re-supplies and water replenishments. He called for a mortar mission less than 80 metres from his position, successfully destroying several of the enemy. Sharpe's contribution to the success of the mission, by personal bravery and action, cannot be understated.

MILITARY CROSS
LIEUTENANT ALEXANDER JOHN PHILLIPS
THE ROYAL REGIMENT OF SCOTLAND
Rifle Platoon Commander
Helmand Province Apr – Aug 09

Lieutenant Phillips has conducted 9 aviation assaults since arrival in theatre. Throughout, Phillips' leadership has been inspirational, leading from the front during every dangerous situation he has been in, never letting his men accept more risk than himself. For example, his company conducted an aviation assault into the area of Yakchal to disrupt an insurgent grouping. With the break-in Platoon fixed dealing with an Improvised Explosive Device (IED), Phillips without any prompting, instinctively led one of his sections under fire to launch an assault on the compound. He gave the order to fix bayonets and led the assault through the gate; the aggressiveness and speed of Phillips' counter-attack forced the insurgents to flee. He led his men fearlessly and with conviction in the face of a very real danger and he led, as ever, from the front.

Joint Task Force Afghanistan Commander's Commendation

The Black Watch, 3 SCOTS
Reserve Battle Group (South)

The Black Watch, 3rd Battalion the Royal Regiment of Scotland (3 SCOTS) in its capacity as RBG(S) is commended for its distinguished service in support of Task Force Kandahar from April to September 2009. Under extremely trying conditions and facing considerable and ever present risk, the officers and soldiers of 3 SCOTS displayed exemplary courage, tenacity, and warrior spirit in the execution of their mission, resulting in a profound and debilitating effect on the insurgency in Kandahar Province.

1 October 2009

Jonathan H. Vance, OMM, CD
Brigadier-General
Commander, Joint Task Force Afghanistan

Stan Stapleford, CD
Chief Warrant Officer
Task Force Sergeant-Major

Abbreviations and Definitions

ACOG	Advance Combat Optical Gunsight
AK-47	Avtomat Kalashnikova, Russian designed assault rifle
Al Echelon	Forward Logistical Support Grouping
ANA	Afghan National Army
ANP	Afghan National Police
ANSF	Afghan National Security Forces
BC	Battery Commander
BG	Battle Group, operational organization formed around infantry unit and includes attached arms such as artillery and engineers
Boardwalk	Central meeting place in Kandahar Airfield consisting of shops and fast food restaurants
Boilie	Sweets found in UK rations
Brecon	Town in Wales that hosts Infantry Battle School where promotional infantry course are conducted, also nicknamed Junior or Seniors
BRF	Brigade Reconnaissance Force
BSN	Camp BASTION, Task Force Helmand logistical node
Buffalo	A warm fleece lined jacket
Casevac	Casualty Evacuation
CO	Commanding Officer, Lieutenant Colonel in command of a battalion
Contact	Term describing initial engagement with enemy forces
CP	Command Post
CSE Show	Combined Services Entertainment, a variety show that includes comedians, musicians and other performers
CSM	Company Sergeant Major
Dasht	Arid ground beyond the irrigated rural areas along the green zone
Dicked	Term used to describe insurgent process of observing ISAF soldiers
D Day	The day on which an operation is to be initiated
Dragunov	Snayperskaya Vintovka Dragunova, Russian designed sniper rifle
ECM	Electronic counter measures, used to combat improvised explosive devices
FLOT	Forward Line of own Troops
FLSG	Forward Logistical Support Grouping
FOB	Forward operating base
FOB Price	Danish Army operations centre
FOB Wahid	Patrol base established in Babaji by Bravo Company
FSG	Fire support group, a small mobile sub-unit that provides heavy calibre weapons such GPMG, Javelin missiles and snipers
FST	Fire support team, involved in coordination of indirect fire
FUP	Forming up Point
GBU	Laser guided munition
GIRoA	Government of the Islamic Republic of Afghanistan
GMG	Grenade machine gun
GMLRS	Guided Multiple Launch Rocket System
GPMG	General purpose machine gun
GPS	Global positioning system, a global navigation satellite system that allows the user to identify his exact location
Green Beans	American coffee shop franchise, found on the Boardwalk
Green Zone	Irrigated agricultural region lining significant rivers
H Hour	Operation start time
Hesco	A means of creating a defensive wall, by filling a cage with rocks and soil

HLS	Helicopter landing site
HQ	Headquarters
IDF	Indirect Fire
IED	Improvised explosive device
In contact	Prolonged period of engagement with enemy forces
IO	Intelligence officer (primary use), or also influence officer (secondary use)
ISAF	International Security Assistance Force
ISTAR	Intelligence, surveillance, target acquisition, reconnaissance
ISTAR Platform	Term used to describe the vehicle employed to conduct ISTAR observations
Jackal	4 x 4 vehicle, fitted with heavy machine gun, general purpose machine gun, and automatic grenade launcher
JNCOs	Junior Non Commissioned Officers
JTAC	Joint Tactical Air Controller, controls air and aviation assets
KAF	Kandahar Airfield
KIA	Killed in action
Kinetic	Term used to denote the use of force
LASM	Light anti-structure munition
LHour	Landing Hour
LMG	Light Machine Gun
LS	Landing Site
LUP	Laying up Point
MAOT	Mobile Air Operations Team
MASTIFF	Armoured fighting vehicle designed to be resistant improvised explosive devices
ME	Main effort, a commander's focus of activity and resources
Med Centre	Medical Centre
Mensurated grid	An exact three-dimensional target location determined through mathematical algorithms and satellite technology
MERT	Medical Evacuation Response Team
MFC	Mortar Fire Controller
MSST	Military Stabilisation Support Team
Monging	Term used by UK soldiers to describe a lapse in concentration of a fellow soldier
MT	Motor Transport
Murder hole	Small opening made in compound wall that insurgents used to fire weapons through
NATO	North Atlantic Treaty Organization
NAV	Navigate
NCO	Non-Commissioned Officer, encompassing ranks between Lance Corporal and Warrant Officer
NDS	National Directorate of Security
NVG	Night Vision Goggle
OC	Officer Commanding (Company Commander)
OMLT	Operational Mentor Liaison Team
Op	Abbreviation for operation
Ops Box	Three dimensional area in which a unit operates, all movement through is controlled and authorized by unit headquarters
OPTAG	Operation and Training Advisory Group, provides basic training package to commanders in order to prepare and advise for operational tours
OP	Observation Post
OS	Offensive Support
OSPREY	Body armour used by UK forces
PB	Patrol base, smaller in size to forward operating base
PID	Positively Identify
PKM	Pulemyot Kalashnikova, Russian designed general purpose machine gun
Pl Comd	Platoon Commander
PRR	Personal Role Radio

QM	Quarter Master
R & R	Rest and recuperation, a two week period out of theatre
RAMC	Royal Army Medical Corps
RBG(S)	Regional Battle Group (South)
RCMO	Regimental Careers Management Officer
RC(S)	Regional Command (South), NATO Divisional Headquarters in Command of Southern Afghanistan
Red Illum	The darkest part of the night in which even image intensifiers provide no help
RPG	Rocket propelled grenade
RMO	Regimental Medical Officer
RMP	Royal Military Police
ROC Drill	Rehearsal of Concept drill, a tool used by commanders to synchronize, align and coordinate their forces on a model
Rolex	Term denoting a planned delay to an operation
RSM	Regimental Sergeant Major, senior soldier in a battalion
RV	Rendezvous
SAF	Small arms fire
Salvos	Simultaneous barrage of artillery or engagement by multiple direct fire systems
Sangar	A protected defensive location
Shura	A meeting of senior Afghan leaders and tribesmen
SITREP	Situation report, used by commanders to provide timely and succinct updates
Soak	The use of ISTAR for an extended period of time to observe a specific area
SOPS	Standard Operating Procedures
Subaltern	A young officer, generally commanding a platoon of 30 men
SUSAT	The infantryman's rifle sight
Tabbed	From the abbreviation 'Tactical Advance to Battle', meaning patrolling in full equipment, ready to react to the enemy
TAC/TAC HQ	Commanding Officer's mobile tactical headquarters
TACP	Tactical air command party that controls all air and aviation assets in support of an operation
TACSAT	Tactical satellite radio system that allows users to speak over vast distances
TFH	Task Force Helmand, British Commanded NATO Brigade
TFK	Task Force Kandahar, Canadian Commanded NATO Brigade
TFL	Task Force Leatherneck, USMC Commanded Brigade
TF Thor	Task Force Thor, US Army counter improvised explosive device unit
TIC	Troops in Contact
Tim Horton's	Canadian coffee shop franchise, found on the Boardwalk
TOS	Tam-o-Shanter
UAV	Unmanned aerial vehicle
UGL	Underslung Grenade Launcher
UNODC	United Nations Office on Drugs and Crime
USMC	United States Marine Corps
VCP	Vehicle Check Point
Viking	All terrain armoured vehicle
VP	Voice procedure, deliberate and short language used on radios
VP	Vulnerable Point
Wadi	A small valley or dry riverbed
WIA	Wounded in action
WMIK	Weapons mount installation kit fitted to British Land Rovers
Y Hour	Time of take off
9 Liner	A procedure used to request emergency first aid, in particular support helicopters
50 cal	50 calibre heavy machine gun

Nominal Role of Battle Group

REGIONAL BATTLEGROUP (SOUTH), OP HERRICK 10, APRIL–NOVEMBER 2010

BATTLEGROUP HEADQUARTERS (AUGMENTED BY TROOPS FROM 209 SQUADRON AND 14 REGIMENT, ROYAL CORPS OF SIGNALS)

Lieutenant Colonel Cartwright
Major Hempenstall
Major Lindsay
Major MacAskill
Major Shaw, Adjutant General's Corps
Captain Anderson, Royal Army Chaplain's
 Department
Captain Baddeley
Captain Bunce
Captain Collis
Captain Colquhoun
Captain Colville
Captain Duthie, Adjutant General's Corps
Captain Harvey
Captain Hawkins
Captain Hood
Captain Morgan, Adjutant General's Corps (Army
 Legal Services)
Captain Waterman, Royal Engineers
Captain Wythes, Australian Army
Lieutenant Goodall, Adjutant General's Corps
Lieutenant McCorkindale
Lieutenant Bonner, Intelligence Corps
Lieutenant Donaldson
Second Lieutenant Eastwood, Intelligence Corps
Second Lieutenant Rivington, Army Air Corps
Warrant Officer Class One McDougall
Warrant Officer Class Two Duff MBE
Warrant Officer Class Two Gray, Adjutant General's
 Corps
Warrant Officer Class Two Theyers
Warrant Officer Class Two Wann
Colour Sergeant Allan
Colour Sergeant Burns
Colour Sergeant Campbell
Colour Sergeant Ferguson
Colour Sergeant Pratt
Colour Sergeant Ward
Staff Sergeant Seaton, Royal Signals
Staff Sergeant Wilson, Army Physical Training Corps

Sergeant Dempsey
Sergeant Murray
Sergeant Tollan
Sergeant Wright, Adjutant General's Corps
Corporal Barr, Royal Signals
Corporal Braid
Corporal Currie
Corporal Diss-Evans
Corporal Durrand
Corporal Gibson, Adjutant General's Corps
Corporal Martin, Royal Signals
Corporal Meade
Corporal Meredith, Adjutant General's Corps
Corporal Nadolny
Corporal Paynton, Adjutant General's Corps
Corporal Rowan
Corporal Russell, Royal Signals
Corporal Smart
Corporal Winton
Lance Corporal Blackey, Royal Signals
Lance Corporal Burningham, Royal Signals
Lance Corporal Cassidy
Lance Corporal Cochrane
Lance Corporal Horne, Royal Signals
Lance Corporal Johnson, Adjutant General's Corps
Lance Corporal Monaghan, Adjutant General's Corps
Lance Corporal Pardoe, Royal Signals
Lance Corporal Qalobulawasakabara
Lance Corporal Ratakalou
Lance Corporal Stewart
Private Alexander, Adjutant General's Corps
Private Danks
Private Donn
Private George
Private Gonsales
Signaller Haxell, Royal Signals
Private Holliday
Private Hynd, Adjutant General's Corps
Private Jones
Private Lackie

Private Rankine
Private Simpson
Private Smillie
Private Smith
Private Stewart
Private Thompson
Private Thorp, Adjutant General's Corps
Private Whittaker

ALPHA (GRENADIER) COMPANY

Major Munro
Captain Newson
Lieutenant Colquhoun
Lieutenant Gorrie
Lieutenant Parsons
Lieutenant Wallace
Second Lieutenant Eltringham
Warrant Officer Class Two Colville
Colour Sergeant Easton
Colour Sergeant Eaton
Sergeant Buchanan
Sergeant Nichol
Sergeant Noble
Corporal Bavadra
Corporal Boila
Corporal Brady
Corporal Clark
Corporal Duncan
Corporal Koro
Corporal McLeod
Corporal Natui
Corporal Nawacalevu
Corporal Pardoe, Royal Signals
Corporal Patterson
Corporal Sharp
Corporal Welshman
Corporal Wrigley, The Yorkshire Regiment
Lance Corporal Boot, The Yorkshire Regiment
Lance Corporal Connell
Lance Corporal Devine
Lance Corporal Forrester
Lance Corporal Graham
Lance Corporal McFadden
Lance Corporal McKenzie
Lance Corporal Munjoma
Lance Corporal Nicholson
Lance Corporal Ormiston
Lance Corporal Rae
Private Bernard
Private Berry
Private Betts
Private Black
Private Boa
Private Brown 00
Private Brown 28

Private Brown 89
Private Brown 10
Private Burrows
Private Byrne
Private Carson
Private Chisholm
Private Connolly
Private Craggs
Private Craig
Private Curr, The Yorkshire Regiment
Private Donaldson
Private Dye
Private Easson
Private Edgar
Private Ellis
Private Gray
Private Gurlay
Private Harrop
Private Hooper
Private Kenneway
Private King
Private Laidlaw
Private Landells
Private Lawson
Private Leslie
Private Lindsay
Private Logan
Private Maiyale
Private Mboge, The Yorkshire Regiment
Private McAuley
Private McDermott
Private McHugh
Private McKay
Private McLaren
Private Methven
Private Miller
Private Mitchell, The Yorkshire Regiment
Private Mitchell
Private Murphy
Private Newell
Private Nino
Private Nisbet
Private Raoba
Private Rewadai
Private Ross
Private Salter
Private Scott
Private Simmons
Private Smith
Private Spring
Private Stevens
Private Stewart
Private Supharee
Private Thompson
Private Todd

Private Uluilakeba
Private Ure
Private Vakalala
Private Van Niekerk
Private Vuase
Private Walton
Private Watson
Private Weir
Private White
Private Wright, The Yorkshire Regiment

BRAVO COMPANY

Major Steele
Captain Colquhoun
Lieutenant Halliday
Lieutenant Mill
Lieutenant Pearce
Lieutenant Phillips
Second Lieutenant Woods
Warrant Officer Class Two Dargavel
Colour Sergeant McSeveney
Sergeant Buist
Sergeant McCready
Sergeant Robertson
Sergeant Weir
Corporal Bruce
Corporal Copeland
Corporal Dowdles
Corporal Ferrier
Corporal Gillon
Corporal Innes
Corporal Kane
Corporal Roy
Corporal Scroggie
Corporal Wells
Corporal Wilson
Corporal Young
Lance Corporal Cameron
Lance Corporal Clark
Lance Corporal Edgar
Lance Corporal Hodge, The Yorkshire Regiment
Lance Corporal Keatings
Lance Corporal Kyle
Lance Corporal Mackie
Lance Corporal Martin, The Yorkshire Regiment
Lance Corporal Metuisela
Lance Corporal Millar
Lance Corporal Olivant
Lance Corporal Paterson
Lance Corporal Pearson, The Yorkshire Regiment
Lance Corporal Richford
Lance Corporal Simpson
Lance Corporal Taroga
Private Anderson
Private Atkinson, The Yorkshire Regiment

Private Bain
Private Belton
Private Blair
Private Blake
Private Brand
Private Brechin
Private Brownless
Private Bruce
Private Cameron
Private Campbell
Private Clark
Private Collins
Private Connor
Private Courts
Private Crawford
Private Crooks
Private Dempster
Private Durie
Private Fraser
Private Gasaudra
Private Gasaucalayawa
Private Goldworthy
Private Greer
Private Hamerton
Private Hannah
Private Hart
Private Johnston
Private Lackie
Private Longbottom, The Yorkshire Regiment
Private MacBain
Private Marshall
Private McFarlane
Private Mackie
Private McIlroy
Signaller McKenzie, Royal Signals
Private McPake
Private McTurk
Private Moir
Private Nasilasila
Private Nicholls
Private Nightingale
Private O'Neil
Private Paterson
Private Pattie
Private Purce
Private Reid
Private Ritchie 09
Private Ritchie 66
Private Robertson 70
Private Robertson 17
Private Robertson 73
Private Rodger
Private Rodgerson
Private Scroggie
Private Shields

Private Smith
Private Sovui
Private Sutherland
Private Teleyko, The Yorkshire Regiment
Private Thomas
Private Thomson 59
Private Thomson 03
Private Turner
Private Vasu, The Yorkshire Regiment
Private Vunediyaroi
Private Wallace
Private Watson
Private White
Private Wilson, The Yorkshire Regiment
Private Wood 58
Private Wood 50
Private Wood, The Yorkshire Regiment
Private Wynne
Private Yeaman

JACKAL GROUP

Major Cattermole, Royal Scots Dragoon Guards
Major Whitelegge
Captain Gladstone
Captain Kerr
Captain MacPherson
Warrant Officer Class Two Lambert
Warrant Officer Class Two McConnell
Warrant Officer Class Two Parker
Colour Sergeant Blyth
Sergeant Gray
Sergeant Holbrook-Woodthorpe, The Yorkshire
    Regiment
Sergeant Lightowlers, The Yorkshire Regiment
Sergeant McManus
Sergeant Mitchell
Sergeant O'Brien
Sergeant Robertson
Sergeant Taylor
Corporal Baxter
Corporal Couper
Corporal Feeney
Corporal Herd
Corporal Lindsay
Corporal McLaughlin
Corporal Millar
Corporal Pasiful
Corporal Polus
Corporal Pow
Corporal Pratt
Corporal Reynolds
Corporal Tod
Corporal Trickovic
Lance Corporal Arnold

Lance Corporal Bain
Lance Corporal Beveridge
Lance Corporal Bruce
Lance Corporal Caird
Lance Corporal Duthie
Lance Corporal Gonsales
Lance Corporal Green
Lance Corporal Hanway
Lance Corporal Hattan
Lance Corporal Hume
Lance Corporal Jose
Lance Corporal Lawaci
Lance Corporal Lowe
Lance Corporal McCarthy
Lance Corporal Moceivei
Lance Corporal Palmer
Lance Corporal Pollard
Lance Corporal Ratumaisese
Lance Corporal Reddington
Lance Corporal Sims
Lance Corporal Smith
Lance Corporal Soqeta
Lance Corporal Tabua
Lance Corporal Tawayaga
Lance Corporal Walker
Lance Corporal Williams
Lance Corporal Winters
Private Barnes
Private Brown
Private Carmichael
Private Carpenter
Private Cassidy
Private Chalk
Private Crawford
Private Durcan
Private Elliott
Private Fenton
Private Fraser
Private Green
Private Hunter
Private Johnstone
Private Jones
Private Kidd
Private Lyon
Private Mackie
Private Marshall
Private McKenna
Private Muir 18
Private Muir 21
Private Mulase
Private Murray
Private Roberts
Private Russell
Private Scott

Private Siata
Private Smith
Private Stevenson
Private Stewart

MECHANISED TRANSPORT PLATOON (AUGMENTED BY TROOPS FROM 19 COMBAT SERVICE SUPPORT REGIMENT)

Captain Robb
Staff Sergeant Kirton, Royal Logistics Corps
Colour Sergeant Pearson
Sergeant Cunningham
Sergeant Halliday
Corporal Anderson, Royal Logistics Corps
Corporal McGuinness
Corporal Panton
Lance Corporal Blackburn, Royal Logistics Corps
Lance Corporal Cruickshanks
Lance Corporal Donaldson
Lance Corporal Ellis
Lance Corporal Fleming-Scott, Royal Logistics Corps
Lance Corporal Pugh, The Yorkshire Regiment
Lance Corporal Richardson
Lance Corporal Wishart
Private Burrows, Royal Logistics Corps
Private Clunie
Private Dobson, Royal Logistics Corps
Private Eaves
Private Kilpatrick
Private Mackie
Private McCartney 66, Royal Logistics Corps
Private McCartney 65, Royal Logistics Corps
Private McNally
Private Morgan
Private Murray
Private Myles
Private Naisaramaki
Private Ramsay
Private Stroud
Private Williams
Private Wills, Royal Logistics Corps
Private Wray, Royal Logistics Corps

LIGHT AID DETACHMENT

Staff Sergeant Searles, Royal Electrical and Mechanical Engineers
Sergeant Martin, Royal Electrical and Mechanical Engineers
Corporal Smith, Royal Electrical and Mechanical Engineers
Corporal Taylor, Royal Electrical and Mechanical Engineers
Lance Corporal Goodwin, Royal Electrical and Mechanical Engineers

Lance Corporal Loughridge, Royal Electrical and Mechanical Engineers
Lance Corporal Procter, Royal Electrical and Mechanical Engineers
Lance Corporal Sim, Royal Electrical and Mechanical Engineers
Craftsman Fortune, Royal Electrical and Mechanical Engineers
Craftsman Montgomery, Royal Electrical and Mechanical Engineers

MORTAR PLATOON

Captain Mack
Warrant Officer Class Two Scott
Sergeant Masson
Sergeant Millar
Sergeant Porter
Sergeant Reilly
Corporal Emslie
Corporal Mason
Corporal Muirhead
Corporal Ramsay
Corporal Rock
Corporal Steele
Lance Corporal Little
Lance Corporal MacKenzie
Lance Corporal Thomson
Lance Corporal Vasunikasi
Private Coulter
Private Glen
Private Gow
Private Harrison
Private Johnson
Private Lekutu
Private Lowson
Private MacPherson
Private McGuinness
Private McIntosh
Private McMillan
Private Mudunavosa
Private New
Private Robertson
Private Ross
Private Sinuleleiwasa
Private Tamata
Private Tawake

MEDICAL SECTION (AUGMENTED BY TROOPS FROM 2 REGIMENT, ROYAL ARMY MEDICAL CORPS)

Captain Charlton, Royal Army Medical Corps
Captain Wood, Royal Army Medical Corps
Staff Sergeant O'Keefe, Royal Army Medical Corps
Sergeant Cooper
Corporal White

Lance Corporal Barron
Lance Corporal Ellerby, Royal Army Medical Corps
Lance Corporal Hardie, Royal Army Medical Corps
Lance Corporal Mokuchedi, Royal Army Medical Corps
Lance Corporal Pasifull
Lance Corporal Quinn, Royal Army Medical Corps
Lance Corporal Scally
Lance Corporal Vorster, Royal Army Medical Corps
Private Fullagher, Royal Army Medical Corps
Private Hassall, Royal Army Medical Corps
Private McCarthy, Royal Army Medical Corps
Private McLean
Private Miller, Royal Army Medical Corps
Private Trott, Royal Army Medical Corps

QUARTERMASTER'S DEPARTMENT

Captain Cooper
Warrant Officer Class Two Duffus
Warrant Officer Class Two Houston
Colour Sergeant Anderson
Sergeant Brown
Sergeant Salmond
Corporal Benson
Corporal Wilkinson
Lance Corporal Harris
Lance Corporal Pratt
Lance Corporal Vunibobo
Private Finlayson
Private Garioch
Private MacDonald
Private Reid
Private Stewart

38 (SERINGAPATAM) BATTERY TACTICAL GROUP (ATTACHED FROM 40 REGIMENT ROYAL ARTILLERY)

Major Sharpe, Royal Artillery
Captain Banks, Royal Artillery
Captain Bartholomew
Captain Dachtler, Royal Artillery
Captain Groves, Royal Artillery
Captain Quin, Royal Artillery
Warrant Officer Class Two Greenhalgh, Royal Artillery
Staff Sergeant Brown, Royal Artillery
Sergeant Carlisle
Sergeant Collins, Royal Artillery
Sergeant McBride
Sergeant Stobbs, Royal Artillery
Corporal King, Royal Signals
Bombardier Hopson, Royal Artillery
Bombardier McAulay, Royal Artillery
Bombardier Munro, Royal Artillery
Lance Bombardier Biggins, Royal Artillery
Lance Bombardier Ewens, Royal Artillery

Lance Bombardier Price, Royal Artillery
Lance Bombardier Rees, Royal Artillery
Gunner Barker, Royal Artillery
Gunner Boateng, Royal Artillery
Gunner Coburn, Royal Artillery
Gunner Freeman, Royal Artillery
Gunner Jones, Royal Artillery
Gunner Mewett, Royal Artillery
Gunner Olive, Royal Artillery
Gunner Robertson, Royal Artillery
Gunner Seaman, Royal Artillery
Gunner Shield, Royal Artillery
Gunner Thorpe, Royal Artillery
Gunner Venter, Royal Artillery

ENGINEER TROOP (ATTACHED FROM 25 SQUADRON, 38 REGIMENT, ROYAL ENGINEERS)

Lieutenant Paskell, Royal Engineers
Sergeant David, Royal Engineers
Corporal Miller, Royal Engineers
Corporal Pattenden, Royal Engineers
Corporal Patterson, Royal Engineers
Lance Corporal Blake, Royal Engineers
Lance Corporal Carder, Royal Engineers
Lance Corporal Craig, Royal Engineers
Lance Corporal Ljewski, Royal Engineers
Lance Corporal Lythogoe, Royal Engineers
Lance Corporal Magill, Royal Engineers
Lance Corporal Taylor, Royal Engineers
Sapper Baskett, Royal Engineers
Sapper Brady, Royal Engineers
Sapper Burton, Royal Engineers
Sapper Cranshaw, Royal Engineers
Sapper Dixon, Royal Engineers
Sapper McIntosh, Royal Engineers
Sapper McKelvie, Royal Engineers
Sapper Monaghan, Royal Engineers
Sapper Peebles, Royal Engineers
Sapper Pocock, Royal Engineers
Sapper Rabeka, Royal Engineers
Sapper Rowe, Royal Engineers
Sapper Williams 02, Royal Engineers
Sapper Williams 62, Royal Engineers

PROVOST SECTION (ATTACHED FROM 173 PROVOST COMPANY, ROYAL MILITARY POLICE)

Staff Sergeant O'Connor, Royal Military Police
Corporal Mackness, Royal Military Police
Corporal Simpson, Royal Military Police
Lance Corporal Davis, Royal Military Police
Lance Corporal Motley, Royal Military Police
Lance Corporal Richardson, Royal Military Police

THE BLACK WATCH 3rd BATTALION THE ROYAL REGIMENT OF SCOTLAND TROOPS DETACHED TO OTHER DEPLOYED UNITS

DELTA (LIGHT) COMPANY – OPERATIONAL MENTORING AND LIAISON TEAM 3

Major Philp
Major Jordan-Barber
Captain Elder
Captain Harrison
Captain Lever
Captain McVey
Lieutenant Doughty
Lieutenant O'Sullivan
Lieutenant Kennedy
Lieutenant Stanning (transferred to Bravo Company mid tour)
Second Lieutenant Hieghton-Jackson
Warrant Officer Class Two Davidson
Warrant Officer Class Two Shaw
Colour Sergeant Beaton
Colour Sergeant Dunn
Colour Sergeant Smith
Acting Sergeant Binnie
Sergeant Connington
Sergeant Hodgskins
Sergeant McLeod
Sergeant Ritchie
Sergeant Watling
Corporal Mather
Corporal Miller
Corporal Ross
Corporal Watson
Corporal Whyte
Lance Corporal Brady
Lance Corporal Brown
Lance Corporal Brown
Lance Corporal Coll
Lance Corporal Everett
Lance Corporal Fraser
Lance Corporal Forbes
Lance Corporal Gilmartin, Adjutant General's Corps
Lance Corporal Gordon
Lance Corporal Hutton
Lance Corporal Milne
Lance Corporal Morgan
Lance Corporal Nisbet
Lance Corporal Rabonu
Lance Corporal Riddock
Lance Corporal Watt
Private Balfour
Private Calderwood
Private Chambers
Private Cain
Private Jamieson
Private Kelly
Private Lavery
Private Peebles
Private Roy
Private Seath
Private Warren
Private Woodward

BRIGADE RECONNAISSANCE FORCE

Captain Johnson
Sergeant Blackley
Corporal Mason
Corporal Sharp
Lance Corporal Blake
Lance Corporal Davidson
Lance Corporal Forsyth
Lance Corporal Strathearn
Lance Corporal Thain
Lance Corporal Young
Private Taylor

AFGHAN NATIONAL ARMY NON COMMISSIONED OFFICER TRAINING TEAM, KABUL

Captain Dunnigan
Sergeant Buchanan
Sergeant Early
Sergeant Ritchie
Lance Corporal Lang

HEADQUARTERS TASK FORCE HELMAND

Lieutenant Colonel Tait
Private Hobson, Adjutant General's Corps

BASTION JOINT SUPPORT UNIT

Warrant Officer Class Two Stewart, Adjutant General's Corps
Sergeant Knowles, Adjutant General's Corps
Sergeant Pyle, Royal Logistics Corps
Lance Corporal Alexander, Royal Logistics Corps
Lance Corporal Chavi, Royal Logistics Corps
Private Patterson, Royal Logistics Corps
Private Rapacha, Royal Logistics Corps

JOINT FORCE MEDICAL GROUP

Lieutenant Colonel Diack, Royal Army Medical Corps

PERMANENT REAR OPERATIONS TEAM, FORT GEORGE, INVERNESS

Major Bruce
Captain Campbell

Captain McClelland-Jones
Captain Murray-Knight, Adjutant General's Corps
Warrant Officer Class Two Anderson
Warrant Officer Class Two Gow, Royal Logistics Corps
Warrant Officer Class Two Stacey
Staff Sergeant Goudie, Adjutant General's Corps
Staff Sergeant Henderson, Royal Logistics Corps
Colour Sergeant Taylor
Sergeant Cessford
Sergeant Fitzpatrick
Sergeant Howlett, Adjutant General's Corps
Sergeant Paton
Corporal Buchan, Royal Electrical and Mechanical Engineers
Corporal Cumming
Corporal Dennis, Royal Logistics Corps
Corporal Dick
Corporal Hamilton
Corporal Hemens, Adjutant General's Corps
Corporal McIntyre
Corporal McKeown, Royal Logistics Corps
Corporal McNamee
Corporal Morgan, Royal Logistics Corps
Corporal Naldolny, Adjutant General's Corps
Corporal Peacock

Corporal Pratt, Adjutant General's Corps
Corporal Quigley, Royal Logistics Corps
Corporal Thomas
Corporal Wainwright, Royal Logistics Corps
Corporal Wallace
Lance Corporal Brockbank
Lance Corporal Cross, Royal Logistics Corps
Lance Corporal Davies, Royal Logistics Corps
Lance Corporal Dodds, Royal Logistics Corps
Lance Corporal Dilnutt, Royal Logistics Corps
Lance Corporal Montague
Lance Corporal Whiteley, Royal Army Medical Corps
Lance Corporal Thompson, Adjutant General's Corps
Private Akerman, Royal Logistics Corps
Private Fraser
Private Kerr, Royal Logistics Corps
Private Nasnja, Royal Logistics Corps
Private Sinclair
Private Simpson
Private Sullivan, Royal Logistics Corps
Private Smith, Royal Logistics Corps
Private Tullis
Private Watts, Royal Logistics Corps
Private White

Tour lengths are not shown. The Black Watch, 3rd Battalion The Royal Regiment of Scotland had a number of personnel permanently attached to it from other Corps of the Army. It received further attachments specifically for Operation HERRICK 10. Unless otherwise denoted, all personnel listed above are members of the Royal Regiment of Scotland (including augmented troops from 1st, 4th, 6th and 7th Battalions).